1986

FAMILY MAN

ALEXANDER HUMEZ &
KEITH FITZGERALD STAVELY

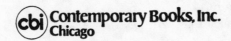

cbi Contemporary Books, Inc.
Chicago

Library of Congress Cataloging in Publication Data

Main entry under title:

Family man.

   1. Fathers—United States.   2. Sex role.
3. Father and child.   I. Humez, Alexander.
II. Stavely, Keith.
HQ756.5.F35   1978   301.42'7   78-57437
ISBN 0-8092-7764-6

Published by Contemporary Books, Inc.
180 North Michigan Avenue, Chicago, Illinois 60601
Manufactured in the United States of America
Library of Congress Catalog Card Number: 78-57437
International Standard Book Number: 0-8092-7764-6

Published simultaneously in Canada by
Beaverbooks
953 Dillingham Road
Pickering, Ontario L1W 1Z7
Canada

For Andrea and Jonathan

Contents

Acknowledgments

Many hands besides our own have labored to create the following pages. We cannot thank by name those to whom we owe the most: the men who allowed us to interview them. They answered our questions more candidly and fully than we had any right to expect, not defending themselves against our invasion of their privacy, but instead graciously inviting us—and our readers—to bear witness to their lives. We can acknowledge more directly the many friends and interested bystanders who either helped us find the men who talked with us, or helped us write down what they said, or both: Britt Colbert, Nancy Colbert, Debbie Crose, Roz Feldburg, Alfred Fengler, David Hildebrand, John Hildebrand, Annette Holman, Louis Howland, Harry Johnson, Paul Johnson, Steven Keese, Susan Middleton, Bill Riggs, Jan Riggs, Diana Smith, Linda Stavely, Tony Stavely, Howard Zinn, and, of course, our editors at Contemporary Books—Sydelle Kramer, Judith Weber, and Eugene Zucker. Finally, we are grateful to the members of our own families. Kathy Stavely Fitzgerald and Jean McMahon Humez have given us practical assistance of every kind—from leading us to several of our speakers, to correcting our editorial blunders. If *Family Man* succeeds in being faithful to the humanity of its fourteen family men, this is due in no small measure to them and to the two children to whom it is dedicated—Andrea Humez and Jonathan Stavely.

Introduction

This book is dedicated to our two young children, ages four and seven, because it originated in our experiences as their parents. We had both been led to believe that these experiences were unusual because they didn't conform to conventional definitions of "male roles." One of us had devoted, from the time of his child's birth, as much time to her care and nurturing as had the child's mother; the other began to do so when his child was three years old. About two-and-a-half years ago, after we had both been closely involved with our children for several months, we discovered each other—discovered that we had good and useful things to tell each other about dealing with small children, and about the quizzical or suspicious reactions we had gotten from people who saw, or were told, that we were doing "women's work" with our kids: "And what are you doing this year?"

"Well, I'm raising my kid and doing some other work part time."

"Oh, really? Hmmm, that's nice."

Each of us had come to our child-care situations for different reasons, and each of us responded differently to society's message that those situations were rather strange and surprising ones for male parents to be in. We have different temperaments, different personalities, and different notions about how the world works; but when we talked with each other, we found out that we had several things in common. One was that we were both eager to talk about our experiences as sons, husbands, and fathers. Another was that our conversations helped and bolstered both of us. We felt aided and supported partly because we were talking to each other at all about our family lives and partly because each of us was fascinated and stimulated by what the other had to say. Both of us had felt that our everyday dealings with our children were normal, natural, and human, and that our changing diapers, or whatever, had seemed odd or unusual to us only to the extent that the larger culture had encouraged us to perceive it that way.

All the elements we had in common enabled us to see each other as more human and substantial than the prevailing cultural stereotypes of American men allowed for. We were sure we could find plenty of other men with stories to tell at least as interesting as ours, and we were also sure that anyone who heard or read these stories would be fascinated and stimulated by them just as we had been when we talked with each other. So we decided to try to put together a book in which men of diverse social backgrounds and domestic situations would present themselves, in their own words, as men in America today.

Since we knew from our initial encounters with each other how woefully inadequate the standard categories were for the "private lives" of men, we did *not* set out to find only "untraditional" men who were "unusually involved with their children," as we were alleged by these categories to be. We knew there was an enormous difference between the "new husband" (as one recent book has called people like us) and what we were really like, and we expected a similar disjunction between the "old husband and father"—supposed breadwinner and taciturn, remote disciplinarian—and those actual men who saw their kids mainly in the evenings or on weekends and vacations. We went out and found men in all situations—fathers who spent a large part of their time with their children, fathers who had chosen or had been forced by economic necessity and social convention to spend less time with them than their mothers, and men who had no children.

We began by talking with people whom we knew as friends. They suggested others who might be interested in speaking with us, on or off the record. Not everybody whom we approached was interested, of course, but many—most—were, and they too made suggestions as to where we might turn next, both in terms of whom to talk to as well as what to talk about with them. The result was that the people we interviewed ranged from close friends to not quite total strangers, and the topics we discussed varied with each interview.

Most conventional social scientists might cock an eyebrow at our method of selecting "subjects." For example, the group of people we interviewed, while certainly diverse enough, could hardly be said to have been chosen at random. And while we had carefully worked out a standard set of questions to ask our interviewees, we didn't stick to it with any kind of scientific rigor, choosing instead to pursue what seemed to be the most intriguing strands of the conversation at the moment, and returning to the question list only when this seemed to help the conversation move along naturally. The extent to which both of us were active participants in the discussion, injecting our own personalities into the interviews, also went against the conventional rules for a project of this sort.

This methodological madness was, of course, not without its motives. We neither are nor have ever been conventional social scientists, and this was never meant to be a conventional book. We both felt strongly from the start that the conventional methods of lining up and checking out a random sample of the population would simply be inappropriate. Indeed we felt that one of the major reasons that there wasn't a book like this already available was that the conventional rules had made it impossible. Most people would not wish to talk about the sorts of things we wanted to discuss in detail in a conventional interview situation.

We wanted the men whom we interviewed to be as much at ease and as open as possible about things that were generally felt to be taboo for them to talk about, and we felt that previously established social ties, however tenuous, would help do the trick. These ties were also helpful in minimizing the constraints naturally imposed on the free flow of conversation by the knowledge that the interviews would be published. And our own emotional involvement was always on the line, which made it easier for everyone to speak more candidly than might otherwise have been possible. Not relying on a standard list of questions had, then, two related motivations. We felt that the conversations could be more freewheeling if they were not so constrained, and we wanted to minimize the distance between interviewers and interviewees that such a list invariably produces.

The people whom we interviewed ranged in age from their mid-twenties to their mid-sixties—from old enough to have started juggling the ideas of marriage, family, and career in earnest, to old enough to have reached the age of grandparenthood and retirement. As for their backgrounds, our interviewees came not only from different eras but also from different parts of the country and different social and economic classes (predominantly middle and working class). Some came from large families with many siblings and resident members of three generations, while others came from nuclear families of one, two, or three children. Most of the men were, or had been, married, and most had at least one child. Some had grandchildren. Some had jobs they liked, others weren't so sure, and some were unemployed. One was being held in prison on a murder conviction.

With the exception of the interview with Randy, which had to be managed through the mails because the prison authorities made it so difficult to see him, let alone interview him with a tape recorder, the interviews were conducted ·in a generally relaxed and open atmosphere, usually in somebody's living room. They were tape-recorded and later transcribed. We then edited out the interviewer's questions, the asides, false starts, interruptions, and dead ends, smoothing the transitions and otherwise leaving the interviewee to speak for himself freely. We eventually chose to have 14 interviews appear in the book. We settled on this number because of our conviction that a relatively modest number of thoroughgoing interviews would make a decidedly more substantial and significant book than would a larger number of shorter, and therefore less revealing, interviews. A book of 14 interviews, we felt, would give each speaker enough room to emerge as a distinct personality, someone with a reasonably coherent and well-integrated point of view—a real person, in short.

Real persons, it seemed to us, were scarcely to be found in the books and articles on men and their family lives that were beginning to appear in larger numbers when we originally undertook this project. Instead of being about people and their lives, most of these writings spoke primarily of mysterious concepts such as "role models," "role expectation reversals," and the like. Such publications either reinforced the old trivializing categories or concocted new ones equally trivializing. We felt that there was a definite need for the book we had decided to put together, one which would allow real people to speak for themselves about recognizably human frustrations and satisfactions.

We knew that the price we would pay for a book full of real people would be the loss of the neat clarity and consistency apparently achieved by the conventional expository format of the "fathering" literature. But this was a price we were quite willing—indeed, eager—to pay. We expected that our real people would sometimes be inconsistent, or inarticulate, when they struggled to express complicated thoughts or ambivalent feelings. We were not surprised when someone speaking to us by letter from solitary confinement in prison now and then forgot what he had been talking about at the end of his last letter when he came to write his next one. Nor did we consider it a weakness of those letters that they were written in a distinctive, onrushing style that violated the canons of literary prose. We decided to publish Randy's letters from prison pretty much as he wrote them, irregularities and all, in order to encourage readers to do more than simply "get Randy's point." We also wanted them to endure vicariously the conditions of prison life which give his ideas their compelling force and integrity.

The same principle guided our editing of the other chapters.

In preserving as much as we could of each man's characteristic speech patterns, and in including as much as we could of his total life context as he expressed it, we sought to present not disembodied intellectual positions but human beings making sense of their own lives. We hope that our readers will find both of the chief rewards of all reading about people and their lives: that of meeting the sympathetic stranger who lives and looks at the world the way the reader does, and that of being confronted with real and significant human differences, instead of empty stereotypes.

Ben

Ben is a teacher in his late thirties. He lives with his wife, Susannah, and their three daughters, Saundra, Erica, and Helen, aged eight, seven, and four.

Having serious discussions like this interview right now, what one inevitably does is begin to hear oneself making up all these things to say. It's just like sometimes when you find yourself in an argument, and all of a sudden you're hearing yourself—this great, flowing polemicist. A group session or an interview like this one is supposed to be something very emotional, and here you are sounding like somebody out of a soap opera, just doing the same thing, as if you were writing a script as you go along and just sort of falling in love with your own verbiage. Although what one says probably has some relationship to something, you are partly bending thought. But who knows? Maybe you even think some of the things you say you think.

Ben's Younger Days

My father died when I was in my late teens. He was not a

happy man. He liked me and so forth, but he was not any sort of disciplinarian, although, for some reason, I didn't seem to need discipline much. I was a very straight kid with some feeling of needing to succeed in certain ways, perhaps because my father was also not a strong person, not successful at all, and in fact drank too much. He was not the sort of father who creates a feeling of security.

It wasn't a particularly happy childhood. There was all kinds of warmth there, but still—there's a sense that all children get at a certain point, I'm sure, that their parents are somehow crucially inadequate or unacceptable socially, if not intellectually. In my case, I always felt that my father was a very smart man but that he had been crucially disappointed in the way he had handled things at a certain point. I still think that's true.

But there were a lot of positive things about him, and when I had my own children, I didn't at all think of him as a negative model. I remember once in my late teens coming home perfectly drunk, thinking, "This is really something I should not be doing," rolling on the floor and puking into the toilet, with my father standing by. He just said, "Can't hold it, huh?" and walked away. I thought that was a really good way to handle a situation like that. He knew the lesson was already there, no eloquence of his could possibly improve on it.

I had a brother five years younger than I. I'm sure he was as bright as I was, but he just had a feeling that whatever I had done—and of course it was always said that the things I did were done well—he would not or could not do. Not that he rebelliously refused to do certain things, but he had trouble in school. Finally he found something he could do—acting. It's a curious thing. He was someone who clearly had a feeling of not measuring up in comparison with me, yet he could project himself very confidently into the roles he played as an actor. Before I had my own children, he was my main source of ideas about what young kids are like. Our relationship was difficult. Whenever I would do things like help him with his schoolwork, it would always end up with my saying, "Don't be so simple, man," and his growling back at me resentfully.

I was never spanked as a child. My brother was, but I wasn't.

Of course, I was a really funny kid. I had all sorts of incredible depressions, sense of wrong, and I had this incredible conscience. I can't believe the kind of conscience I had as a kid. I remember doing something wrong once and just sort of being in utter misery until I confessed that I had done it. No one would ever have known. It wouldn't occur to me to do that today.

Having Kids

When I got married, I assumed that I would have children. That was not something that came as an extra idea. It was the sort of thing I was getting myself into, I assumed, just because that's life. We did natural childbirth with all three kids, so I was in the delivery room every time. It was very nice, partly because Susannah had no trouble delivering babies. The main hassles were with the hospital and the nurses and the doctors, whether they were going to demand that you do something silly, like take an enema. We didn't go to natural childbirth classes with our first child because Susannah didn't have time. She read a book about how to have a baby, one with great pictures of women in 1940s underwear doing exercises. I think Susannah was still reading it in the labor room. It's a very funny book, written in an extremely rapturous style. I had a hard time getting it out of the university library because it was in the sociology library, in the locked case.

We had our first child, Saundra, about a year and a half after we were married—sooner than we had planned. Susannah's gynecologist said she had an ovarian cyst and that it would be best for her to have a baby as soon as possible if she wanted to have children. Another gynecologist later told us that this was a highly unlikely diagnosis, especially since it was made only on the basis of a routine examination. He said the earlier guy was probably trying to drum up business. In any case, Saundra came along while I was a graduate student and Susannah was finishing up her undergraduate work at the same school. In fact, she was born a few days before Susannah's last final exam. The exam was in a required course, American Institutions—you had to get a noncredit B in it to graduate—which Susannah had never gone to. So she bought the notes for the course and I summarized them for her the hour before the exam.

There was a fair amount of excitement involved with having the baby. Having a first child is not the sort of coolheaded decision one is apt to make about having a third child, which may be insane anyway. The first child is such an unknown. It's like getting an automobile when you've never had one before—you wonder how it will change your life. Of course, we hadn't been married long enough to really need another change of life right at that point. Although the truth is that getting married doesn't change your life that much, but having a child does. There's something more nearly irrevocable about it.

Shortly after Saundra was born, we moved across the country to where my first teaching job was—a job I still have, as a matter of fact—and then a few months later we discovered that the second child was on the way. Erica was not planned; it was just faulty methods of contraception. We had a lot of talk about how we were going to handle it and whether it was going to be good having two children close together. They would be just 16 months apart. We said, "Oh, yes, they'll be great friends," or "It'll be just horrible having two children in diapers," and so forth. We had to move because of Erica. The apartment we were in wouldn't have been large enough.

We never considered not having the child. By that time, Susannah had decided she was going to have more than one child anyway, and that was OK with me. We thought, looking on the bright side, "Well, why not now rather than later? We'll get them all out of the way at once." We also figured it was better from the kids' point of view to have more than one. We were both from families with two children, and we had a sense that to complete your experience you've got to have a sibling. Otherwise, you'll grow up seriously disturbed.

Of course, getting both a brother and a sister turned out to be hard since we ended up with three girls. The third child was more of a decision than the other two, and part of it was the idea that we would have a boy. We got a book on how to have boys and pursued its advice to the letter—you abstain and wait around for all the circumstances to be propitious, and then you rush upstairs. We had to rush upstairs once when my mother and grandmother were staying with us and we were having dinner. We made some incredibly feeble excuse about a sudden illness which lasted half an hour.

I felt the need of a third child a lot less than Susannah did. Susannah found that she really liked children, liked having them around, liked them as babies, and was faced with the idea, "Either I have a third child now, or I don't have any more children." And for her, I think, the prospect of not having any more children was a sad one. All the experiences with the births and with the young children had always been very pleasant for her, despite all the crap of sleepless nights and so forth. And I guess the decision was finally just that she wanted another child much, much more than I didn't want another child. I can't say positively that, all other things being equal, I would have said, "Yes, let's have another child." I probably would not have.

The question of having a boy was not paramount. It was part of the argument, but there was always the possibility that it would be a girl. I'd think to myself, "Chances are if you've had two girls, you'll probably have three. But if you're trying to have a boy, as we are, then your third girl will be a genius, because the sperm has to survive an incredible series of obstacles." I had a moment of shock when I first saw the baby, Helen, in the delivery room, a slight feeling of "failed again." But it didn't last long. Despite my theory of "everyone needs one of everything," I don't feel that my life is diminished by not having a son.

If I were to sit down and work out an ethic at this point, I think I would say, "Yes, I certainly would get married; yes, I certainly would have children." But someone whose oldest child is only eight really isn't the final word on that, I think. You should really talk to some people with children that are grown up, simply because after they are out of the house and gone, people sometimes ask themselves, "Have we sort of falsely filled our lives with these children? Now we're left to rattle around and wonder what the hell we're doing." Of course, this is perhaps more a problem with women than with men, for obvious reasons. Thinking that way is tricky, though, because you're partly wishing your kids out of existence, and there they are. It's a question of what you allow yourself to think.

The Kids

I'm not very analytical about what the kids are like, partly perhaps because I don't have a clear sense of what *I'm* like. On a lot of kid-related issues, I'm all in favor of not rocking the boat. It doesn't occur to me to worry about things like how the kids are doing in school, so I don't worry about them, the same way it didn't occur to me to worry about having children at all until I had some.

Saundra's not a terribly aggressive girl, I discover, although she seems that way at home; she's more aggressive at home than she is outside, apparently. Still, she's the oldest and most combative, and I'm perhaps instinctively more guarded with her than with the others. But that's great fun, to break down the guard at times when she'd quite clearly love to do something with me and "have a hug." But if she's dissatisfied, she's the one who's most apt to come right out and say so.

I sense the middle child is physically somewhat different, softer than the other two, and I think somewhat more insecure— wants, needs to be liked by more people. When we were in England, for instance, Erica was up in her room practicing how to sound like an Englishman. Right away, you know, she'd spend hours saying "Wawtah, wawtah." And she's apt to be very demonstrative with adults when they come. When a baby-sitter comes, Erica will always go out of the way to show she's glad to see the person. She wants to be liked by her teachers, and the way she gets them to like her is by showing that she likes them. She's so eager to be loved and approved of that you—you don't stand off, but you sometimes say, "OK, that's enough."

Helen is enough younger that she gets more leeway. She is not treated as being as reasonable as the others, or potentially as reasonable. That's a good deal, though now that she's toilet trained she's starting to become quirky in other ways. She's very cute and funny to watch because she's young and she's just saying things that are funny, the kinds of things you can tell people about and feel they will be amused. Like yesterday, we were going up on the sand dunes not far from here. They're very high and open, with a huge cliff. We climbed up there, and Helen looked around and said, "I want to go someplace smaller."

When people see the children in public—at other people's houses or whatever—they tend to say that our children are well behaved. They don't strike us as particularly well behaved at home, which doesn't bother me, really, except for its annoyance value. Quite the contrary, I think I'd be worried about them more if they were sort of sheepish and went around being too good.

Of course, with three of them there are constant squabbles. Somebody gets something, and there has to be a sense that everything has been doled out equally. The complaint is always, "Saundra always gets this," or, "Erica always gets this," or, "You do this with Erica, and you don't do it with me." Saundra and Erica occasionally complain that Helen gets away with a lot more than they do. Erica was lecturing us on it the other day, that we shouldn't let Helen get away with so much because she was going to get spoiled. It wasn't good for children to say yes to them too many times.

We don't have any evidence of serious animosity between any of them. The two older ones are generally very good with Helen, very interested in her. They're very conscientious about keeping track of her, washing her off, reporting if anything's wrong with her. And they don't do it because we've asked them to do it. They're quite solicitous, and at this point in their lives they're quite willing to have Helen sort of run around with them—three steps behind. That may change in a year or so, as Helen gets older, but for now they're quite tolerant of Helen's eagerness always to do what they're doing.

When does a child become a person? It's very funny—do you answer that by saying that a child never becomes a person until it ceases to be a child? To some extent, that's true, because as long as you have a sense of him or her as a child, he or she is never completely independent, and that always colors your sense of who they are. On the other hand, from the beginning here is this person there, squalling and shitting in his pants, who's got to be dealt with. And you think, "This is not me over there; this is somebody I can afford to get pissed off at." I suppose a clear point would be when a child can talk, is clearly making up things and has some kind of sense of its own mind, is saying things to you that you have not said to it. That quickly turns into sort of—politics.

I guess the stage of child development I've gotten the biggest kick out of is the point at which children are just beginning to sort of ape human beings and they're sort of cute. Helen's just getting to the end of that period where it's really fun to watch what she does. Except for the diaper problem, kids are a lot of fun from about the age of nine months to three years. I guess I do feel it's sort of a loss when they stop being cute and they start growing up, start being independent in one way or another.

Saundra has become very sort of guarded about many of the things that she does. She was telling me the other day that she wouldn't take her shirt off when she was hot because that was being a hippie. I asked, "What is a hippie?" She wasn't quite sure, but she did not want to be one. It's interesting about sex roles, too. I don't really all that often think of them as girls. Of course, I sometimes think of them as girls and I enjoy the fact that they're pretty little girls, and that sort of thing. I say things to them like, "You don't have to be a nurse, you can be a doctor," and it's very surprising how they have a sense of role that comes from the woodwork or somewhere. I mean, I ask, "Why can't you be a doctor?" and the answer comes back, "Well, I don't know. Men are doctors. Women aren't doctors." They never saw a woman doctor, as it turns out. I think children are often dogmatic in their feelings about how they should and should not fit in. Of course, it all changes with a great thunderclap, I suppose—at least, the dogmatism may turn around. They become dogmatic about other roles that they're required to play. So far, Saundra and Erica have both said that they wanted to be like Mommy. They want to get married and have children. Saundra has recently suggested that maybe she was not going to get married. She thought of staying with us.

As for me, I would like to see the girls learn to play musical instruments very soon so we can have a band. Susannah took up the recorder seriously a couple of years ago, and I began playing harpsichord last year. I'd always played piano a little bit. The girls used to come and interrupt us, and we came down very hard on them about that. We said, "At least you have to wait until the movement is over." So now they come down and breathe down your back until the movement's over. If we're playing and Helen really wants something, she tends to start walking around Susannah in a circle, which makes it harder to concentrate on the music. But this is changing. Erica is keen as the devil on playing the cello because I told her that's a great thing for her to play—it's just what we need. Certainly something the family might conceivably do together besides watch television is play music. But by the time the kids are old enough to play very well, they'll probably want to cut themselves off from what we're doing.

Otherwise, I don't have any specific designs on their futures. My assumption is that if they're bright, they ought to do something with their brains. And I suppose there are certain things that would disappoint me. I mean, if they became stars of porno movies, for example, I would find that upsetting. Or if they married people I thought were real schmucks, I would find that hard to handle, although I probably wouldn't say anything openly or directly about a son-in-law. I don't feel any jealousy about my children's affections for other people, although this may come later, when I'm forced to share my daughter's affections with a pimply-faced freak.

I do have a lot of anxieties about being the parent of adolescent girls. The idea of having a teenaged child at all is sort of horrifying, and to have three in the house at once, all girls—the mind boggles. I find myself being fairly reactionary in my protective instincts towards my children, mainly, I guess, because they're girls and I'm scared of what'll happen with them sexually. I've joked about that sort of thing since Saundra was two or three, and I hope I'll continue to joke about it. One jokes about the things one is secretly ill at ease with. I tell myself I'm more worried about the other sort of irreversible dangers of adolescence that are around today, like drugs and so forth.

Another part of it is that larger children can be so boorish and rude. I see this in part just from looking at my students. Many of them are the sort of people that I wouldn't want in my house. I mean, it strikes me that the adolescence of one's children may be the next great stumbling block, suddenly to have kids that overnight are becoming people in the most annoying sense of the word, and there they are in your house!

I've had adolescent baby-sitters that have lived with us for a week in the summer a couple of times, and I found it very distressing to have them around. There seemed to be nothing wrong with them, and they were taking care of the kids and everything, but they spent so much time sort of sitting around and looking sad. There was some kind of great grayness that had settled on them. I found myself trying to cheer these people up!

Of course, my kids may turn out to be absolutely charming. But that's another challenge. If they're very charming, I'll want to be friends with them all the time, and I may find out that they don't like me. I know lots of people who are charming and witty and beautiful and don't like their parents.

Being Parents

I think our assumption is always that the children are shared, but my tendency is to defer to Susannah's wishes in most matters concerning the children. I think her wishes are usually reasonable. I don't always agree with them, but Susannah's not an unreasonable person, and most often I can certainly see why she wants one thing as opposed to another.

I think in every family there's got to be one parent who's slightly overprotective and one parent who's slightly "underprotective." It doesn't necessarily have to be split up between the mother being overprotective and the father being the other way—I know a family which is just the opposite. But in our family it tends to be Susannah asking, "Does this child feel feverish?" and my saying no. I put my hands to the forehead and feel it's not. That's just sort of an accepted convention. There's always one pull in the direction of rushing off to the hospital and another saying, "No; just let the child alone; it'll be OK." And what often happens is that we delay rushing off to the hospital, and then when we finally take the child to the doctor, it's about well. I come back saying, "Well, that was a waste of time." In another area, Susannah's very particular about what the children eat. I would not be so particular. But she's particular about what she eats, too, and I'm not very particular about what I eat.

We handle discipline differently, too. I spank the kids now and then. I have on occasion just sort of, you know, bang! and the kid has really felt it. And Susannah's been mad at me about that. I never felt that I struck any of the kids without justification, but sometimes I have felt that I should not have struck the child as hard as I did, although I've never bruised one of them or anything like that.

The idea of hitting children is a horrible notion, certainly, for lots of people, but it doesn't strike me as being particularly worse than other kinds of discipline. It usually just amounts to a slap on the bottom or something, which has a kind of symbolic value if nothing else. You don't have to hit a child hard if you want to insist that this is where the buck stops. That's the only thing that Susannah has openly complained about to me—"You shouldn't be so violent." I think that probably is a failing on my part, that I should be so ready to lay on where there's no threat of retaliation. I don't go around hitting my colleagues.

It seems sort of a natural thing to do, spanking. I say to the kid, "Look, please do this," or, "Don't do this." The kid does it, and I say, "If you do that any more, I'll hit you." I make it perfectly clear, and then when the kid does it again, what do you have to do? You have to hit her. Susannah rarely strikes the kids, but she's often quite strict with them. She scolds them, yells at them, takes things away from them, requires that they go to their room, things like that.

I have sort of relegated the job of finding people to sit for the children to Susannah, and I think she resents that to a certain extent. We belong to a baby-sitting pool—the families who belong to it sit for each other—and it's become more or less a pool convention that the women do the calling up. I can see why she resents this, because the reason I don't do this is that I find it an absolute pain in the ass to call somebody up to ask them to baby-sit, or to call anybody up for any reason, for that matter. I don't really believe in innate sex roles, but sometimes, as in the responsibility for baby-sitting, I'll lapse into a male chauvinist attitude for my own convenience. I tend to do more of the actual sitting than Susannah does, though, because I can usually get some work done while sitting. If it's a question of sitting for a very young child, Susannah will usually do it. I would rather she dealt with that, and she seems more willing to than I am. That sort of situation does not put her off particularly.

It's the same way with the kids' school. Susannah has some idea that the worst thing that could possibly happen in school is that you might learn something. I'm not sure where she gets this idea. What she means is that schools should not put pressure on children—at least not at an early age—to achieve in some sort of dazzling way. But I think she goes to extremes. It's quite true that the things you learn in school are 90 percent things that you forget, but the idea that you are learning something seems to me important. There ought to be courses with substance for children. If they learn to read, they are learning something; if they learn math, they're learning something; if they learn a language, they're learning something. So much of what they get taught in school seems to be without a subject. There's no *thing* out there, just a kind of waffling around. I suppose they're learning how to learn things—at least, I'm sure that's what Susannah thinks is more important. In any case, Susannah has paid more attention to what kinds of teachers the kids get and whatnot than I have. She tends to think I'm utterly indifferent to anything that's happening to my children at school. And it's true I don't go to PTA meetings, and I tend not to go to interviews with the teacher about the child. Somebody has to go, so Susannah goes. I don't know why; I guess I just assume that as long as the kids are not complaining in obvious ways, they're doing all right.

Occasionally we're played off against each other by the children. Mommy says no, and they come down and ask me, or vice versa. If it's a clear case of a child obviously knowing what she's up to—even if I had said yes when the child came down or Susannah had said yes after I had said no—we just say, "Well, look, you shouldn't have asked the second parent after the other said no. You can't do it. You don't get a second opinion." Of course, they do get a second opinion sometimes. Sometimes there are obvious examples of two opinions that they can see being arbitrated, and they just wait to see how it turns out. And I think by and large it turns out to be what Susannah says more than what I say.

Having children puts a premium on being alone with your spouse, which is something that gets to be hard to do and something which you have to work at. We were traveling in Europe with three children for a month last year, and the kinds of pleasures we could seek out were clearly very limited. For instance, no nightlife to speak of. We'd run ourselves ragged during the day, so we'd go to bed at nine o'clock anyway. When we were thinking of going, I had a vision of its being a total horror, which it might have been if the children had gotten sick, for instance.

It's hard for me to imagine what our marriage would be like without children, since we were married for such a short time before we had our first. We have great affection for the place we went to school, and I think we've idealized it partly because it represents to us the childless state. You know those two pieces of folklore about the effect of children on marriage—that they put a strain on the marriage or that they cement the marriage— they're probably both true of all marriages in different proportions. They're both true of our marriage.

Living and Working

At one point, we considered a sort of communal living arrangement with another family. The idea was that it would be nice for the children to have a number of adults and other children to relate to. But we never did it, and perhaps it's just as well. I'm not a great proselytizer for suburban living, but in the neighborhood we're in there are a number of adults around with children, and our kids certainly know these adults and spend a lot of time at their houses. The adults just treat them in that sort of extended-family sense, without the enforced intimacy of always being in the same house.

For instance, one of the neighbors' kids, a little boy, stays at our house every morning for half an hour or 40 minutes because his parents have to go off to work before it's time for him to go to school. His parents sit for us one afternoon a week in recompense. I think probably we are closer to this little boy than to any other child besides our own. He's like one of the family, and he seems to like us a lot. Occasionally he becomes oddly demonstrative about it, will come up to Susannah or me, give a kiss, and say he loves us. He feels that way about us because he's around us a lot and we treat him like one of our own children, which includes scolding him when he does something we don't like. He's a pretty good kid. I sometimes think he's the noisiest kid in the world—he seems to be unable to keep it down—but he's good natured.

I think it would be a real problem to live in a neighborhood where there weren't any other children of the same age. That's a really necessary thing from the age of five or seven—that a kid's able to get out of the house and meet the gang. A friend of mine was telling me about how he really disliked this one suburban neighborhood he lived in when he was a kid. He'd moved there from someplace else, and in his old neighborhood he'd had all these kids to play with. All his memories of that old neighborhood were of being outdoors. At the new place, he took his little wagon out the first day and "there never was anyone." It wasn't a neighborhood where there were any kids.

I would venture to say that I am around the house more than most fathers that work in more ordinary ways. Since I'm a college teacher, I don't go to work nine to five, five days a week, and when I am working at home I can be, and usually am from time to time, called upon to do something with the children. I was involved in the everyday stuff from the beginning. Susannah nursed the babies at first, but I also fed them. And as far as cleaning them up went, I certainly did my fair share of that. I've been a good father in that sense.

I suppose the time I get to spend with my kids is conditioned to a large extent by my job. Even if it weren't, I think I probably would not want to be with my children all the time. I would want to be able to have free blocks of time in which I was not responsible for the children, as does anyone. Susannah certainly does, too. If you have any kind of family, children or not, there are always conflicting demands between your job and your family life. Even before we had children, there was studying. You were always doing certain things that had no particular connection with your mate, things that could, if one were in the right frame of mind, be set up as a force opposed to your marriage. You were doing this instead of sharing something with the person you were married to—in other words, you were doing something independently. All the romance magazines suggest that one's idea of marriage is sharing, but there are certain things that are shared and certain things that aren't.

Susannah tends to feel it more quickly than I do when my job is interfering with our family life. One's idea is that you are being paid to do something, that this is your job, and, in fact, that some of what you're doing you like. Your spouse will not be entirely sympathetic to all this. I have on occasion had to sort of cry, "Work! You don't realize how hard I work!" It's a load of shit, of course. Everyone thinks of how hard they work, who works the hardest, and the truth is usually that it's six of one and a half-dozen of the other.

From time to time I do think of my job as relief from the children, particularly in the summer when I'm doing my own work and not having to teach a class every day or so. Then I like to go off and just sort of fuck around in the library, not really doing anything except wasting time. I mean, one feels a certain pleasure in being alone, apart from anyone, for a certain amount of time, and this again is something that has to be worked into the idea of a family. However, I don't put an absolute premium on my work, and I have a sense that time spent with my family is not time lost.

I don't think my family has caused me to be less compulsive about my career. In fact, if anything, getting married sort of jolted my ass out of graduate school. I'd been hanging around for six years or something, and you know, just like the storybook says, it made me grow up and say to myself, "I gotta do something now; now or never." I felt I had committed myself to some kind of forward progress in life, that I was no longer just a bachelor and graduate student ad infinitum.

Still, I don't have any sense of having pursued my career with any kind of miraculous energy. I did take a little time a couple of summers and redo my dissertation, which did get published by hook or crook, and then they gave me tenure. That's about all, you know. I felt worried about not getting tenure, partly because of having a family. But it wasn't that the family was really making me do anything differently than I would have done anyway. I wasn't churning out an article a month or something. You know, I was spending time with my family.

A Family Man

It doesn't usually occur to me to measure my performance as a father in various parent-child situations. I have, on occasion, said to myself, "Well, you know, I almost blew my top then, but I didn't. It's probably just as well." Or, "I must be in a particularly good mood this morning, because on some mornings that would have sent me through the ceiling."

The only time I can think of that it occurred to me that I was being a good something in relation to a child was once when I was baby-sitting for a boy who must have been about four. I'd never sat there before, and when I got there the kid wasn't in bed yet. His mother was sort of solicitous and sort of eked her way out the door, then kept coming back to assure me that everything would be all right. I said to myself, "Woman, get out of here and leave me with this!" She finally left, and the kid started doing something annoying, obviously in order to see what I would do. He already had his pajamas on, but he said he was going outside. I said he couldn't, so he didn't and went over in the corner and sulked. I wondered, "Now what'll happen?" But I went over and started kidding him, or said something. I don't know what the hell I said, but it seemed to be the right thing. He was going to clam up at having been disciplined, but was willing to have some transition made back into a friendly relationship—and it actually worked. I remember at that point thinking, "Gee, I must not be entirely unacquainted with children."

As a teacher, I consciously play a role and measure my

performance, but as a parent I don't. With the students I do two things which are absolutely inconsistent with each other. One is that I'm ultimately forced to present myself as someone who knows a great deal more than the students do. I make myself an authority. But at the same time I also very frequently pretend I don't know things that I do know, so that the assumptions they have about my authority won't completely stifle any kind of conversation—although that sometimes backfires. With my children, on the other hand, I don't make myself an authority; I sort of feel that I *am* authority. There's no conscious role playing involved in my being a father. I mean, I don't feel that as a role that I have to get up for an occasion.

Anyway, there's always a problem teaching people that you have any kind of emotional connection with—teaching your wife or your girlfriend or your kids. You immediately get into this thing where your "pupil" feels you're continually trying to torture her in some devious way. I've read with the girls a little bit, but not much, because it quickly became clear that they found me oppressive. The kids have trouble sounding out words, and when I'd be reading with Erica, my tendency would be to make her work as hard as she possibly could to get the word. After about ten minutes of reading with me, she'd say, "That's enough."

Images of the "ideal father" have, I would imagine, mostly negative characteristics—that is, a good father does not do the following things. I suppose mainly the good father is not a tyrant. However, one discovers very soon that the occasions and the inducements to tyranny are many. I find that children are very strong in their likes and dislikes, and right from the first it's clear that they're able to reduce you to their level of emotion about certain issues. Being bigger, stronger, louder, and so forth, one's response is to become tyrannical. I suppose a very even-tempered, saintly person could be repressing this response—indeed, perhaps he wouldn't even have it—but that's not me exactly. I think perhaps it's a mistake totally to repress what your actual response is, though that may just be rationalization. Since I can't do it, I'm saying that it's all right to shout or even strike a child from time to time, in some modified form.

These situations usually develop when the child insists on wanting something that you don't want her to have, or the child insists on doing something that you have told her constantly not to do. As I said earlier, more than occasionally I have felt, after behaving "tyrannically," that I have overreacted. The way the girls have responded has changed as they've grown up. They tend to cry, Saundra less easily than Erica. Erica tends to dissolve more, whereas Saundra, now at the age of eight, maintains a sort of hostility over half an hour or so that she cannot be talked out of. If you make initial gestures of shame and repentance to Erica, she's willing to accept your apologies.

When children are not rational, there's a tendency, I think, to impel you as the parent into that irrationality. I mean, I can quite understand people who are habitual child beaters—though I am not one, I'm happy to say. There's a real person there, a person about whom you have certain assumptions: i.e., you are the father, you are the master, they are the slaves, in a way—though, on the other side, they're the beloved objects, too. I think it's true of male fears of women, also, that when the beloved object seems to assert its independence in some way, your sense of self is crucially diminished and you get quite peculiarly wrathful about it. You're beloved on certain terms. That sounds terrible, but I think all relationships have their norms, which create security. In a way, you know, the tensions are normal, too. They perhaps exist for some reason.

One should not be absolutely permissive with a child; the child doesn't seem to want that. Although I must admit that we are rather permissive with our children. One thing that's often said about being a good parent is that you have to be absolutely consistent. Well, anyone who thinks he can be absolutely consistent in his behavior toward another human being is just crazy. You can't be consistent. The children realize that you are not consistent, so they seize upon your inconsistencies as a sign that you can be bargained with, which, in fact, you can. I think that's a fair thing for children to be doing, although it annoys the hell out of one. No does not mean no, absolutely, until no is up to the tenth power and is accompanied with a whip being brandished. And even then the kids may think to themselves, "Perhaps we can get the whipping and end up with what we want anyway."

One of the frightening things about being a parent is that one really doesn't know what's bothering children. They don't really tell you anything, and one can't be sure there isn't some sort of deep-seated feeling behind some kinds of behavior. The children don't have tantrums very often any more, but there was a period some years ago when Saundra was starting off every morning with the same fight about what she was going to wear. Nothing would work. One tends to make threats in a situation like that, but it's not a good idea to keep them, because they're made in the heat of the moment. They imply long-term punishments, which is also not such a hot idea. It's better to have a fight that flares up and then cools down than to have Daddy going around all day saying, "I'm really pissed off at you," and, "Don't talk to me," and that sort of thing. That's for the child to do, after all. If you set up a jail, you have to be the jailer. It's terrible to have a good feeling about a child and not to be able to express it because you have said three hours ago, "You are in the dungeon. You are not allowed to approach the august presence." When all is said and done, the children are not afraid of me—they are not afraid of anybody in the family. They're not afraid to argue, particularly Saundra.

I tend to kid the girls a lot, a lot more than I discipline them or get angry with them. It occurred to me that often when I'm kidding them, they don't understand that it's a joke, although as they grow older they seem to enjoy it more. It's a way of keeping your own sanity from time to time. I mean, you have a lot of jokes at the expense of the child, and if the child doesn't understand, I suppose it isn't hurting her. Nothing pleases kids more than to think they have made us laugh with a joke. Susannah was pointing that out to me the other day. I think that probably comes from the social sense that what one does in a sort of harmonious situation is make some fun. That's the only way to keep people sane, I think, although it has that double edge that somebody's always being made a joke of. I think one has to do that from time to time with people you're living in close contact with. The hardest person to live with is the humorless one.

One thing I've done with the kids a couple of times is pretend to cry in response to their crying. I've always wondered whether that was a bad thing or a good thing. The first time I ever did it, there was utter shock with each kid. They would be crying and bawling, and I would pretend to cry. I don't know whether they think to this day that Daddy is someone who cries. They either go along with the gag, or they get mad and say, "No! No!" or they just stop crying in utter disbelief. What you're assuming when you do something like that, I suppose, is that they can see when there's a parody of their behavior going on.

I think when you're teasing someone, what you're doing is taking things that are sources of tension and trying to convert them into a sort of social harmony. But there's always the danger that the person just doesn't feel like treating that particular thing at that particular moment in that particular way. It's some kind of comic accommodation that we make.

It never occurred to me that I was getting points from anybody else for being a father. I have felt like a father from time to time when I've been in public dragging three kids around. Someone's looking at me and saying, "That man is the father of those children." It depends on the situation. When we were in Europe, I was dragging a port-a-crib and luggage and three kids, and I was thinking, "People are looking at me and saying, 'That man is a crazy person, an absolute fool.'" That's exactly what I recall doing when I was in Europe on my own and I'd see somebody dragging his family around. "Why he must be out of his mind!" But on the other hand, you know, I'll be going for a walk with Saundra or Erica or somebody, we'll be walking along holding hands, and I'll feel like I would if I were out with a pretty girl. I'll imagine people saying, "That man's got a nice-looking daughter."

I think it's important that you like your children, that they feel you find them important to have around, at least sometimes, and that they feel you like to talk to them sometimes, or touch them. Our kids have a great sense of Daddy and Mommy being busy doing other things which they're not supposed to interrupt. On the other hand, I don't think that they feel cut off from our lives. They sort of take us for granted, and around, and sooner or later available. From my side, I think having children has been fairly positive for me. They're part of my life, certainly a positive part of my life, although I don't go around thinking to myself how great it is to be a parent. Nevertheless, when I see them, I'm more apt to feel good about them than to think, "Jesus, not *you* again!"

When I didn't have a family, I used to spend all my time either absolutely, unashamedly goofing off, or working. Now there's this sort of no-man's-land where you are "living" with your family. It's sort of deceptive—you don't notice it—but there suddenly is this other thing. There's not work/play any more; there's life. When you leave your first family, where you're the son, you really do get sort of pushed out into the world where you have plenty of time to do whatever you want to. Even before you're pushed out, everything's done for you and your time's pretty much your own. It certainly is in college. And then you really become radically socialized the minute you take on a family with children in which very different kinds of demands are made on your time. That's what "life" is, but apparently many, many men don't accept this sort of socialization as an inevitability. I don't think I quite fall into that category, although I'm sure I fall into it more than Susannah would wish I did.

I haven't yet stayed awake nights worrying about the future. It's a weird thing—I've gotten away so far sort of not pushing myself too hard, sort of taking things as they come. Nothing's gone terribly wrong for me yet that I can remember, at least not in a long, long time. I don't even know if I could deal with a real crisis. I graduated from high school, and I graduated from college, and I got a job, and the things I was working on did get published, and I did get tenure, and my kids were all born, and they were all healthy, and my wife and I still get on. When you turn 40, everything surely must fall apart.

Sid

Sid pursued a career in show business for a few years after World War II. He is now his own boss—a partner in an office furniture supply business. At 56 he has been married for 26 years. He and his wife have no children.

Childhood

My father came from Russia when he was five or six years old—my mother was American-born. I was born in 1922, the youngest of four children, and I grew up in the largest neighborhood of the city. My father was a musician, a drummer. I don't think he was ever educated in musicianship, but I found out later he was one of the best musicians around here—he played the timpani, xylophone, anything to do with the percussion part of life. During the 20s, he actually had his own jazz orchestra, and it was very popular. But when the Depression came, musicians were one of the first things that were cut out—orchestras went from ten guys to six or from 20 guys to 16—and eventually my father was out of work. He got into the music part of the

WPA program and did small gigs for several years, and then during the war, he joined up with Frankie Green and His Oldtimers and played drum with them for about 25 years, until he retired.

My dad was very punctual. In the drumming business, you have to keep the beat, and, my God, that was exactly the way my father was! He would get up every morning around 7 or 8 o'clock, have breakfast—of course, by that time I had gone off to school—and go down to the Musicians' Union, where he would sit around and play pinochle or gin rummy or pool while he was waiting for a job to come in—I used to shine shoes there at the union hall sometimes. If he got a job, he'd be working from 8 in the evening until 1 in the morning, so he wouldn't get home until 2. But he'd still get up the next morning at 7 or 8. He kept up this routine even after he got on with Frankie Green, up every day and down to the union. He didn't get into drinking and drugs and really irregular hours, like some musicians. He was just very dedicated to music.

We all grew up with music and show business in our background, and my sister became a professional dancer. My oldest brother got killed in World War II, but my other brother Joey did some entertaining on the side—he had a hillbilly singing and guitar act, and he played the dollar joints around here for awhile. But neither my father nor my mother acted like those backstage mothers you hear about. They didn't push us into show business—in fact, after we were grown, Joey once said to me that they didn't do enough to get us started in show business. Joey and I aren't close at all, and I certainly don't agree with that. When we were seven or eight years old, Joey and I did appear on this sort of community auditions radio program. We had this little routine of imitations—I used to do the low voices like Bing Crosby or whoever, and Joey would do the high stuff, Kate Smith or Morton Downing. The emcee, Uncle John or Uncle Eddie, whatever his name was, liked us so much he had us on every Saturday.

My dad was a good father. He was very strict about coming to supper on time, sitting at the table and eating the right way and everything like that, but he wasn't mean—he certainly didn't slap me around or anything like that. He didn't bug me. He used to bring us presents, and on Sundays, which was his one day off, he would take us to a football or baseball game or to the park.

My mother was great, a real nice person. The first emotional shock of my life was her dying, which happened when I was a young man. She was very sick with cancer for about nine months before she died, and that sort of took the life out of me. She wasn't educated as far as college was concerned—we didn't think of college back in those days—but she was very bright, very knowledgeable about music, for example, even though she'd never played anything herself. And she was an easy person to talk to. You could sit and talk to her on a one-to-one level, even tell dirty jokes in front of her—we were that kind of family. Part of the reason for this was that we were a very young family. My mother was married when she was 16, and she was a grandmother when she was 33. There wasn't that much age difference among us, all the way through the whole family, and that made it easier for us to get along with each other and talk to each other.

There were some things about my childhood that I didn't realize at the time. I didn't realize how much my parents were struggling to support us, especially during the Depression. When Fran and I started going with each other, I used to drive her crazy, because every time we were driving around anywhere, I would always be pointing out places and saying, "I used to live there." "I used to go to school there." We lived so many different places when I was a kid because we always had to be skipping out on the rent. It was like a dream—they'd wake us kids up at 2 o'clock in the morning, there would be a van parked in front of the house, they'd put us in the car and drive away somewhere. And I never realized—my folks were poor, and I didn't know it. All I knew was that we had clothes to wear and food on the table—chicken soup three times a week. Sometimes they had to tell us we couldn't have a lollipop or another pair of shoes, but I don't think that made much of an impression on me—although maybe it kept us from being like those kids you see today in the stores, screaming at the top of their lungs, "Oh, I want that, Mommy!"

Another thing I found out about only later was some of the tensions in the family. My mother opened up to me a few times after I was grown up and told me she didn't like it at all, the crazy hours my father had to keep. And after she died, I found out that my father was tough to communicate with and a little bit selfish. He had no car, so he used to get me to drive him to his jobs and come back and pick him up when the jobs were over. But a union musician gets extra money for transportation, so he was taking advantage of me. I finally told him I wouldn't drive him around any more. I think my oldest brother, the one that got killed in the service, had a couple of big run-ins with my father—I wasn't really aware of how serious it was, but I do remember being upstairs in the bedroom and hearing the yelling—I think my father thought he was hanging around with the wrong crowd. I think both he and my sister thought my father was too demanding, because they both left home very early in life, when they were 16 or 17. But like I said before, I wasn't really aware of this stuff at the time, and I wasn't antagonistic towards my dad like my brothers and sister were. Maybe he treated me better because I was the baby of the family, sort of the favorite. Or maybe he was just too exhausted from the other three.

Starting Out

I went in the service when I was 19. I was a "Flying Crew Chief"—that's someone who takes care of the airplane while it's in flight. But I was stationed stateside, because I was mostly supposed to be a teacher, teaching other people how to do this job. I had this bug about show business then, so during my free hours, I was in the special services—they used to have shows every week for the servicemen, and I had a little comedy act. Then when I got out of the service, I went to dramatic school in New York. Fortunately, I had an uncle in the restaurant business there. He let me sleep upstairs and threw me a few bucks to keep me going, and, when I wasn't in school, I helped out in his restaurant. It was probably a bad time to break into show business then, right after the war. There were very, very few plays on Broadway, radio wasn't that popular, and television hadn't come yet, so your chances of getting a job were very, very bad.

I did meet a fellow from around here at school, and he and I put an act together, a Martin and Lewis kind of thing—I was Lewis and he was the straight man, Martin. We stole most of our material—most comedians do—took a little bit from this guy and a little bit from that guy and staged it all our own way. I guess the biggest influence on me at the time was Danny Kaye. I can be a little conceited about this, but I had an amazing memory. I could go to a show and see Danny Kaye or Milton Berle or any comedian and get the act down verbatim. But because there were hardly any jobs around, our act didn't work out, and I finally got out of show business. I do have some regrets about it—I'm still a frustrated actor really—but I lost my feeling for it . . . not so much my feeling, but once you're knocked down a few times, you're afraid to go back again. You know, "Hey kid, call me in a couple of years," or, "Don't call me, I'll call you." So I gave it up, except for amateur stuff. If one of our local temples or synagogues was doing a show, I would help them out, but that was about it.

I moved back here from New York and went to work in a supermarket. I'd worked in this place before the war, doing pushcart stuff—taking orders from the customers and then delivering the stuff later on at night. Now they put me to work as a cashier, but after a month or two, one of the company big shots offered me a job as a manager of the dairy and frozen food department in one of their other stores. The money wasn't that much different—$37.50 a week—but it was a big promotion, and I took it.

I met Fran while I was working for the supermarket. I used to work Friday nights. After work, some friends and I would go bowling, and then we'd go to this big delicatessen in my neighborhood for a cup of coffee. It was a big community place, very famous—the local politicians used to go there, and President Roosevelt even campaigned there, because he wanted the Jewish vote. The young crowd used to go there too—though not the bad kids. It was called the S & S. Well, I met Fran one night at the bowling alley. She was bowling the lane next to ours—I said a few things, and she said a few things, we invited her and her friends for coffee at the S & S, and that's how I met her. Yeah, I more or less picked her up.

The supermarket had a yearly show, and I signed up to do impersonations in it. I invited Fran to go to the show with me, but I didn't tell her I was in it. We went and ate and everything, and then when it was time for the show, I said, "Oh, excuse me Fran," and slipped off to get ready. I guess I was trying to surprise her, and I think I did. I don't think the act I did that night was what won her over—I think I did impressions of Charles Boyer and Jimmy Durante and Edward G. Robinson and James Cagney, all the ones that were easy to imitate—but I do think that she originally liked me because I had a good sense of humor. I liked her for the same reason. I always liked people that had a good sense of humor.

We went together for about a year and a half, maybe two years, and then we got married in '51. I quit my job at the supermarket just before we got married, because I was unhappy with my boss. Fran's people weren't too happy about my quitting—they said something like, "How can you marry a guy that doesn't have a job?" But she just said, "Oh, he'll be all right. I got a job anyhow, and I'll take care of him." She was getting a big $25 a week or something back in those days working in a very high class women's clothing store. But I did get another job within a month or two, still before we got married, as a shipper in my uncle's garment business.

Fran and I were probably kind of unique in the fact that we never discussed having children before we were married. I know a lot of my peers did discuss this, you know, "Oh, we're going to have 2½ kids and 1½ cars and live in a house with a white fence around it." But with us it just didn't come up, even after we were married. Fortunately we thought the same way—it probably wasn't important to either of us. You hear about people who don't talk about it until after they're married, where it turns out that she wants a kid and he doesn't, or vice versa. But for us it didn't come up at all until the third or fourth year of marriage. I think maybe Fran said something like, "Oh, your aunt wants to

know when we're going to have a kid." And I think I probably
said, "Well, if you want to have the kid, it's up to you. If you
don't want one right now, that's okay with me too." I found out
later that she was working on a sort of five-year plan. She was
saying to herself, "Well, when five years go by, I'll think about
it." So we didn't decide to have a kid after this first four or five
years. Then when the second five years came around, it was she
more than me who said, "This isn't a bad life the way we are.
Why bring someone else into it?" And that was pretty much it.
We never had any long or heated discussion about it—we just
sort of evolved into not having kids.

There wasn't much pressure on us to have kids, even though
this was in the 50s, the big time for Mom and Dad and the kids.
As far as my mother and father were concerned, they were not
pressure people—they let us live our lives pretty much as we
pleased. Fran got a few little innuendos from my family, and
myabe a few from her mother—"Aren't you bored with work?
Wouldn't you like to stay home?" But her mother was like my
mother, not one to interfere with your family life. Again, a few
of her aunts would give her a little *schtick*, as we say in
Yiddish—"All your friends have children." And there was this
one uncle who said to us once, at a Bar Mitzvah or a wedding or
something, "Here's 5 bucks for the baby carriage, for Christ's
sake." But that was about all we got from the relatives.

Our immediate friends didn't give us any trouble either.
Sometimes at cocktail parties, people we didn't know would be
introduced to us. They'd say, "Oh, you married long? How many
kids do you have? None? Oh, that's too bad." As if there were
something wrong with us. Of course, the general "pro-ma" stuff
was always there on television and everywhere—give a girl a
doll when she's very young, teach her how to feed it and all.

But that stuff never really bothered us, because we're both
very independent people—maybe Fran felt it a little more than I
did, because the woman gets that pressure more than the man.
But as for me, if anybody ever said anything about it to me, I'd
tell them to go screw themselves. It's none of their goddamn
business. Or, I'd just ignore it, and people would never bring it
up again. I made the pressures go away so that I wasn't aware

of them. As I say, I always was an independent person. I make my own decisions. If you interviewed another family, they might say, "Oh yeah, we had pressures all the time." But we just didn't recognize the pressures, or we fended them off so easily that nobody ever raised the subject again.

Every once in awhile, I say to myself, "Gee, I wonder if I would have had a better kid or raised a kid better than my buddy down the street." That's about the extent of my parental thoughts.

Family and Freedom

I got married later in life than most of the gang I grew up with—I was 29 when I got married, but they were 21 or 22. So when we went to visit these people after Fran and I were married, they already had children that were maybe 5, 6, 7 years old. We found after a while that we were losing social contact with our friends who had kids because we didn't have much in common with them—all they wanted to talk about was their children. We'd be driving home after an evening with some couple, and Fran would say, "My God, all I heard tonight was the cost of diapers and Pablum." Fran and I naturally wanted a little more intellectual conversation than just talking about children. Let's say we were socializing with 20 couples; after awhile it probably narrowed down to about three couples, and those three were the ones that didn't talk about their kids all the time. Johnny would show off his report card, and then it would be, "Okay, screw, you go to bed." And then you could sit down like adults and talk about something else, like the Vietnam War. Another thing we would run into was if you wanted to see a play with people who had children, they would say, "Oh, I don't know if I can get a babysitter. Let me call you back." Or, "I'll call my mother and she'll call me back." It became this big hassle, and we began to feel, "Screw you, I'll go to the play without you." So our social life did get to be out of the perimeter of people with kids.

We joined a group for people without kids a few years ago, and one of the things we liked about it was that we didn't talk only about not having children. We talked about anything, literature, music, you name it. Most of the people in the group were educated, college graduates, which Fran and I are not—a great many of them were teachers. Fran and I said to each other, "My God, we've been hanging around with those dodoes who're always talking about their kids. This group is a lot more interesting."

How did we get into this group? Well, one day on the TV morning news, this woman was promoting a book she'd written called *The Baby Trap*. The book was saying, "Don't get trapped into having a baby just because somebody else wants you to have a baby." We thought it was nice to hear somebody who thought like we did, because nobody in our crowd talked like that—they all had children. Then about two months later, there was an ad in the newspaper saying, "If you want to talk about not having babies or if you're being pressured into having children, call this number. We're having a meeting at such and such a place and time." So we went, and it was very enjoyable.

Most of the people there were a lot younger than us. They'd only been married a little while, and they were getting all these pressures to have children. They either weren't sure about having them, or they didn't want to—they were concerned about overpopulation, or, with the Vietnam War on, they were thinking about not raising children to be cannon fodder. Everyone had to say why they'd come, and when we told about ourselves, how long we'd been married and everything, we became the big attraction. We'd been married 20 or 21 years and we'd survived all these pressures. Everyone wanted to come over and talk to us. I think that's why we were invited to be on TV too—we're like living proof that you can *not* have children and still have a happy marriage.

It's not a group that's against children. We just want to let people know that there's a choice. If you want to have a kid, fine, but don't rush into it, and don't let all these subliminal pressures bother you. Children are okay for some people, but maybe not for others. We even have some members who have children. They're with us because they don't want to raise their children like their parents raised them—they don't want automatically to train their children to become parents, to get married and have children.

When I go out and talk to young people, I try to bring out the point that you can't undo having a child, so think about it first. I think it's difficult to ask people about their reasons for having children, because if a guy or a woman realizes that he has three kids and he doesn't want them, he's never going to admit it. I guarantee you most parents aren't going to give you an honest answer, because they're too defensive. But I really would like to know what motivates people to have children. I would like to believe in the idealistic thing, where they want the next generation to be better than the last generation, but I don't think many parents think that. You hear people make statements like, "Oh, I want to have a kid to play football or baseball with, or to go hunting and fishing with." Or even, "I want someone to take care of me in my old age." What kind of a stupid statement is that? Some kid's going to take care of you in your old age?

We may not know what motivates people to have kids, but parents do want, as a child grows up, something to be proud of— "My kid went to Harvard." "Look what Johnny did today." People live their children's successes vicariously. I think if I had a kid, I would try not to do that. It's nice for a parent to be proud when their kids are young and they show goo goo pictures and stuff like that, but when a guy or a girl is 18 or 19 and their parents go on and on about, "She's got a PhD and a BSS and all this," it just shows that the parents are trying to make something of their dull lives. There's the story about the Jewish mother going down the street with the two children in the baby carriage. A woman passing by says, "Oh, what cute little children! How old are they?" And the Jewish mother—I say Jewish mother because that's the way the joke was told to me— the Jewish mother says, "The lawyer is 3 and the dentist is 2."

Parents talk more about the pleasure they get from their children's achievements than they do about having fun just having their children around. I really wonder how much pleasure any parent gets out of his child. If you try to measure pleasure against disappointment and anxieties, you've gotta have an awful lot of pleasure. When kids are little, you get a kick out of watching them start to walk and talk. Fran and I still have a good time looking at a baby picture—the kid googling and everything. I think parents miss that kind of fun, when their children get to be a certain age—"Now they're grown up, they're not fun any more." I can only think of one friend of mine who says he can't stand kids until they're 5, 6, 7 years old. He doesn't want to bother with the diapers and all that—he wants the kids to be active and viable. But most parents don't say that.

Once I was asking this friend of mine how his family was, and he said, "Boy, lately we're having a great time." It happened that for one week in his life, none of his kids were at home—one was in college and one was here and one was there—and he was having the greatest time. His wife called him one day and said, "You know the kids aren't going to be home this week? Wow, we can do anything we want and say anything we want. Let's go to a movie, and let's go to a play." He was very honest—when the kids came back home, he didn't like it that much. They were inconvenient now! I don't know how many times I've heard people from my old gang who have kids say, "Oh, I can hardly wait until that daughter of mine is married!" Or, "Jesus Christ, when he goes off to college . . ." They're waiting to get rid of these kids. All their lives, they're bringing these kids up, and yet they can't wait to get rid of them. So, when someone says to me, "Gee, you don't know what you've missed," I think of all the times I've heard, "What a pain in the ass! I gotta go down and get the kid out of jail," and I usually come back and say something like, "*You* don't know what *you've* missed."

I have nieces and nephews, but they all live far away from here. But Fran and I have been Aunt Fran and Uncle Sid to a lot of kids—I think that's what we are to many of the people in our "non-parent" group. I'm not conceited, but I know there is some kind of touch that Fran and I have with children. I find that children gravitate towards me, and I like talking to them— in fact, I love children. Maybe it's because I've sometimes seen parents do it that I don't talk down to children. And I tell them when I don't like something—if I'm having a drink and talking to somebody and a kid interrupts me, I tell him off. I think kids respect that to a certain degree.

Fran has a female cousin that has 3 boys, and we lived with them once for a couple of years when I was out of a job—I guess the boys were 7, 8, and 9 years old. We babysat for them and everything, but the main thing was that I did things with them that their parents didn't do, like telling jokes, drawing, and etching. I would draw a funny picture and the kid would say, "Let me draw one." When we moved out of there, this one boy—5 or 6 years old—was in tears, and he wrote us letters for a while.

I'm sure there are a lot of Uncle Sids and Aunt Frans around, that take an interest in children. But of course it's easy to be an aunt or an uncle—children remember the two hours with you better than the other 22 with their parents. When I tell funny jokes and stuff like that, the kid may say, "Aw gee, my father never does that," not realizing that his father can't do that kind of thing 24 hours a day. I hope the good relationships I have with kids hasn't made any breach between me and their parents, or made my friends jealous of me. There was one time when I was over visiting one of my best buddies. I liked the way he raised his kids—it seemed there was a nice balance between him and the mother. He and I were having a drink and rapping about golf or something, when his boy came in and said, "Oh, Uncle Sid, look at what I'm entering in the contest." And he brought out this model racing car that he'd carved himself out of balsam and painted and made the wheels and all that. I said, "Gee, that's terrific. That's something I always wanted to do, but I never had the patience. That's really terrific." After he left, I looked up at my friend, his father, and he had a very funny look on his face. I said, "Is something wrong?", and he said, "He never showed me that car." The kid had been working on it for two or three months, and had never shown it to his father. Boy, I felt like going right through the chair. That incident made me wonder about other times when the same sort of thing might have happened. I've never seen it go the other way, where the parent was glad his kid was getting some kind of stimulation from me that the kid wouldn't get from him. I would tend to think that most parents would be kind of upset if they thought Uncle Sid was Number One over them—almost as though their kids brought their report cards to me and not to them.

I've had a very diversified career. After nine years in the garment business, I quit, because I was having problems with my boss. Then I spent ten years in electronics and quit again—I just lost my taste for it. I scrounged around for awhile, and then—at a time when I had about $75 in the bank—I borrowed some money from Fran's brother and became partners with this guy selling office furniture. I think one of the things about being child-free is that you're able to have a more diversified life. If I'd had kids, I probably would have had to stay at that garment business job, because I had to support a family, and I probably would have been unhappy the rest of my life. Without kids, it's a lot easier to tell the boss to take his job and shove it, a lot easier to do things like travel—Fran and I have been across the country three times, been in almost every state in the union. Fran's had a lot of different jobs too, left jobs she didn't like, the same as me.

Fran and I do not take in a lot of family social functions. We went to a few when we were first married, but we both found it a drag, so we stopped going. We're both independent people, and we like our privacy—even more than me, Fran likes to have her quiet times, as she calls them. We like each other's company— we're fortunate in that. After 26 years of marriage, we still enjoy each other and like each other and can still be friends. I think that's quite an accomplishment. Fran said once that our friendship had grown over the years. Maybe that's because we haven't had children. We're the only two we have, so we'd better be good to each other.

Frank

Frank has been an active participant in the trade union movement since he first went to work during the Depression. Married shortly after World War II, Frank and his wife, Alice, have shared both their involvement in the union movement and the raising of their five children.

A Worker, a Fighter, and a Father

I'm 59 years old, and I have five children and one grandchild. I was born during World War I, and I got married when I was 29 years old, right at the end of World War II. I got out of high school during the Depression. My mother and father were determined that there was going to be one kid in the family to go to high school, though it happened that my older sister went first, so the two of us went. The other kids, as soon as they were 16 years old, went into the CCC camps—that's the Civilian Conservation Corps—because they had to help out the family. My father was in the WPA, earning $12–$14 a week.

When I got out of high school in 1935, I couldn't find a job, so I sold newspapers. I'd go down to the commuter train depots every morning around eight o'clock to catch the businessmen getting on the trains with their attache cases. Naturally the strictly conservative paper was the best seller there. I made about seven or eight dollars a week, and I turned it over to the family. It helped feed us—you figure my father was bringing in $14, so another $8 made a big difference.

My father was working as a night watchman at a lumber company, and he finally got me a job at the same place. I started there working 54 hours a week, making $10 a week, and I was glad to get it. There were no taxes taken out in those days, so I gave my mother $9 every week and I kept $1. With that dollar a week, I bought a typewriter on time, because I wanted to be a writer.

It's quite a different world when you come out of high school and you go into a shop. In high school you get taught, "What a wonderful country we live in," and "We've got a wonderful government," and "We should all be very happy that we live here." Then suddenly you get thrown in this jungle. You've got a foreman cursing and swearing at you, and you're told to work with obsolete equipment. I was working on saws, cutting and sawing wood. Right after I started working was the year of the CIO and sit-down strikes. I guess every worker in every shop in the country was talking union. You'd go to the movies and see in the newsreels that the rubber workers, the steelworkers, the automobile workers—everybody was on strike. And there was this Swedish Socialist who worked where I did who used to pass around Jack London's books and Upton Sinclair's. He got me interested, influenced me to see that workers needed a union. Of course, like I said, I could see this by experience too. We had a foreman there that used to actually kick people. We knew that if we wanted to, we could organize that shop. The CIO wasn't active around here yet, so. we signed up with the Teamsters. When the boss started firing people for joining the union, we went on strike, and after a week the company gave in. Our pay doubled, went up 100 percent, and we got dignity. We couldn't be sworn at and kicked around anymore, because we had the right to bring up grievances and go to the Labor Board if necessary. My wages went up to about $20 a week, and I felt rich. I went out and bought a car.

I stayed at the lumber company for eight years, and we kept getting good contracts and raising our wages. It was all so nice and secure that I got kinda bored. I wanted to quit and try something new, but it was during World War II, and jobs were frozen. You had to get a release from your employer, and even though I was a thorn in my boss's side from being active in the union, he didn't want to give me a release, because it was hard to get experienced, trained workers. By that time I was an experienced tallyman—I could just look at a piece of wood and tell you how many square feet of lumber was in it. So the boss wouldn't let me go, and I had to raise hell to get my release. What I did was I got on the loudspeaker on Christmas weekend, and I started ridiculing the company for not giving us Christmas bonuses. The next day the boss came out and gave me a release.

I got fired from my next job because I was trying to organize the place, and I had trouble getting another job because by this time I was blacklisted in this neighborhood—over the years I'd written a lot of letters to the local paper and had gotten a reputation as a radical. My father even had trouble getting a job because he had the same name as i.e. So I went to another part of the metropolitan area where there were a lot of leather shops—I heard that they never asked you anything about your background in those shops. And it was true—the first shop I went into, they hired me. All they cared about was that I was husky-looking, because it was a rough job. They put me down in the beamhouse, pulling leather hides out of the lime pit. It was really rough—the hides weigh a hundred pounds or more, and you have to wear a rubber uniform and rubber gloves, because of the burns. You pull the hides out of the pit, and you shake them, and you still get burns on your face. But I was going with my wife then—I met her while she was working as secretary for the packinghouse union—and we wanted to get married, so I had to take any job I could get.

My wife quit her job when we first got married. She stayed home, and that's when we started raising children. We had our first kid, Chris, in 1948. We both loved children, and we both talked about having a dozen kids before we had any. We both came from big families: five kids in my wife's family and five in my own. Maybe it was because of the Depression, but we both felt that big families seem to help each other more—with a big family, maybe one or two of the older kids can help support the family.

Around 1949, after Hank, our second son, was born, I got laid off. Plastics were coming in, and the leather shops started sinking, going out of business one by one. For the first time in my life I had to collect unemployment, and because I couldn't find a job, my wife, Alice, went back to work, this time for the United Furniture Workers Union. So for a year I stayed home with the kids—I was sort of the father and mother. That was very interesting. They were both practically babies, so I got a lot of experience helping raise them. I'd feed them, give them their baths, make their formula, generally take care of them during the day. It was a fascinating experience, and I loved it. It was interesting seeing children develop, change, and start to talk.

It didn't bother me at all, doing this. I'd read about how they were fighting against male supremacy in the Socialist countries and changing the roles of women. I felt women had the right to work the same as men. And why shouldn't we men be fathers and have our share of taking care of kids? I loved it. I got to talking with the housewives in the neighborhood, like mothers do. I'd put the kids out in the sun at the playground, and the other housewives would be out there with their kids. I don't know how the men in the neighborhood felt about my staying at home with my kids, but the women were very cordial. They'd say, "Gee, I wish my husband would help out like you are." They'd talk about their kids, and I'd talk about ours, while the kids were playing together.

That year I was helping bring up those kids was valuable. I was able to get some good experiences. When they're that age, you go through a lot of worries: they break out in a rash, and you look it up in Dr. Spock's book—that was our bible in those days—or you call the doctor. I didn't ever feel trapped. Maybe if you have to stay home with kids for a long time, maybe you do get to feeling trapped, but when Alice would come home from work, I'd go out and do my political work. I was active in the Civil Rights Congress—I had no union activity then because of my layoff status, but I did other things. Besides the civil rights work, I was learning photography, taking shots of the kids, learning how to develop and print them and how to make vignettes. And I watched the baseball games on TV while the kids were asleep. We had a little ten-inch TV—we really couldn't afford it, but it was cheaper than going to the movies all the time. I can see why people today on welfare have TVs—what other outlet do they have for enjoyment? We didn't have a car either, so we didn't get out very often, but we had a lot of friends and relatives in the same boat as us, with little kids. We'd get together and help each other out that way.

After about a year of this, I was starting to feel funny. I was having fun taking care of the kids, but it seemed like Alice still had to do a lot of the housework. A man doesn't do all the things a woman does. She'd work hard all day and then come home and do the cleaning and ironing and other things. We both did cooking, although I usually prepared supper—I still do if I get home early enough. I like to cook, probably because I like to eat.

Anyway, I was feeling funny about it, so Alice suggested I try to get a job in a meat-packing plant—she'd worked for the meat-packers' union before we were married. It was the summertime, when they do a lot of hiring—they sell a lot of hot dogs then at the ball park and the racetrack, places like that. But when I got in line to be interviewed, I saw that as each person got to the front and was interviewed, he was told, "No, we're not hiring." When I got there, the woman who was doing the hiring called over her supervisor, and she started whispering to him, "Hire him, he's husky, he's a husky guy." They interviewed me and hired me, and that was the biggest mistake they ever made. I was the only one hired that day, and I thought I'd get the heaviest job in the shop, because they said they wanted a husky guy. But they gave me a little instrument that looked like a screwdriver and told me to go "test the shoulders." This instrument is called a trier, and what you do is stick it in the marrows, pull it out, and smell it. If it smells sour, then the meat is rotten and you're supposed to throw it out. When pork turns bad, that's where it starts, in the marrows. I was amazed that I had such an easy job—you get paid for smelling.

Of course, there was a catch to it. They didn't really want me to throw out the sour meat. It was just a routine for the government inspectors. All they'd do was go through and see if the meat had been poked with the trier—they didn't really check to see if the meat was rotten. Occasionally there was an honest inspector, but most of them weren't. But I took the job seriously. I couldn't see sending rotten meat out to other working-class families, even though it might not kill them. So I really did throw out truckloads of shoulders that were sour, and the company got mad and put me on another job—a harder, heavier job, lifting 80-pound boxes of meat up on flats. But it wasn't that bad. They transferred me instead of firing me, because they were afraid I would go to the inspector and squeal on them.

After I spoke up a few times about conditions in the plant, I got elected chief shop steward of the union there, and a little while later we had a really big strike. In fact, it was the longest-lasting strike in the history of the state—lasted 14 months, from October '54 till January '56. It was about a new contract. The old one ran out. There had been an understanding among the local meat-packers that their workers would get the same wages and benefits as the workers at the Big Four companies in Chicago got. But they decided to stop doing this. I guess they figured they couldn't afford to pay as much as the big guys did. But we couldn't stand for that—it would have been the beginning of the end—and we went out and stayed out for 14 months. Probably the local packers were financed through the strike by the big companies, who maybe figured they'd make a test case out of it and break the union. It was a big operation. They hired private guards and used all kinds of injunctions and Red-baiting.

The two oldest kids were about eight and seven during the strike—the next one, Judy, was just a baby—and a lot of times I'd leave those two off at the union hall while I was on the picket line. I wanted them to see what was going on, why Daddy wasn't home much—sometimes I would spend 24 hours on the picket lines. Sometimes I'd bring them to the hall for meetings too. I'd get up and make a report, and one of the kids would get up and stand by me like he was going to make a speech. Everyone got a big kick out of it, and they got a big kick out of marching around in the hall, eating the doughnuts and sampling the coffee, and being made much of by everybody. I wanted them to know what I was doing and why I was doing it, that it was to help the family. So those two at least were brought up in that atmosphere of being on the picket line—I took them there sometimes when I was pretty sure there wouldn't be any trouble—and around union halls and watching scabs go in and knowing what scabs were.

During the strike I saw the kids, of course, on weekends and in the evenings too. I usually tried to get home in time to read them stories. That was my job—read them a story and put them to bed. I used to improvise on the stories, and they enjoyed that. I'd get released from strike duty, and I'd take them to a circus or something else special. I wanted to be close to them—I didn't want to become a union stranger. I didn't want them to turn against unions because they never saw their father. And I think they understood.

We eventually won the strike, after a long, hard struggle—got most of what we asked for as far as wages and benefits were concerned. One thing we got was medical insurance, though for me and my family this came almost too late. We'd already had three kids—Chris, Hank, and Judy—without any insurance to pay for their births, and our next one, Mark, was born right after the strike was settled but before the union benefits were starting to come in, so we were saddled with that bill too. Freddy was born two years later, and he's the only one that the insurance completely covered. He was the last.

I stayed on at the meat-packing plant for about 15 years after the strike was settled, and I was also chief shop steward during most of that time. Then in 1970 I got arthritis, and my asthma kept getting worse. I felt I wasn't doing my best work—you know, you take pride in your work, especially if you're active in the union, because you don't want the company to be able to use your sloppy work as a point against the union. So I quit. I'd had experience putting out the union newspaper in the plant, so I was able to get a job editing a paper for the local Model Cities Program. I raised hell with that for a while—used the pages of a government-financed paper to tell people that U.S. Savings Bonds were a lousy buy, things like that. But then the program got wiped out when Nixon cut the funds. After that I got a job as an organizer for the hospital workers' local here, and that's what I'm still doing now. I fool around with writing too. I'd like to do a history of the local labor movement, interview people for it.

All through the time when the kids were being born and were little, my wife, Alice, was working to support the family too—mostly factory jobs. It sure was tough on her. She'd work the second shift, 3 to 11. I'd get out of work at 2:30 or 3:00, so we'd have a girl from next door come in and stay with the kids for an hour or so until I got home. Then I'd take care of the kids in the evening—feed them, put them to bed, tell them stories. The only time we could all be together was on the weekends. Alice's jobs would only last for a while—she'd get laid off, or she'd have to quit when the next child was due. Of course, she couldn't work all during the strike either. When Freddy was about 12, she got a job as a bookkeeper, and she's had it ever since. She's been a union fighter wherever she's worked.

Just to bring you up to date on all the kids. Chris is a mailman, and he's active in their union. He feels kind of left out, because the other mailmen aren't very militant, but they've had some struggles and some successes. He's also writing for a community activist newspaper and fighting for rent control. Hank's doing what I did—working in the packinghouse. And he's going to community college at night, going for a degree in social work. His wife is an RN, and they're the ones that gave me the grandchild. They're doing what we did in that way too— she works at night, and Hank takes care of the baby on the nights he doesn't go to school. Judy's an apprentice at a big company and a steward in the union there. She's married to an organizer for the same hospital workers' local that I work for. Mark's a sheet metal worker and a welder, and he's learned about the need for strong unions from his own experiences. Freddy, the youngest, is going to college this fall. He's a sports nut—tennis, basketball, softball. He's not too interested in politics and unions yet, just sports and girls. But he's a good kid. I'm pretty happy with them all—they all seem to be doing worthwhile things in their spare time. None of them married the boss—or the boss's daughter.

Loving Kids and Showing Them What the World's Like

When times were especially tough, we tried to keep from having more kids. But the birth-control devices wouldn't work, we'd find out Alice was pregnant, and we'd say, "Oh, my God, what did we do wrong?" But when the kids came along, we didn't get mad. Once the babies're born, they're beautiful and you love them. Even while they were growing inside their mother, I just couldn't wait to see what they'd look like, how they'd develop, how quick they would learn. And I was amazed to see how completely different each one was from the others, in personalities and everything.

If you put Chris in a playpen, for example, he would just stay there all day, examining his toys and playing with them. He might stand up and look around, but he'd stay quiet. Hank was the adventurer. He'd want to get out of that playpen. To him, it was a prison. He'd work on the spokes until he broke them, and he'd get out and go down the street. Chris would never go out, even if there was a hole open for him. As they grew up, it was exactly the same. Hank was the one who was more militant and aggressive, getting into trouble all the time and investigating things. Chris didn't want to get into trouble—he associated with peaceful guys, never went to barrooms or places like that where there might be a brawl. And when he got older, he wanted a nice, quiet civil service job. Hank was more extroverted, but Chris was an introvert. He had some temper tantrums. We had to get some psychiatric help for him when he was about 12. The doctor said I should be mainly responsible for him, because he and Alice didn't get along too well. He made her high-strung and nervous. Chris got over it though, and he's fine now. It was a temporary thing.

Judy was different from both of them. Both of them would get crabby when they were hungry, or they wanted to be changed. But she was so peaceful, it seemed like she was never unhappy. She'd wake up in the morning singing, instead of crying for something to eat. She was pleasant and wonderful and feminine, just a lovable person.

Mark engaged in pantomime from the time he was a little kid. He was a born mimic, an impressionist. In those days Sid Caesar was our favorite comedian on TV, and we thought he'd grow up to be a comedian too—he was so good at describing things with his eyes and hands. For example, he'd look out and he'd see lightning flashing in the sky. He'd say, "Mummy," and then he'd go like this with his hands and blink his eyes, describing what lightning seemed like to him. He was so funny, we'd just sit down and roar at everything he did. He had trouble in school, though—reading problems—and it turned out that he had dyslexia, although no one knew it until he was in high school, and by that time it was too late. But he learned a lot and absorbed a lot orally, by listening to his teachers. Also, he had good manual dexterity, and he went to trade school.

You could see what Freddy would be like from how he was when he was little too. He was always the athletic type from very early—he was always swinging and jumping up and down. He couldn't keep still, always doing exercises and running around. So they were all different, and they were all wonderful. I loved them all, and I tried not to have favorites—that was a mistake my mother had made.

One thing I kept reminding myself of, when I was raising my own kids, was how my own parents—especially my father—were never politically conscious of what was going on. They never told me that unions were good things and that maybe some other countries had some things that we could learn about and use to improve our country. In fact, when I was 18 years old and starting to get interested in unions, my father would criticize me. I'd bring home radical papers, and he would tear them up. My mother thought a little differently by then, and she'd say to him, "Now you leave Frank alone. He knows what he's doing. He has a right to his ideas." But my father would say, "What's he always reading for? He's always got his nose in a book. He's going to get in trouble reading all those books."

They were ordinary working people who loved their country and believed in God and went to church. They certainly didn't believe in getting into trouble. My father had started in the coal mines when he was 12, and he'd just always had to work hard. When he was still pretty young, he'd gone to a mass meeting and heard Big Bill Heywood speak, when they were trying to organize the IWW. But he wasn't impressed. He also went to hear the Ku Klux Klan—he thought they were crazy and extreme, even though he was more or less anti-Catholic. That feeling goes back to the old country—some of his ancestors were from the North of Ireland and were Orangemen. But the main reason for my father's antiunion feelings would come out when he would say, "I remember the unions after World War I, and how they got smashed in the open-shop days, and the Red Scare, and all that. Don't get involved. If the rest of them want to fight in the union, OK, but you stay out of it."

I felt ashamed when he said things like that, and for a while I even hated him. I couldn't really understand why he thought that way. I thought then that when I had my own family, brought up my kids, I was going to tell them what the score was. I wouldn't set it up so they would have to do what I had to do—meet other people outside the family and read books in the library in order to learn the truth about the world. I wanted to bring my kids up to fight the same battles I was fighting.

One night I was drinking beer with a friend, and I said to him, "I hate my father. I can't stand him, because he represents everything I hate. He's against everything I do." This friend of mine was older and more mature than I was, and he said, "You never hate your own father like that. He grew up in a different generation, and his experience taught him different things. He saw the unions smashed after World War I, and he has no faith that the unions can win in this system. You gotta look at it that way. He's been beaten down for years—every time they talked union, he saw the unions get smashed." Well, hearing that helped to change and mellow my attitude. I didn't hate him anymore. I just looked at him and thought, "Here's a guy that worked hard all his life to support me. How can I hate him? He must have loved me, because he took care of me and sacrificed for me. He took all kinds of rotten jobs during the Depression to help bring me up."

Besides, I lived to see both my parents change. They were anti-Catholic, but they voted for Kennedy and got rid of all their anti-Catholic prejudices. And when their son married a Jew—Alice is Jewish—they accepted that. In fact, Alice became a favorite of theirs. In her old age, my mother worked for all kinds of progressive political candidates—imagine that, an 80-year-old woman going out to all those political meetings! And my father was a member of the UAW for the last 20 years of his working life. He retired when he was 80 and got a good pension through the union—my mother still gets money from it.

I'd still have to say that my father was a negative model for me, as far as his antiunion attitudes were concerned. But I took him as a positive model when I thought about how he worked hard to support us. I wanted to be like him—sacrifice things and not just live for my own pleasures. He really did live for his kids, his family.

I have tried to teach my kids more things—and different kinds of things—about politics than my father taught me. But I didn't want to do it the way a lot of other people from the Old Left did it—you know, people who were radicals in the thirties—they tried to hammer their ideas into their kids' heads, indoctrinate them: "Read this paper; read that leaflet; I want you to study this." Alice and I both believed in just exposing them, showing them by example—just bringing them to the picket line and into an atmosphere where there are union people around all the time, like we did with Chris and Hank during the strike. They seem to grow politically in that way. Also, I wanted them to see just the work I was doing. When we had open house at the meat-packing plant, I brought the kids and showed them the machinery and everything. Of course, they'd always get an idea of my work, because I'd come home with the smell of meat on me and with spots of blood that had soaked through onto my clothes from my uniform.

One thing we did talk about a lot with the kids was economics. That would come up because they couldn't understand why they couldn't have some of the things that the other kids had— whether it was toys, or why I couldn't run out to the ice-cream man every time he came. We told them that we were working people and we couldn't afford all those things. They were brought up on powdered milk—sometimes we'd get a quart of regular milk and some powdered milk and mix them up. That's the sort of awareness of economics that we tried to get them used to. And it's funny—when we could afford to get the whole milk, they didn't like it. They were used to the taste of powdered milk.

The only time when there was much conflict with the kids— about politics or anything else—was the age Freddy's at now, between 16 and 18, when they're trying to assert their independence from the family. Mark used to make a joke out of it. He'd say, "I'm going to be a scab when I grow up." And his mother and father would say, "Well, if you are, you'd better not live here." But all of them except Judy did seriously threaten to move out. You know, "I'm going to move out of here as soon as I can. I can't do this, and I can't do that." We tried to keep them aware of the economic part of it during these battles. For instance, if they asked for the car, to use the car, they'd get it. We were pretty liberal with them—but they had to earn the money to pay the difference on the automobile insurance. You know, it costs more if drivers under 25 use the car. And they had to be responsible and bring the car back at a certain time.

Chris had some trouble in school because of my politics. One of his teachers—this was when he was in high school—was an extreme right-wing person and used to harass him a lot. The teacher would say things like, "There are people that go right here to this school whose fathers and mothers are being investigated as subversives. I hope none of you kids grow up to be that way." He would attack unions specifically. Chris was put under a lot of pressure because of this, and I think his marks suffered as a result of it. We tried to deal with it by explaining that there were people in this country who believed that we were evil people and that some of us were spies for a foreign power. The kids could see that that was ridiculous, because they knew that I was in there fighting the boss for better conditions, not going around finding secrets to sell to another country. Common sense could usually reach the kids.

I was pretty pleased with the way Chris and Hank dealt with the Vietnam War, which was sort of the same thing for them as the Spanish Civil War was for me. When the American involvement started, we let the kids know that we felt this was a war our country shouldn't be getting into. But we didn't want to force Chris or Hank into doing anything they really didn't believe in. Working-class kids don't usually become conscientious objectors, but we talked about that. But you have to explain why you're opposed to war, and you have to have a religious affiliation, which they didn't. It was just a political war they didn't like. We said that if they wanted to try being COs anyway, they'd have our support. But they both decided they wanted to go into the Navy, and that seemed good to me, because there they'd be less likely to kill anybody or be killed themselves.

The kids learned a lot about the struggles at the meat-packing plant, because I'd come home and tell them things. A lot of it was funny, crazy stuff—you know, stories about the rules concerning the length of bowel movements, and about how foremen would try to seduce women on the line. But I was still a little worried about the younger kids because they hadn't gone through the turmoil of the big strike, like the older ones had. When Judy was about 11 or 12, I started taking her to political events. I took her to a "God and Country" rally downtown one time—that is, I took her to join the picket line that the NAACP had set up against the rally. I think she was very proud to take part in that demonstration. We'd always had black people visiting our home, so she knew that racism was wrong—she always used to argue against kids that used words like *nigger* and *kike* and *wop*. So politically, she didn't really miss out on much. She became pretty progressive, and when she was in high school she took part in peace demonstrations.

Like I said, Mark learned for himself about the need for good unions. At his first job there was no union at all, and he saw how lousy the conditions were there. His next job was at a place where there was a union, but it was a lousy, weak union. Where he is now, the union is stronger, and they get good contracts, but it's corrupt. He's learning a lot about the corruption of union business agents working there, and he listens to what we say about it too.

We're a little worried about the youngest, Freddy, but I think he'll be all right. I'd like to see him work, take a job, so he'll know what it means to be a worker, even if it's only for a year or two or during the summer or just working part time—so he'll be better able to sympathize with the struggles of working people. He did work one summer two years ago in a bookbinding shop, and he hated it there. The boss was always yelling at him, telling him he was doing things wrong, and he didn't like that at all. So we said, "See, that's why you need a union." So when we asked him to get a job the next summer, he said, "You don't want me to work in a scab shop, do you? Get me a job in a union shop." Then last summer I wanted him to get a little more exposure, so I got him to go with me to a local hospital where I had some organizing stuff to do for the hospital workers' union. He helped me pass out leaflets—he took one side of the front steps, and I took the other. Right away, the hospital guards came running up, grabbed both him and me, and threw us off the property. They called the police, and we had to go down to the station. We weren't arrested, just warned that we were trespassing on private property. I thought that was a good educational experience for Freddy. His education into the class struggle is more limited than I'd like, but he's had some. He thinks a lot of Judy's husband—the guy who's also an organizer for the hospital workers—so that's a good sign.

All in all, I'm pretty pleased. I guess the kids feel they've learned something from me, because they come and ask my advice about problems they have with their work or their unions. They don't always take my advice, but they still ask for it.

Alice and I pretty much agreed on how to raise the kids. She's always been just about as prounion as I am. I guess if there was any difference, it was that I had the biggest influence as far as ideology was concerned, and she was more concerned with manners and morals. Maybe part of it was that she was Jewish, and Jewish families place a higher value on education. We both thought both things were important, but I tended to emphasize getting a class education in the shop and the factory, while she talked a little more about bettering yourself by going to college and getting a degree.

We never had any problem with sex roles in raising our kids. I mean, Judy played ball and sports just like the boys, and the boys loved teddy bears and dolls as much as she did. They all wanted things that were nice and soft to touch. Judy certainly never got the idea that her future was to get married and stay home. Like with everything else, kids learn by example. They saw that their mother was working. They saw me washing dishes, cooking, helping to dress them and change their diapers. They knew that it wasn't only Alice that did all the dirty, monotonous work around the house. And they knew that there wasn't any work that was definite male work. In fact, Alice was a welder, you know, and she's better than me at some types of work. Her father was a cabinetmaker, and her brother's a tool-and-die maker, which is a highly skilled trade. It must run in her family, because she's very good at fixing things around the house. I envy her those mechanical abilities, because I'm not mechanically minded myself. Anyway, the kids always knew that she wasn't "just a housewife."

I think the home atmosphere we had was pretty good for the kids. We used to have parties every Saturday night—all kinds of people would come in, both black and white. We'd get together over a few bottles of beer and sing union songs and have a really good time. The neighbors thought we were crazy, but we didn't care. There was this one black woman psychiatrist that used to visit us a lot. One day, one of the neighbors came over and said, "I see you've got a black woman doing your washing for you." That was the kind of thinking that went on. But the kids knew what we believed in. For a while we lived in a cottage that some abolitionists had lived in. It had been part of the Underground Railroad—slaves on their way to Canada would stop off there. We felt good about carrying on that tradition in our own little way—we were involved in struggles in the community about the rights of black people, gaining equal access to bars and cafes, things like that. I also tried to open the kids' minds up about religion. I'd take them to different services—a synagogue one week, a Catholic Mass the next, then maybe a Quaker meeting—so they'd find out there wasn't just one kind of people in this world. Every year, here at home, we'd have a Hanukkah-Christmas celebration, and we'd have symbols of all the world religions around the house.

Another thing that's been good for the kids, I think, is that for the last 25 years or so we've had a cooperative arrangement here in this house with Alice's sister and her husband. They live upstairs, and we live downstairs. Of course, it's helped us a lot economically. We wouldn't have been able to buy a house at all if we hadn't done it that way, with people. And it especially helped us during the strike, because we saved a lot of money by living cooperatively. But mainly it was nice because we all got along good together. It helped us get across the main thing we wanted to teach our kids: to be happy and love each other and help each other and not exploit or take advantage of people. The kids could look around the neighborhood and compare, see the difference between us and people who are money-mad, see the problems it causes in families when people are obsessed with money and property. The kids also found it difficult to see why other people would be fighting so much, why there were so many divorces and things like that in families we knew. They'd ask, "Why are they fighting? Why can't this one get along with that one?" The kids couldn't comprehend that stuff because of the good cooperative arrangement we had—and maybe also because of all the other things we tried to teach them.

Brian

Brian works in magazine publishing as an editor and at 40 has been married and divorced. He has recently remarried. One of the two children of his first marriage now lives with him.

Brian's Family

I was born in a house—not a hospital—on the second floor, next to a gas station, and I probably lived in most of the lower-middle-class or lower-class areas of the city over the years. We would get evicted a lot. I think all my mother's births were at home. It was probably fairly traditional then, and also I assume there wouldn't have been the money to pay a hospital bill. I suppose it's a lower-class custom. She was pretty old, I imagine, for birthing at that point—probably in her 40's. I was the baby. She had two families: she had had a marriage and two kids and then, a divorce and then three of us, three Coopers.

My father was a guy of, oh, an Irish-American father, several generations removed from I don't know where. His father's father had been a captain in the Civil War. His mother's family,

they were, I assume, Yankees, probably swamp Yankees. They
might have been Canadian—I'm not sure. Their name was Bell,
and there had been Bells who had been boatmakers up in New
Brunswick. Most of them were probably originally Celts. Half
my mother's family was German—that's very prevalent in this
area, German-Irish—so I'm sort of a bastard German-Irish-
Yankee-Irish-Canadian-Scotch whatever.

My father's mother was a lady of unusual and loose charm.
They lived in what was then a summer place, and she apparently screwed around a lot, with a lot of doctor friends, did a lot
of entertaining on boats in the harbor. And, in fact, my father's
sister, who was a cripple, had been fathered by a friend of the
family's. My father's father was a boatbuilder and inventor. He
apparently at one point developed a bottom paint that was very,
very good—an antifouling paint—but someone stole his idea; and
of course he had never patented it. He was a very nice, quiet,
gentle character, I guess, whose wife screwed around, and he
worked hard and tried to get along—at least that's the way he
comes across to me, even from my mother, who I think was
antagonistic towards that family.

My father, like his father, was a very nice quiet, nebishy kind
of man, a sweet person. He was also a part-time drunk and a
shopkeeper—always somebody else's shop, never his own. I don't
think there was ever any drinking around the house; his wife
forbade it, which was a sick and bad thing, but he would go off
on bats. My stepbrother would go pick him up at a cheap hotel
somewhere—he might have been there for nine days dead drunk,
just trying to obliterate himself. I don't blame him at all.

He was a nonexistent character—I can only remember having
one conversation with him, and that was not long before he died.
He had lots of nice aspirations and very little ability to work
them out. And he had a wife who supported that self-destructive
side of him by making life impossible for him. It was just one of
those classic little marriages where a person marries the wrong
person. My mother was very much like her mother, a very
German woman who drove her husband to an early grave with
her silence and her martyrdom.

For some reason, my father gave me the nickname "Ralph,"

and he always thought Ralph should go to prep school, because he thought Ralph was really bright. And Ralph *was* bright when he was a kid; he read very early and that sort of thing and was adored by all the teachers in grade school because he was brighter than the teachers were, but they didn't resent it because they were nuns and would be guilty of envy. They thought I was a little angel. But anyhow, my father thought Ralph should go to prep school; he wanted to live in a nice suburb; he wanted . . . he wanted to be a WASP, I suppose. He clerked and kept shop for other people. He was not what you would consider a success and he resented it. He did have these aspirations. His biggest success, shortly before he died, in fact, was when he was hired to put together a small retail business for two doctors, and he managed that. But by this time, his episodic drinking was less steady than it used to be and instead, he started popping Nembutals, I think, and he would stay high or low, whichever they do to you, as often and as long as possible. And finally—he was a small overweight guy—finally his heart complained on the street one night. I was fourteen when he died.

Our family was a matriarchy. My mother was a very unpleasant woman who could be charming and funny and witty—witty in a vicious sort of way, which I think is very Irish. And also very Jewish, because the wit I think comes out of the same sort of experience. But she was one of those really classical martyr types, and she played that role beautifully—"Oh, I don't eat; I don't sleep; and I don't have time to go to the bathroom!" She not only reinforced the weakness in her husband, but she also came close, I think, to totally destroying all of her kids: a really bad-ass woman. And she's totally unaware of that, totally unaware.

She would just reinforce whatever negative aspects of your personality, your physical self there were: "You've got buck teeth; you've got a big nose." If an aunt was visiting and the aunt said, "Would you like a piece of fudge?" I would have to look at my mother to see whether it was all right. Nothing could be done without her approval. That's the way I guess she related to all of her kids.

That may be an unfair portrait of somebody, but the only sorts of things I can remember are like breaking a jar of Cocoa-Marsh, which is something chocolate that you put in milk, and she was down talking to somebody on the street, and I almost fainted from fear—literally almost fainted from fear of having to confront that woman about that event. And I ran down three flights of stairs to tell her because I couldn't stand the tension of having to wait for her to come upstairs. And she scolded me for interrupting: "You stupid bastard." How else do you talk to a child?

I was really the baby—my sister was the closest to me in age; there must be six or seven years between us. So as a result, I never learned anything social from them. I never learned to play from them, and I was living with a very protective mother—I certainly didn't learn how to play from her! In fact, I never learned to play at all. I rode a bicycle I think for the first time when I was about 25. And I never learned to swim—"Oh! Keep the baby away from the water! He'll drown!" I love to sail boats and I can't swim. I was my mother's last chance to really *possess* somebody.

We once lived on the third floor of a double Philadelphia-style threedecker, six-family house. I had my own room in that house—that was where we kept the milk in the winter because it was a very cold room and you didn't have to buy ice—a really terrific room. Behind us was the public library, and I used to spend a lot of time there—when I was allowed to go out. What I really wanted more than anything else was to be a shoeshine boy. There were lots of bathhouses then because people didn't have showers and tubs. I could see one of them from our porch. There would always be shoeshine boys around it, and I thought that being a shoeshine boy would have been the most romantic job in the whole world. My father said, "Sure, let him do it," but of course my mother wouldn't let me. I kept trying to make some kind of connections with the outside world, but she wouldn't allow it. I exaggerate, I know, but I've said it so many times that I believe it now: I spent most of my early life literally with a rope around my waist on the back porch.

Marriage

I got married when I was still in college. I met a nice little girl from a little town, pretty as a picture, sweet and nice and kind. I was in a frame of mind where I was going to save everybody, save everything, including her. She'd come from a broken home. Her mother died when she was young and her father had had a couple of marriages—he was an awful human being, that kind of small mill town person who's genetically poor and intellectually poor and just very sad. He made his daughter quit school so she could work—when she was sixteen years old, he pulled her out of high school. I was really in love with sweet kids, just loving sweetness, and I fell madly in love with her. She worked as a countergirl in a luncheonette I worked in after school. I pursued her for about a year and a half or something and married her.

I was just 21 when we were married, 21 and a few days, and I needed my mother's permission because we had to apply for the license before I was 21. And she was going to withhold it, as usual—Monsterwoman strikes again! It was during that period of time that I almost committed physical violence on my mother. Maybe it wasn't because of the permission, but it was something that was sufficient to make me want to kill her, and I actually held her against the wall and yelled at her very loudly. I felt better then.

We were married for sixteen years, and eventually it was one of those terrible and terrifying things where you just decide that you must reject another human being. I know that very early on I began to think that this relationship had to end in only one way, and that still I didn't want it to. I mean, if there's anything I subscribe to, whether I've been effective in it or not aside, it's that if nothing else, what we don't do is we don't hurt another human being. We may not be swell guys all the time, but what we don't do is we don't purposely set out to do any damage to anybody else. So I literally did a lot of crying. There were times when I was alone—say, driving—when I would become so terribly aware that this was not a viable situation that I would be moved to dissipate that anxiety through tears. I think that for maybe eleven of the sixteen years, I was aware that it was not going to work.

Early on, my wife voiced real anxiety about whether she was bright enough. She would say, "Well, gee, I don't know anything about that, and that's terrible. It isn't fair to you." And I would say, "Well, don't be silly; people change and grow and we all learn; we'll learn together." The fact was that she didn't change and grow and learn, but retreated further and further into the traditional mold of keeping the house, I suppose out of resentment—"Oh, you're ten minutes late for dinner! It's cold!"

It was probably one of those foreordained things—she had a set of problems, I had a set of problems: "Oh, good; let's use them with each other." And really, that's the stuff of which human relationships are more often than not made, until some sort of "maturity" is reached. My problems had to do with the fact that I was a very, very shy person. I could no more sit in this room and talk to you when I was 20 years old than I could fly—because I wouldn't have known you. I stuttered very badly until I was about 22. The first time I had to say my name to anybody at college was when I took the medical exam on registration day, and I couldn't say "Brian." I said my last name first, "Cooper, Brian." And I'm convinced that my myopia is the result of the need to be myopic when I was younger; I'm absolutely convinced of that. It may be horseshit, but it makes some kind of emotional sense to me. After I graduated from college, I took a job in a library, and I made myself stay in library work, encountering scores of strangers every day because I had to stop being terrified of people. I made myself do it; and what made that possible was that I loved dealing with books.

I guess this was a classic relationship where the male who has a very weak ego picks a female for whom he can provide everything, and then as the male gains confidence, the male says, "Who is this dull thing sitting next to me?" I think that's the major overview of the relationship fairly objectively viewed. We both had our serious problems. It turned out that my wife wasn't nearly as fond of sex as I was; she wasn't crazy about the outdoors, and I was. We were total opposites in a lot of important things. I remember how I described the relationship to a friend of mine after it got really lousy, after I was able to verbalize it: She had these little flat shoes like ballet slippers, and she had the prettiest damn feet and ankles. I loved her feet in those shoes. As soon as we got married, she threw those shoes away.

What finally happened was that one day I was feeling really terrible. I was working in the library, and the head librarian, who was a surrogate father or something, said, "What's wrong with you?" We were in the elevator going upstairs, and I just burst out crying and said, "I can't stand this fucking life any more; I just don't know what to do." His brother was a friend of mine and a psychologist, and he sent me to this psychiatrist who specialized in talking to people who didn't like each other any more. I went out and talked with him—alone—and then my wife and I both went out to see him. We talked together for a little while and we decided that I would leave. . . .

No; I know. What precipitated my leaving was one of these wonderful unconscious acts—you write a letter to the doctor and leave it where someone else will find it: "She's a really nice lady. I don't want to hurt her. But I can't stand her." This was a terrible rejection. Things got really ugly, and she said, "You've got to leave." So I went and lived in a roominghouse in town for a long time, but then I came back, and in the meantime, we met with this psychiatrist and we kept talking. From my point of view now, I think the guy was taking an advocate position. Maybe he was a sentimentalist—I don't know. Maybe he had the point of view that it's really important to keep people together rather than let them come apart. Anyhow, I decided to lead, as Thoreau said, "a life of quiet desperation." I resolved that Brian Cooper would thenceforth lead a life of quiet desperation.

Then there would be periods when my wife would get into really dark troughs that I would have to say were close to clinical paranoia. I couldn't deal with that, so I did all kinds of symbolic things. I had taken off my wedding ring at one point, and she had discarded hers, so I bought her a new wedding ring. It was sort of pitiful in a way because I was doing things that I didn't want to do. I was going to parties with other suburbanites who I didn't really enjoy. I learned to care about professional football and all that sort of thing. I was beginning to put on weight and I was sitting around watching television. I was doing all this because it was a way of filling up time and trying to get myself into a state of mind that would allow me to "fit in" with this suburban society as a sort of typical husband and father. Meanwhile, she would get into these depressions where she would say, "You don't love me; you don't respect me," and I would try to reassure her—"Oh, I do, I do." But I'm sure that I'd telegraph my real feelings. I would never be good in a public relations department because I don't have that public relations personality. People generally know when I like them or I don't like them. Because she would be upset, I would say, "Well, let's go to a counselor." We spent a lot of time and money doing that—we couldn't afford it—but it was very important to do. Things would go along and we would try to make it—and real darkness would descend. I thought at least that I was willing to make the commitment that I'd decided to make, but it wasn't allowed—it just wasn't.

Finally, one summer day, I was lying in a hammock in the back yard reading *Decline and Fall* by Evelyn Waugh—which is very funny and also very sad and also about marriage—and I wound up crying and crying and crying. I asked my wife to come outside, and I said, "Okay, we're going to end this." The thought of having to say "No" had made me weep for years, but I finally saw that something bad, something really worse was going to happen to me than might happen to my family because of a separation. I was under siege and I was going to turn into something that I did not want to turn into—one of those suburban men who sat around and watched football all weekend and a guy who drank too much. And I wasn't particularly interested in either one of those careers, so I decided that I had to do something about the marriage. I think that that whole mystique is mistaken anyhow, about the importance of the solid family, because from what I've been able to glean over the last year or so, the studies that set out to discover that there are all kinds of problems among families of divorced parents are preordained—the results are preordained. When you compare studies that are done with the rest of the populace, you generally find that they often wind up with very much the same results. I think I was laboring under the delusion that there would be a lot of destruction because of my action vis-a-vis my marriage—destruction to the kids.

We sat down with the kids and talked with them. I guess my wife said, "We've been trying to postpone this, but it isn't going to work out. . . . And I've asked him to leave." They were not particularly surprised—they were about thirteen and fourteen at the time. I guess my wife and I had decided what would be the most practical way to do all this—she wanted to stay in the house, and the kids were in a suburban school system that was reasonably good, so they all stayed out there and I moved to the city. We told the kids, "Later on if either one or both of you want to live with your father, you can make that decision, but for the time being, he's going to be moving and settling down, and he's going to have to find a place to live, and there probably won't be room for you right away. You'll probably want to finish school here." We probably just talked it out. We had done enough preliminary discussing that we probably knew which way the dice were, and indicated that it would be a reasonable solution for them to stay where they were. They felt it was a good idea to stay—they still feel that way about it. I suppose my daughter was just in high school, and my son was going to be in a year or two, and they were having a good time. It did dawn on me that here I was, "abandoning" my kids just at the same time that my father had abandoned me—at age fourteen.

I knew that I would have a really hellish period, not being with the kids and not growing with the kids, and not watching them grow and influencing their growth in the way that you can when you live with somebody. I wondered about what kind of effect that would have; I always wonder about those things—I do now—and I probably won't ever answer or resolve them. It was a painful situation: suddenly my hand was no longer over the fire; it still hurt like a son of a bitch but it wasn't directly over the fire.

Separation, Remarriage, and the Kids

After I moved out, I would go visit the kids, though as they grew older, they really didn't want to see me every goddamn weekend! I probably wound up spending a lot more time with my son than I did with my daughter simply because she elected to spend not as much time with me. I mean, "What do you do with this guy? Wanna play ball?" What does *anyone* do in a suburban town? I would go down there to the house, and those visits were difficult, you know. If a piece of furniture had been moved, I felt the compulsion to want to put it back where it *used* to be. The fact that maybe after a while some other man had been spending time in this house and with these children—that was always the hardest thing to think about.

Most parents try to overcompensate at the beginning. I made a very conscious effort to try not to do that, because I think it's ludicrous. You wouldn't try to make every weekend into a special event because it isn't fair to the kids and it isn't fair to the other parent—"Look what *I* do for you"—because the other person has to take all the day-to-day stuff, which is a bastard of a job. Sometimes we'd go off to the movies—I remember going to particular movies with my son. Maybe sometimes we would go off to the theater—things I probably would have done if I'd been married to somebody else. What I tried to do was avoid evaluating those times because I think that that's where you really get into a bind. If you say, "Okay, here is a special time. How did it go?" you put pressure on everybody involved in the process—it's like everybody's got to perform.

I would call my son once in a while, if I had something very specific to say to him. And we'd have a short conversation or a long one, depending on what kind of mood he was in. I let him pretty much call the shots. All he needed to know was that I love him—that's all that ultimately matters, as far as I'm concerned. He knows if he wants or needs something, if he wants to talk about something, he's got total access to me.

I changed jobs around the time we separated, moving from the library to magazine editing—that's a pattern you see a lot of people fall into, one life change and then another right away. Elspeth was my secretary at the magazine, a sort of nondescript pudgy Vassar girl. I had zero interest in her for a long time. Then we began to talk to each other, and we eventually moved into an apartment together—we've been married for two years. I like her a lot and we get along extremely well all the time. She's 28—12 years younger than I am—and she's solid and dependable and thoughtful. She's about the most mature person I've ever met—she was probably already completely mature when she was 12. It's really spooky sometimes. She had an enormously happy childhood; she adores her parents; just sort of solid middle-class midwesterners. Good taste, good sense of values—just terribly decent characters. She's really exceptional.

I certainly didn't want any more children, but the hardest thing in a way was coming to terms with *her* not wanting children. I'd think, "Is there anything to this nesting instinct? What's wrong? Is there a vacuum somewhere?" And I decided that she'd just evolved into a true rationalist and had made a decision that she would make a terrible mother because she'd be worried all the time about her children.

I was always a very, very involved and concerned father— overly so, I think. I spent a lot of time with the kids. Having grown up and gone to school when the sociologists were talking about the suburban family and the father being away, and having moved in fact to the suburbs, still I was going to spend a lot of time with the kids. And I did. I did everything with them; everything, really—although I probably did less with my daughter than with my son. Since I certainly didn't want to take my own family as a model, I'm sure that my view of marriage and family was probably based on film as much as anything else. I'm sure that film has had a profound effect on our attitudes, films of the 40s and 50s. I worked a normal 40-hour week, but all the weekend time would be with the kids.

My son is 17 now and my daughter is 18. He is Mr. Anal, like his father. His room is very funky—in an orderly way, if that isn't a contradiction. Everything's in place, he can put his fingers on everything. He's never scratched a record. He's a very resourceful and I think he's unfortunately a very tense person, but he loves to do what he loves to do. A lot of what he loves to do is foreign to me, like hunting and fishing. When I was a young kid, I really adored the idea of that sort of thing, but I never had any experience.

My son's the tall dark silent stranger in an old John Wayne movie. Last year, he decided he didn't want to finish school, the school he was in; he wanted to go to a private school. So we went off to look at this place in Vermont that he'd heard good things about. We spent the day up there and he didn't say anything all the way—it's a long fucking ride and it was stinking hot. We drove up and spent the day and we drove back, and finally when we got home, he said, "I don't think so." And that was that. He went back to the public school system he'd been in.

My daughter is a butterfly, pretty and bright. She haunts me—marvelous, good, charming kid who is like a throwback to the 1940s—she's got to be something out of my past. She's incredible. She doesn't speak the language; I mean, she drops her "ings," she doesn't complete words, she doesn't complete thoughts. She has a lot of social grace; that's always been her great strength and also, I think, in the end, the thing that has served her not very well at all. Because when she's in a situation that demands some sort of real solid resolution, she's able to float around in it. This is typical of kids who are learning disabled—she was diagnosed as l.d. at one point—they develop terrific social skills. I mean, there are all these wonderful survival mechanisms. Well, she's extremely good at that sort of social stuff.

Both my kids have really hated school. In fact, my son's going to take a year off after graduation and get some sort of "shit job," as he calls it, before making a decision about further education. My daughter quit high school early in her junior year. She had been cutting up and cutting class. We went to school several times and discussed this with guidance counselors and the staff psychologist and all this. I didn't want her to leave school, but they said, "Let her; she'll come back." And we let her, and she didn't go back. She's living with me this year—she goes home to see her mother on weekends—because she's going to a school here in the city. She's going to vocational school and given what I had hoped for her, it is just very hard for me to cope with.

I think that if their daddy really investigated it long enough and hard enough, he'd find some roots in his own attitudes toward school that move his kids to hate school. I might have pushed school too hard. Also, the kids may have said, "Okay, Mommy's not so bright and Daddy's putting her down. I really sympathize with Mommy. Sometimes we get put down and we don't like to be put down." They may indeed have made an identification with their mother and made an unconscious judgment. I think we are *all* of us—no matter how much we're working on a rational level as much as we think we are—we're operating as animals who are sensing things a hell of a lot more than we're really rationally receiving things. I think kids are aware on that level. They're not necessarily intellectually aware, but later on maybe they intellectualize things. I do think that my daughter identifies with Mommy very strongly. I don't intellectualize it very often, probably because it isn't very pleasant, but I think she has made a moral and ethical judgment about rejection and has decided that what I did was not defensible, that the things that matter to me don't ultimately matter; that the things that matter to me are externals and that basically her mother's a good person who got screwed by someone's shallow value system.

When I wasn't living with the kids any more, the hard part was not to cry sometimes at night when I would realize that, yes, this isn't a temporary situation. There were a couple of times when I would go into depressions of four or five days. I would come home and I would make something to eat and then I would go and I would sit in a hot bath and I would just be as close to having nothing in my mind as I could imagine. I was just vacant, just totally vacant, unable to feel anything emotional. Those were the worst times, when I really thought maybe that I was deep-ending. The downs, while they lasted, took another form with Elspeth: sometimes I would actually try to terminate our relationship—sort of a mercy-killing. I would suggest to her that maybe she should be marrying that 28-year-old guy from Yale who had a very good law practice. But now I think about my son's graduation from high school which should be this June. It will be peculiar to be in that place, at that time, and at that event without having been as involved as other fathers, not knowing those other boys as I would have otherwise. I don't have a context to live in in relation to them, and that bothers me a little bit—I feel sad for both of us.

Phil

Phil, now in his late twenties, comes from the heart of a major Northern urban black community in which he has been an active organizer. He and his wife, Sally, are divorced. They have two children, Meaghan and Habib, aged eleven and eight.

Phil and His Father

I had a chum-type relationship with my father, which was part of a larger thing that went on in our family. My parents and most of my relatives dealt with me more as an adult than as a young person. I was the second oldest. My sister was five years older, but she was the daughter. I was treated as a son for a short period of time; then I was brought in on the decisions and that shit. Even today I get calls from members of the family in other parts of the country who are a lot older than I am and who have always put me in that kind of role. I would never want that done to my kids because it does some very heavy things. It puts you in a very difficult and compromising relationship with your parents, where they're not really the type of parents that you want them to be, because you can't be the type of son, or whatever, that you want to be. There are just too many other things happening in the relationship.

They were all treating me like I was their contemporary. It started around the time that my grandfather died, when I was about 11, and it was great, because here the adults were treating me like an adult. But it became heavier and heavier as time went on, because it meant that I couldn't in some ways be the kind of kid that I wanted to be. There was all this sense of responsibility, and that prevented me from dealing with my own life, my own problems, my own shit that I wanted to get together.

It wasn't an abdication of responsibility on my parents' part. There had always been a feeling that decisions and stuff should be shared. But this was more than just decisions. It was people in the family coming to me, almost for advice, about stuff that I had no fucking idea about. I mean, come on, you know—"I'm a kid." My younger brother and my older sister didn't get any of this treatment, but man, I got it.

Mostly because of this stuff, I left home when I was 13. I was very close to my family, loved them very much, but I didn't feel that I could handle all that. So I split, worked—I had some money saved up because I had been working before. I lived down the street for a while—had some relatives down there. I paid my way, as much as a 13-year-old can. And I was away from home for about three years—pretty much really away from home, not just living down the street and coming back and eating and shit. I came back for a couple of months when I was 16, and I've been away ever since.

Part of the problem was that there were a lot of similarities between my father and myself. It was very hard for two egos that size—two stubborn people, which we both are—to coexist. My feeling was that if I wasn't going to be given the same kinds of privileges, I didn't want the same responsibilities as my father had. They thought I should accept that kind of weight and not worry about having the privileges which would have allowed me to deal with my own stuff. So I said fuck 'em. And we fought, my father and I—we fought physically. A lot of it was a process of demystifying him on my part, my defining who I was within that context. I remember thinking in the midst of it, "Yeah, at some point we'll be friends, but right now we can't get along." It was really a heavy time. My mother definitely stayed out of our battles. I mean, we used to slug it out, and for her it was, "Hands off! I hope they don't kill themselves."

Now my relations with my family are very, very tight. I think it was after my son was born that there was peace again in the family—not because of my son, but just that by then I had changed to a certain extent in the way I was dealing with stuff, and so had my father.

When he was a lot younger, my father was involved in some trade-union stuff, and he was a member of the Communist Party for about three years. I also have an uncle who was deported from this country for political reasons in 1952—that was the whole McCarthy period. He was a black Communist trade unionist, and they didn't like that. When *I* started getting involved in radical politics, my father didn't really understand what I was doing. It was a world that he had sort of stepped aside from, you know, and here I was back into it. I guess he was very afraid I was going to get crushed.

Conceiving Communities and Kids

I've been involved in community organizing since before I was a freshman in high school. I did not graduate from high school. When I was a junior, we were just beginning to put together what we called an Action Center around the campaign of a black person that was running for Congress. Toward the late summer, which was also toward the end of the campaign, I became director of the Action Center. Because the voter registration drive was coming to an end, I was in the process of turning it into a community organizing project, and I just started doing that instead of going back to school. At that point that sort of work was a lot closer to where my head was at than another year of vocational high school. I decided I didn't want to deal with college or high school for a couple of years. There was some stuff I wanted to get straight in my head, so I went out on

the streets and started doing it. I've never gone back to school as
a student, but I've been back in terms of putting together
courses and programs in urban planning and community needs
at two different universities.

I worked for a while in community programs at an Episcopal
church. With a special grant from the Episcopal diocese, we set
up a day-care program that was staffed by welfare recipients.
After that, we began to think about a school—an alternative
school. Lots of the youth whose parents were involved in community action at that point were having some serious troubles in
school, being identified as behavioral problems and blah, blah,
blah—which we're still hearing, right? What this meant was
that some had serious problems being in a classroom with 45
kids, some had problems dealing with teachers that were racist
and were really tired of being teachers. That's all those people
knew for the last 150 years. At the same time, we were involved
in fighting for hot lunch programs in school—this was in '65, '66,
and '67—fighting against corporal punishment—which also still
exists in schools—and against the old textbooks. When my
brother was in school—he's a year and a half younger than I
am—he was using a textbook that I had used, and when I had
used it, it was over 50 years old—a history. We might have
raised hell with working-class history, too, but just the way that
book depicted black people was so bad. If you come out of that
kind of system, you're usually pretty fucked up just in terms of
your own self-worth. So we got involved with some of the
parents in some of the schools, PTAs and stuff, and decided,
essentially out of the requests of some of the kids, that we'd set
up a school.

We were willing to take anyone in that school. It was mostly
community kids, but anyone that the school system identified as
a behavioral problem was welcome because we knew we could
make it work. Our attitude was that the parents, especially
welfare recipients—who were constantly being told that they
couldn't teach their kids, they being irresponsible—were in fact
the best teachers around, that parents are responsible for the
education of their children over a long period of time, more so
than the five hours a day or whatever it is that the schoolteacher

has them, and that if they weren't decent educators, there was nothing that could happen in that five hours a day that would make much difference. Since we knew that most people in our community had gotten at least some of their personal shit together, we were sure that we had a lot of good educators running around, good educators who didn't realize how good they were. So we began to instill that in people—a better sense of their own worth. And we did it. Our school was the first alternative community school in town.

We ran it with only one teacher—licensed or master teacher, that is—because that's all you needed to be legal. All the other people were parents, either welfare recipients or working mothers. We started with three grades—K-1, K-2, and first grade. I was teaching first grade along with a bunch of other people: myself, one mother, and one "community aide," a teenager. That's the type of team we tried to work out for each of the classes.

We attracted a lot of attention; very quickly, a lot of people wanted to get involved with us. And we had a lot of fights with the public school system, where they were happy as long as we took people that they didn't want, but when other people started coming to us, they were very upset about it. At the end of the first year, they came to administer tests to our kids. Remember, we didn't even deal with the standard curriculum. We just decided at the beginning of each month what course areas we wanted to deal with and how we wanted to deal with them. They found that our kids in K-1 were operating at first-grade level and that our first-grade kids were handling third-grade material. So they came in with their guns, prepared to blow us away, and had instead to give us a written evaluation that said we were doing a dynamite job with teachers who had, on the average, a seventh-grade or eighth-grade education.

Now the school has become an end in itself, but originally we did not see ourselves as being primarily outside the school system. We were a place where some good stuff could happen, an example and source of encouragement to welfare recipients and parents, saying to them, "You can do this." When the school board came along and told them that certain things were impossible in terms of education, they could point to concrete examples now and answer back, "You're full of shit!"

My daughter, Meaghan, was born in 1965. She's my adopted daughter, not my "daughter" daughter. But I was involved with her family from before she was born until the birth and afterward. She doesn't remember her biological father at all. During the first years of Meaghan's life, I was working with kids at the community school—I'd worked with kids since I was eight years old—and I saw my being part of Meaghan's growing up and my work at the school as all part of the same thing. At first I'd been scared of the responsibility and did not see myself in the role of her father, nor did I even expect that we'd be together all that long. But at some point I made a decision to stay involved, because I dug Meaghan. I had in fact been her father for a while, had become very much involved in her life—as much as I was involved in Sally's, her mother's, life—and I did not see myself being anyplace else. My hesitations about the whole responsibility trip just dissolved as I went along dealing with stuff.

In '67, the black community blew for the first time in about 20 years—around a welfare action. The welfare commissioner had recommended to the state legislature that it not approve a cost-of-living and clothing allotment increase for welfare recipients that year. So we decided we were going to protest that by locking ourselves in the welfare building, chaining all the doors. The mothers went in on a Wednesday. Myself and three other black males from the Party went into the building and joined the action later the next day. Friday, the police came in and the shit went down. The deputy commissioner walked in with a bullhorn and said, at the top of a whisper with the bullhorn turned off, "I order you all to leave"—said it three times. None of us heard it until the third time, just as they were coming at us with bolt cutters. There were a lot of injuries, including a pregnant woman who died as a result of being stomped.

As I was being put into a police van, somebody threw a gallon or half-gallon glass container of milk and hit a police officer on the side of the head with it. After that, it was shit. They immediately pulled out the guns and started firing in the air, and people split and then came back stronger. The individual who threw the milk bottle was reacting to the way they were treating both the men and the women—pulling people by the heels down the steps and shit, over cut glass. By the time we got down to the station, the police were putting on their riot gear. But we were not released for about three hours, so we had no idea what happened during the first few hours of shit that went down. When I came out of the station, I couldn't walk.

We made a decision to have our son, Habib—and it's interesting that he was conceived the next day—the day after I got out of jail in 1967. There were a lot of things involved in that decision that Sally and I didn't talk about for a while. Mainly, it was sort of a feeling of the moment that we didn't want to squander all that revolutionary fervor. We'd been thinking for a while about whether or not we were going to raise a family larger than Meaghan or whether we were going to deal with just one child, and we figured that a three-year spread was about right. So we did it, and it had to be that night after I got out of jail. It was a trip because that was also a very heavy year politically for our community, and Habib ended up being born two days before Martin Luther King, Jr., was assassinated. So from his conceiving to his actual birth, it was just that kind of turmoil. It was something that we very much wanted, that we planned and thought out. We didn't expect to have the hassles that we had later on.

Phil and Sally

I come from a working-class family and had developed a working-class perspective very early on, I'd like to believe, though I couldn't put it all together because my world wasn't big enough yet. But I had some very serious problems working with certain kinds of people—with white people in particular. At one point, I was in this situation where I was working with a lot of white people, responsible for their everyday goings and comings and work assignments and all that shit, and there was one person that bugged me more than anybody else. She wanted to work, do this, do that. I'd send her out to the roughest housing projects to do tutorials and stuff, and she'd do it, right? And I'd be saying to myself, "This person can't be for real!" After a while we became involved with each other, which was very irritating at first, not in terms of my working-class perspective, but because of my racial outlook.

She was one of the white college students that were coming into the black community then. Man, we were buried with them. But I found out that she was a decent human being, and over a period of time most of my racial stereotypes about white people got broken down.

She was from a working-class background herself—that's where her family started. By the time she got to college, through some breaks or whatever, her family had begun to be upwardly mobile. But her father was more proud of his working-class background than the fact that he had a house and a car and all that kind of bullshit. He was a printer, a proud pressman, and he would have been happy if he'd stayed that way. But his wife was the person that was very much going someplace else. She was a teacher and wanted to get this and that.

My family thought I was crazy. I did too in a way. They understood that proximity breeds certain kinds of relationships, that if you work with somebody long enough, you begin to develop either a feeling of aversion or a feeling of affinity. And a feeling of affinity—who knows where the fuck that's going? They'd seen me involved in lots of other relationships, with blacks, Asians, from the political work that I was doing, because I came in contact with just a tremendous amount of people from all over the world. So they had no idea what I was going to end up being involved with or married to, whether it was even going to be human! I mean, seriously, I got some very heavy raps from those folks. But they did feel that I had fairly good judgment, and in spite of other things that were going down, I myself felt that I had fairly good judgment.

We didn't get married until almost just before we broke up. Most of the time that we were living together, in fact, we weren't even planning to get married. We didn't feel it was necessary, you know—all the traditional arguments. And we had a fairly together relationship during a good part of that time.

We were both involved in community stuff—Sally was working in the tutorial program and at the community school.

But there were a lot of problems. We had a tremendous amount of trouble with her parents. I had appeared in both the *New York Times Magazine* and in the paper—pictures and shit and a couple of articles. Once while I was helping the Panthers set up a political education program—the Party was doing that across the country—my picture was taken at a Panther demonstration in New York. Sally's parents clipped it out of the paper and sent it to her, saying, "Now we know what he does." All during this time they had this whole beef about, "What actually does he do? Where's the money coming from?" They were very, very uptight about that shit. The father wasn't quite so bad, because I had been a printer; I was a union organizer, and he was a solid union man. But he didn't like the fact that I was black. The mother was the worst, though. As a schoolteacher, it was inconsistent in her mind that I had dropped out of school, yet I was giving lectures and stuff at colleges. She couldn't understand how I could have helped design two college programs and set up a community school. She kept saying, "Well, if you can do this, why don't you finish school? Why don't you make that little box complete? But if you can't finish, how can you do all this stuff? It doesn't work right."

At one point, they threatened to take away the kids because we weren't married. I didn't have any legal claim to them, and the argument was that Sally was an unfit mother until she came to her senses and came back home. I flew up there, sat down with Sally's father, and laid it out to him, told him he was not getting the kids, that he wouldn't be able to get within ten feet of them because he would have to come into my community to take them.

Sally was freaking out during a lot of this. She was very bitter about their reaction, expected them to be able to deal with people. She did once take the kids up there, after our house was set on fire—gasoline bombs thrown underneath the porch and shit. This was kind of hairy with Meaghan around, so she went up there for a while. After she came back, we almost broke up because my manner of dealing with it was, "Nobody's going to

take the kids, no matter what I have to do!" She was caught
between love for her parents and love for the kids and me, and I
was not as sensitive to some of that shit as I should have been.
So one day I came home and she was gone, had gone home.
She'd spent a couple of years fighting her parents, not even
talking to them, and very much needed to touch base with them
again.

We finally got married in '69, and I adopted Meaghan in '70.
Then we began to really have troubles. I was in the hospital a
couple of times after nervous breakdowns, and when I went into
the hospital the second time, we had a big fight about our books.
There were about 3,000 volumes, and they were my whole
education. Over a 10- or 15-year period, I had read a tremendous
amount of material, and I wanted to bring the books and some
other stuff over to the hospital. She wouldn't let me. Before I got
out of the hospital, I found out she was filing for divorce; and
after I got out, she had taken off. I couldn't get into the house to
get the books because the lock had been changed. So when she
came back, we argued about the books. Some of the books were
definitely mine, some we had bought together, and some were
hers. It was hard, because I don't believe that people should own
books, in a sense, but this was like my whole education, and also
it was my resource material for my writing and for the educational work I was doing for the Party. I was very pissed off and
told her in no uncertain words how pissed off I was. *She* was
pissed off that I'd want the books, because I'd read them all and
she hadn't. But I never got the books. She has them today.

The kids stayed behind with her, too, which was twice as
vicious, you know, arguing and battling. After she filed for
divorce, we sat down and talked about how we were going to be
friends and shit, but what ended up going down was that I
didn't see the kids for about four months. Then there was a
complete reversal—I could see them anytime I wanted, and I
began to see them on weekends. Then she began to change her
mind about the divorce, but at that point I decided I didn't want
any. As long as I didn't tell her that, it was easier for me to see
the kids. When I finally did tell her, it became hard again, and
it went through ups and downs until October of last year.

Now things are stabilized. Her situation is better both emotionally and in terms of work stuff. We've begun to work together politically again, which is easier now than it was before. Also the kids are older. She was very uptight at first when the kids began to see me again, because I was with somebody different, but we talked about a lot of stuff straight, the four of us together, when I'd bring them back. It's the first time in about six years, I guess, that I've felt on an even keel with my children, with her and our children. The kids'll call or drop over, and that's allowed now because she's not as uptight about my saying at some point, "Fuck it, I've got them. I'm leaving." Of course, there were reasons on her side for being uptight about a whole bunch of shit, too. I'm not trying to lay it down one-sided.

The two of us had just stopped growing together, were seriously growing in different directions, became almost strangers to each other. When we talked about futures, I talked about taking a course in labor law, something I could do while I went on working and doing political stuff within the black community and the working class. She'd gotten her master's and her teaching certificate and talked about doing something that would guarantee her income, about needing things she could count—a house, a car, trips to Disneyland or Mexico, stuff that had never entered my mind. And I was very insensitive to her needs.

Child Rearing

Sally and I had some disagreements about the kids—for instance, discipline. I felt it was important to be strict, not in the sense of yelling at them and stuff, but in the sense of trying to be as consistent as possible. Sally didn't worry about that kind of thing, and she was not consistent. She'd get pissed off at me and take it out on the kids. There was a certain type of violence about that which was due a lot to frustration about the life we were living. I mean, when she had gotten to college, her family had more money than my family had.

Then there was food, whether the kids ate or didn't eat. I have a thing about throwing away or wasting food—it's something I grew up with, and it just drives me up the fucking wall. I had to get to a place where I was cooler about that, because I didn't want to enforce my kind of dietary restrictions—I don't eat meat now, for example—on the kids.

On safety, my thing was that they could do a bunch of things up to a certain point, and if they messed with things that we had agreed were off limits, then all of those perimeters were moved in. Her attitude was let them go until something happened and they found out themselves about stuff we'd warned them about. To me, that was very dangerous. In the situation I grew up in, there were things you had to watch out for—like when you go across the street, you gotta make sure there aren't any cars coming. Growing up in the city, you dealt with a lot of people, but you had to decide where you were coming from at any given point, whether this new person you're meeting is someone you can deal with or not. In the situation Sally grew up in, you could walk across the street blindfolded and the chance of being hit by a car was nearly nil. There just weren't that many cars around. There weren't that many people around, either, so her attitude was you didn't have to be so careful when you met somebody new. She thought most people weren't going to mess with the kids anyway.

Sometimes we'd resolve stuff by talking about it for three or four days in a row. When the kids were older, we'd do this when they were around. After all, we're dealing with their lives. They might have something to say that changes everything. We resolved some things by one or the other person just giving in and saying, "Fuck it." That happened a lot. The food thing with me was a "fuck it" thing. I was feeling that we were wasting x amount of food a week and we just didn't have the money, but she was not about to change her attitude, so "Fuck it." On the other hand, some of the things I was doing weren't too cool either, like smoking. I was doing about five packs of Camels a day then, and I'd leave them unlit all over the house. It was pretty hairy when I found my infant son chewing two cigarettes.

Even before we got involved with each other, Sally and I spent a lot of time talking about sex roles and shit, about how we wanted to see stuff go differently than what we saw happening around us. There were periods when we were in those traditional roles, and periods when it was reversed, when Sally would be working and I'd be at home doing the work with Meaghan. That was very hard for me to deal with, because in the family I came from, everybody worked. If everybody didn't work, at least the man of the house worked; not necessarily as the sole provider, but just because there were options or jobs available to my father that weren't available to my mother. But often this was reversed for us because of my political notoriety. You can only be in the papers so many times before, when you apply for a job, they know who the fuck you are. You can only be in court so many times and have it written up that you are a member of this and you did that, or you can only have your picture on leaflets so many times and that kind of shit, before the doors close for you. So sometimes I was home with the kids.

As I said, at first I flipped out about it. I'd worked all my life, even when I was very small. I'd never had anybody else take care of me, always been on my own. Remember, I left home when I was 13 years old. So to be in a situation where I couldn't take care of myself was just very, very difficult, in spite of the fact that I was still doing all these other political things. I finally came to peace with it, but it took a long time, and I still have some problems with it. I can be at home with the kids now without going through the entry phase, but I haven't really accepted the situation as something that's compatible with the kind of person I want to be.

It wasn't a sex-role problem at all. My hassle was very much being tied all day to a place that was 13 × 12, 8 × 12, 24 × 12. If I took the kids out, that was fine. We'd go to a park, the zoo, play crazy games outside, draw pictures on the sidewalk, write on garbage cans. That was fine; no hassles. It was just being in the house, because I'm not an inside person. That has a lot to do with what my whole style of life has been. If I had been an inside person, I could have dealt with some other stuff easier. Being inside with kids isn't the same as being inside on a job. I don't look on my relationship with my kids as a job. There's work involved, but it's not a job—it's my kids.

Children of Revolution and Divorce

When the kids were young, there were problems created by the fact that I was in and out of jail constantly and traveling constantly with my political work. I would be sent to Gary, Indiana, for a couple of days and then end up in Bogalusa, Louisiana, for the weekend. When you're on your own, you can do that and it doesn't disrupt anybody else's life. But if you're with other people and you have a family, then it causes certain kinds of problems. Especially with Meaghan. We would be together a couple of weeks, regularly, every day of the week, all the time—I'd take her with me when I was doing my work—and then I would be away for a week or so. It was almost like I was a visiting parent, and it was very hard, both in terms of my establishing a relationship with her, and in her seeing me in any kind of particular role other than that of someone she liked who came into her life off and on. And of course with King's assassination, I hardly saw Habib for a couple of weeks after his birth. If I had it to do over again, I'd try to insure that I'd spend more time with them.

In some ways all this coming and going—both from my political work and from the troubles Sally and I had—has been good for the kids. They can be transplanted very easily, make do very quickly, and one way that shows up is that they're very good with other kids. They know how to organize activities and pull other kids around them in a really dynamic way. The same kind of thing often happens with a kid who gets bused to school. Both Meaghan and Habib are being bused to school now. A kid grows up in one neighborhood, belongs to a gang and stuff, terrorizes the community in general. Then he gets bused and goes to school with kids outside his neighborhood. This means he gets exposed to a whole different set of values, because different neighborhoods have different values in terms of how things are dealt with and how things get looked at and shit. The parents are coming from different places economically, religiously, educationally. So the kid gets injected into his life at a very important age a totally new set of experiences. That, to me, is very important. It's not a matter of disrupting the growth process, which is how most people see it, but of allowing the kid to become richer.

My kids already have that experience from the kinds of lives they've led since they were born. They have a larger sense of community than I had when I was growing up. I only had my own immediate turf, but they've got the whole black community and a large part of the progressive white community, too. They move freely within that whole framework. On the other hand, the kids have run into some heavy shit in their own neighborhoods because Habib is black and looks it, and Meaghan is white and looks it, and they're two people who are very much tied up with each other. It's not so bad now—people learn after a while—but there are still some heavy identity problems there that have to be worked out.

I worry about the fact that they haven't made very many permanent friends. I think that's caused by the impermanence in their lives. They know only two permanent things in their lives besides each other—Sally and me. So, though they have friends and acquaintances all over town, they each have only a couple of close long-term friends. They don't even get involved with other kids the way lots of kids do, fight about stuff—they don't get into too many fights. At school they do, which is just the reverse of the way it usually is. Usually at school you're semicool, and it's only at home that you let it all hang out. When I talk to them about this, they say they just don't see any kids that they like that well. It's kind of scary.

I'm talking partly about the kind of tightness you get in working-class neighborhoods as opposed to the suburbs. If you live in the suburbs, you usually travel by car to work, and your social life is spread out way beyond your neighborhood. Working-class people often walk to work, and their social lives are around there in the neighborhood, too. Whether it's a bowling team or people getting into card games or whatever, it's right there in the community. Anyone who walks to and from work or just walks to and from the store is going to have a different sense of where he lives than the person who builds himself a little castle—either house or car. My kids have a broad turf sense, but the problem is, within that turf they don't have the type of centralized or focused areas and relationships that I think are important.

Another problem that comes from my politics is the way the kids do a hero-worship number about me. I'm thinking about some of the stuff they've written to me, drawn about me. It wasn't just the traditional godlike father figure—but they've pictured me with a fucking gun in my hand and hammers and sickles all over the place, the whole trip, which is going to be very heavy later on for both of them. They always saw people deal with me in a very deferential manner. Organizationally, and within the community and stuff, their father was a big shot. And they still talk about the police, when the police arrested me, beat me up, and all of that shit. They saw me get busted a couple of times, and once they saw me get beaten pretty badly. Meaghan was going to the day-care center down the street then—this was when she was three years old—and there was a young woman who was supposed to help her across the street and take her to where I was working. Then I'd take her to the center. One day, just after Meaghan saw me all beaten up, the young woman didn't show. There was a police officer there, but Meaghan just sat down on the stoop of the stairs and cried, because she was scared to death to ask the police officer to take her to me. She was afraid he might beat me up. That kind of shit is just very, very heavy. They came to a strike I was involved in in '73 and saw some pretty serious violence. The police used dogs for the first time in a labor strike around here. I was one of the organizers of the damn thing, right out in front, and so the kids saw a line of those crazy animals coming at me. We didn't expect that to happen when we decided to bring the kids there.

There are people who talk about me when I'm not there. I've heard some of the stuff, and when I think back on what I was doing during those periods, I was not doing half of what they say. You know, I was not organizing the world. That's the image the kids have, and it's very important to me that the myth gets destroyed, that I become more of a human being to them, less of a superimage.

What I do is talk with them about my anger. They never used

to realize that I got angry about certain kinds of things. I talk about being upset. If I'm upset about something when they're around, and I feel like crying—which is hard anyway—I do it, or I try to do it. I try to be straightforward with my emotions when they're around. I also try to talk about my fuck-ups in the past— the fact that I had some serious problems with drugs there for a while, and that when that got taken care of, then alcohol became a problem; the fact that those things contributed to the mish-mash within our marriage, which is why I said there were two sides to this shit. You know, kids think parents are gods until they reach a certain age and find out that they breed, they cra?, they get down. "My parents don't do that." "Oh, yes, they do. And kids are disillusioned for a couple of years. I'm trying to do that kind of thing with my kids in a manner that doesn't blow them out of the water. But it's difficult, because it means reliving and going through lots of stuff that I'd rather leave buried back there.

Sometimes it's upsetting to them to hear this stuff, and sometimes it takes a while to explain that what I was about or what I was doing was not against them. They've already spent a long period of their lives reinforcing that special image of me, and to some extent that's legitimate because that's the way you put your hold onto something or somebody. So it's hard for them to accept that their father had a whole bunch of problems and still does and is trying to work them out. It's hard for them to accept the idea that they've got to deal with that part of their Daddy, or else what they've got is a memory that has no relationship to reality.

They haven't idolized Sally the way they've idolized me because they've lived with her more. There's not that much of a myth about her. And generally they've been open and natural with the women in their lives. Even if they're women I care about, they haven't seemed to be any kind of threat. They get along fine with the woman I'm living with right now. But the men in their lives—that's always been a very heavy thing. I mean, they have physically gone after some of the men Sally has seen, not dug them, not liked them, not treated them as human beings. That has pissed me off. She's seeing someone now pretty regularly, a dude who lives in the same building she does, and it looks like it's going to be a permanent relationship. The guy's beginning to become very attached to the kids, but the kids are extremely resistant to him. I'm trying not to foster that resistance. What's behind this stuff is the kids' not wanting any part of someone that would threaten the possibility of my coming back. And when it became obvious that I wasn't coming back, they just didn't like any of them because none of them could be me.

For a long time the kids thought, "What did we do? How come you two can't work stuff out? What did we do to make that impossible?" But that's pretty much worked out now. They understand, I think, that you can be involved with someone for a while, and then things hit the point where it's impossible for you to share anything, even the air, with your mate. That's somewhat a foreign concept still, but they can conceptualize it now. And they now begin to understand, through stuff I've done, that the divorce isn't something that I have against them, that it's not even something I have, in a sense, against their mother. I'm very much trying to decriminalize divorce, almost. You feel like a dancer on a hot tin roof sometimes, because you've got to do it in a manner that is straight. They can see the minute you game.

Parents, Kids, and Politics

About roles—and this is connected to the hero-worship stuff, too: Because of some things I could do very well, I was sometimes actually in a very heavy macho role. I used to train people who wanted to learn how to handle themselves physically, and I was also doing a lot of revolutionary security work. It's very wearing when you get a reputation for being that kind of heavy. You spend your life either backing down from that role or defending it. I started trying to put myself in a different place, because it was very dangerous for the kids. Some of the stuff that happened to the house—gasoline bombs and shit—happened because Meaghan lived there, and people thought they could get to me through her. If I could put myself in a different place, that shit wouldn't happen. What I tried to do was change some of the ways in which I did my political work. When you're on your own, it's possible to be adventurous and romantic within traditional male models—rake or whatever. When you decide, though, that you're involved in a relationship with someone, and if there are kids there, that changes; or for me it changed.

One thing I did was, I stopped carrying a gun, which I used to carry all the time. I used to travel, nationally and internationally, with that damned thing. That's not too cool when you've got kids. If you don't return the fire when someone's trying to blow you away, the chances are better that they'll just drop it and split. So I tried not to set up things like that. Even the way I handle speaking engagements and stuff like that changed after I had kids. There are certain ways in which you can make or respond to challenges that are less likely to lead to really rough stuff.

Getting out of that macho role was kind of hard, though, because some of the jobs that I would get would very much reinforce that stuff—for example, working as a truck driver and trying to pull together the rank and file within the Teamsters Union. I'd constantly get pushed and challenged into stupid fighting, just as a stand-up dude. And it was rough, because those fights determined who got loaded first on the loading bay, who got the good help and who got somebody that couldn't carry the weight. It all depended on how you carried yourself and what you did. If you fought against that macho stuff, you might end up getting 50 deliveries to make instead of one big haul, which meant that it took you a lot longer to get the work done and you got less money for it. I'd try to divest myself of all that when I came home, try to be the kind of mellow human being I wanted to be, but it didn't always work. It was because of the kids, though, that I made the effort.

The kids have been in most of the demonstrations that I and my wife have been in. In fact, they've gone on demonstrations that we didn't go on. What I believe in and what my ex-wife believes in are things that they've grown up with. Our politics haven't been forced on them or anything, but they get to look at some stuff their way. I've never told my kids what I wanted them to do, what I wanted them to be—outside of decent human beings—but they pick it up. They pick it up by induction, by how you deal with your own crises, what you want to see happen for you, the kinds of things you get upset about. They begin to feed into that kind of thing, and you begin to feed into it, too, because you begin to feel proud. They're doing things now that I would like them to do, even though I've never said, "This is what I want you to do." And they pick it up from other places, too. It hasn't just been from being around their parents.

At one point, the kids and I played with notions about God and shit, because that's part of the magic that makes the world real to you. Later on they said, "Well, that's something somebody else believes in, that people on the street believe. It's not something that we believe in."

My daughter's gotten hassles in school from teachers when they'd talk about black history or the war in Vietnam, because her perception of how that stuff went down is qualitatively different. My son had a problem with his teacher this past year, a young woman that voted for Nixon and worked on his campaign. Habib hated Nixon with a passion above and beyond anything that we adults ever expressed. Nixon to him was like John D. Rockefeller in the thirties, you know, the little evil man in the cartoons. So they definitely have their own politics. And they're just 11 and 8. I'm very proud of where they're at now.

Having kids didn't stop me from sticking myself out there politically; in fact, it gave me more reasons to, gave me more of a stake in the future. When you're dealing with stuff by yourself, and you go through ups and downs about who you are and what your own self-worth is and whether what you're doing is important, there are times when you say, "Fuck it," and you just stop. Or you say, "Fuck it," and do something that's in fact stupid. You're not always as analytical or thorough in your planning out of stuff as you should be, and it's very easy to give your life for the cause. When you've got a family, it's a lot harder. You've got stuff to live for. So you've got to do the same things, get the same work done, have even more audacity and be even more aggressive in certain areas, and yet be around to deal with things the next day. And that only happens when you have a stake in what happens the next day, and the day after that, and the day after that. I had that stake before, but there's a different type of meaning that your life takes on when all of a sudden another human being is in it too. There's a different type of meaning it takes on again when that other human being could possibly embody all your hopes and dreams for the future.

That gets very heavy. You know that the struggle isn't going to end, no matter what happens. The revolution could be over tomorrow, right? But there's a whole revolutionary rebuilding that has to go on then, and that can be a very messy process. I want my kids to be strong enough to deal with that; at the same time, I don't want them to go through half the crap I went through. So you have a commitment to get as much done as possible, with as solid a foundation as possible. The stakes become different, like I said, when you have kids. It's not just your own life that you're playing around with.

David

David, unemployed at 30, wonders which way to turn next.
Whether or not to have children is a serious and increasingly
pressing question—as yet unresolved—for him and his spouse.

Decision Making

I haven't explicitly decided not to have a child, nor have I
explicitly decided to have a child. It's an unresolved issue in my
mind at this point. And I can tell you why it's unresolved: the
stumbling block has to do with the question of whether I want to
say something now about what I'm going to be doing 15 years
from now. I mean, I think of having children as establishing,
representing—you know, being a commitment to a long-term
relationship with some kind of long-term stability. It's different
from my long-term relationship with Susan, which I'm already
committed to. *That* commitment was made with various kinds of
communication, and it's constantly subject to various kinds of
reevaluation and renegotiation. I think we both are in some
sense or another equal partners in the contract, whereas the

relationship with one's offspring is not quite the same. You foist life and dependency off on the kid without the kid's being able to choose that, and you take on a certain kind of commitment to the kid's future in return.

It's quite up in the air. I have no idea how it will work out. I think that at some point or another we will actually make an official decision, but when that will happen and which way it will go, I don't know. But this state of things is only tolerable within certain limits. There will probably come a point when it's balanced off, for example, against birth-control risks. I mean, Susan is on the pill. There would be the convenience of being able to decide to have a vasectomy if I were not going to have kids.

Of course, even after a vasectomy there would always be the possibility of adoption. Susan's very open to adoption, much more so than I am, although she's opened me up to it as a way of going about having kids. She's interested in adoption partly because one of the things in the way of having a kid, as far as she's concerned, is just plain, simple *physical* anxiety over childbearing. I mean, no matter how enlightened we are, I wouldn't be having the kid at that level, right? I wouldn't be going through the physical dangers, the physical experience of pregnancy. And that's not something that she finds a fascinating prospect—worrying about her safety or having fairly unspecified anxieties over the physical, what-it-means-to-your-own-body kinds of things, coming to terms with the immediate physical aspects of pregnancy, childbearing, nursing.

There's also this other issue for Susan—the other thing that Susan has going has to do with the ideas prevalent in her family about her relationship to a meaningful career, you know, as a woman and all of those kinds of things. I think she might be worried about whether or not having a child was some kind of a cop-out, to the extent that she relied on just having a child as a way to define her role. I think that she would want to have some other realms of achievement.

I have much less of a feeling about satisfying official, external—well, I view them as external; she doesn't—external notions of what's acceptable and how achievement really fits into personal satisfaction. I'm not particularly achievement-oriented, and I think that she is. I can't even imagine my own life five years from now. That's something that both Susan and I are able to accommodate ourselves to, but it doesn't mesh with the image of parental responsibility I got from my parents. They viewed the whole family trip as one of—immediately—$50 bonds in the bank at regular intervals, the college fund, and all that kind of stuff. That doesn't fit into my way of thinking at this point: I have no career in any sense; I have no residence. I just don't feel that I have any kind of long-term *place*.

I have mixed feelings about my own role in the world of work, as my mother would put it, and I'm not sure that I want to be working that out at the same time that I'm getting used to having a kid. And as for the possibility of staying home, say, and taking care of the kid while Susan works, I don't think that she would find that interesting. I mean, Susan doesn't like work any more than I do, and I think that we would *both* enjoy raising a kid. We both find kids really interesting, fascinating, fun, enjoyable. Having a kid would be, if nothing else, access to a status that has a certain amount of fluidity; and to the extent that any kind of life-style issues were resolved by having a kid, to the extent that I had a greater access to the rewards than Susan did, that would be a source of tension between us.

But implicit in what I said before is that while, on the one hand, I don't have any career goals now, I know it's not going to go on like this forever; and in a sense I would like to see how it works itself out before I have a kid. Though, on the other hand, personally—and within my relationship to Susan alone—I think that the drift of my life is organized right now toward somehow or another coming to terms with *not* having a specific lifetime career, which is certainly very different from my earlier images of where I was going.

To a certain extent, I suppose I'll have to come to terms with its never being resolved. And I find coming to terms with *that* to be in contradiction with having a kid. I imagine that it would be easier to have a kid if those things were settled, if you were playing it in the standard way.

Now, on the other hand, I'm aging. I have certain specific

beliefs about one's responsibility to be fairly young when having a kid, so I'm feeling more and more time pressure to resolve the kid issue. From Susan's view, of course, she's a couple of years younger than me, so that's no problem, or it's offset by a couple of years at any rate. I think of it more in terms of early retirement, early retirement from parenthood. I mean, I don't want to say, "Well, I got him through college," and roll over and die. And that has more to do with my feelings about aging than anything else, I suppose. But one of my specific memories about my relationship with my father was that he didn't seem to be as physically active with me as he was with my brother. Now that may just have been my mapping onto the situation certain kinds of resentments. I don't know. But that's another interesting aspect of my whole view of the thing, that I'm now at the age that my father was when I was born. And I'm the younger one. I think about that.

Susan and I have an ideal notion of what we would like to achieve, and it has to do with what we think would be best for us as a couple. Ultimately, what we would like to have is something that didn't require a lot of work and produced a lot of money, and we could work on it together at home and raise a kid and bake bread. You know, the home life kind of thing.

We live in the middle of no place. We don't have any friends for 50 miles around, and we've learned to get a great deal of our social activity and support and reinforcement out of each other. Our lives are pretty interpenetrated, and those times when we get to spend more time with each other tend to be happier than those when we spend less time with each other. And work is viewed as coming between us rather than facilitating anything.

When we were working on our book together, it was great. I mean, that was work and that approximated, except for the friction over the intensity of it, the actual setup: being able to both be working on something that we felt really positive toward, at home together, yet within our different styles. I mean, it wasn't like we had the same desk and typed together or anything like that, but we just had a very loose schedule. I don't know how demanding kids can be on that, but maybe there could be some kind of flow of activities like that that could have child rearing as a part of it.

We do divide labor, and we do have different domains to a certain extent. There are some things that we don't divide, that either can ask the other to do. It's completely unpredictable. I mean, you know, I think that we both recognize that it's unpredictable and that we would assume that we could work something out. We know that we have the skills that are necessary to make some kind of arrangement so that everybody gets as much out of the situation as is possible of all of the necessary kinds of time, time alone and time together. I don't know how much a kid can intrude into that, exactly, how it affects the time budget.

Having a kid or not having a kid would have to be a decision mutually arrived at by both Susan and me and embedded within the relationship. At this point, I would not want the decision to become in any way an issue that could affect—not *affect*, but disintegrate—my relationship with Susan. I mean, I assume it would affect it, but the decision to have a kid is dependent upon or derived from a commitment to my relationship with Susan. I mean, the desire to have a kid is completely subservient to my desire to continue to be related to Susan, though I could conceive of myself as finding it so much more important than Susan to have a kid that it could become a serious point of conflict. I don't want that to happen, and I certainly temper my attitudes in such a way as to not let that happen.

There are a variety of ways of doing that. One of them is the tentativeness with which we discuss that. What we're doing is constantly judging each other's attitudes. So you put out trial balloons, basically. You say, "Well, hey, you know, what if, you know I wouldn't mind having a kid, I mean, you know," and she might say, "Well, I don't think it's a nice idea." And a little while later you come along and say it again and see whether or not saying it in a different form gets a different response, and you just adjust your attitudes to each other over time.

Discussions between us about whether or not to have a kid or when have never been very detailed. They probably wouldn't ever have to be. We might be preparing dinner, for example, and one of us will say, casually, to the other, "Shit, we could easily have a kid here for this or, you know, or not, or whatever," but in fact the actual *details* of what would be involved are not something that we've ever really discussed. What typically happens, I think, is that one or the other of us advocates one side of the coin, and the other one advocates the other for the sake of argument as much as anything else. It flip-flops to a certain extent, although I suppose that I advocate having a kid more than Susan does, although I don't advocate it in any immediate, let's-do-it-now way. I mean, we've never come to that kind of confrontation.

I mean, it never comes up in the form: Should we or shouldn't we have a kid? It always comes up indirectly: work, life-style, long-term relationships—they're all obviously involved, and they're all obviously brought up by the same question. There are many anxieties about things that don't get specifically stated— what I'm saying is that if we had a conversation about children in our life, it would invariably bring up a bunch of other things that, even without the issue of children, are *also* anxiety-producing.

Our feelings are not so much wrapped up with kid-orientation as much as future-orientation, I think, and the unwillingness to deal with it has to do with the unwillingness to come to terms with just total life-style issues. To the extent that the conversations get bogged down or don't really get detailed or elaborate or specific, it has to do with our own anxieties over the way we are, you know, waffling through life in general. And I don't think that either of us is particularly interested in bringing a kid into that situation.

We've been discussing it since long before we got married. I mean, Susan's attitudes about adoption and fear of childbirth, things of that sort, are things that I knew before we got married, ten, ten-and-a-half years ago. We've been married for eight years, and we'd known each other for two-and-a-half years. But I don't think that either of us has ever talked about it as something that might really happen until very recently.

We've been influenced by Paul and Linda in the way we approach this decision. I certainly do think that people look around them and see what their peers are doing. They think, "Hey, shit, you know, if they've thought about having a kid and decided to go ahead and do it, what does that mean about my thinking at this point?" Of course, I think Paul and Linda reached the decision to have a kid in a way, at least from Paul's descriptions, that I would never tolerate. I mean, it seems as if one of them presented the other at some point with some fairly heavy bargaining—you know, an ultimatum. It's very unlikely that either Susan or I would present the other with an ultimatum of that sort. I say that because of our rules about conflict resolution, what kinds of demands one of us can rightfully make on the other and how we deal with that. You can never say, "You give me this, or I leave." No ultimatum which calls the relationship itself into question is ever legitimate. I mean, we know enough about each other at this point to say that there's nothing we want or don't want really, really more than the relationship. That's the primary goal.

The primacy of our relationship also comes up in thinking about our probable areas of disagreement and conflict over raising a kid. We now have conflict resolution techniques for most of the conflicts that we're used to. But with a kid around— the kid being very important and each of us feeling committed to raising it—maybe, you know, all of a sudden we would not have the resolution techniques. There would be new kinds of conflicts which would necessarily involve a very complicated set of political things that are unpredictable. I know about the limits of guilt-tripping and power-tripping now—how much I can get away with now. I don't know how those limits would be changed by the coalitions that would be brought about by having another person in there—I don't know. I certainly know that I don't particularly relish the thought of using a kid against the other person, for example, or of using the other person against the kid. And those kinds of elements, how it would affect the basic relationship between Susan and me, are real imponderables.

We both recognize that all this may lead us by default to end up just never getting it together to have kids. And we don't know what that lets us in for in the long run in terms of, you know, at the age of 60, our looking at each other and saying, "Shit, we really should have had kids, you know," or something like that or whatever.

But I mean, for somebody my age, you know, without a kid, it's one of those things: there *are* final deadlines.

Looking at Friends and Relations

Richard and Tracey are not going to have kids, for example. They've decided explicitly never to have children. So we have friends of that sort. I mean, Tracey says, "We're not going to have kids." I don't know how Richard feels about that. I don't know how he feels about their relationship. And I don't know how, entirely, to interpret that information. In general, I take statements like Tracey's to be a way of fudging the political aspect of the relationship with the other person. Usually, it's one person at a time talking to you about that kind of thing, and I take their statements to be only a gloss on the interaction between that person and the other party. Yeah, and I go home, and I say, "Gee, I wonder what really went on between Richard and Tracey."

I don't need information on how people resolve issues like having a kid or not, because I know how Susan and I resolve them. For the most part, what I look at is the ways in which the kid seems to be affecting the relationship after the fact. I hear the complaints, the bitching, you know, that kind of stuff. And I get a fairly realistic appraisal of the time commitment that's involved, just the day-to-day thing. I'm not so sure that I'm particularly interested in the potential that Susan and I would end up not paying as much attention to each other as we would like to because of the kid—in other words, that we might find ourselves related to each other only by virtue of the fact that we're both related to the same child. I mean, Paul has said things like, "The trouble with all this is that although we both get to see the kid, we never get to see each other any more." Well, I'm not interested in that. That's negative information, but I don't know how to assess it, because I don't think that I would be the same kind of parent.

Paul's relationship to his child is hard for me to interpret outside of the temporal brackets imposed by my comings and goings, but sometimes I view him as being unnecessarily short-tempered, unnecessarily annoyed, flustered, tense. I say to myself, "If Paul weren't so uptight about this particular situation, the kid probably wouldn't be picking up on that and there would be less fuss." I mean, it's hard for me to judge how much of the types of things that he has to cope with on the kid's part are things that in some sense he's set the kid up to force him to cope with. It's something I haven't resolved in watching his form of parenthood.

Susan's sister Laurie, who's another piece of evidence in this whole thing, came along and just had her own thoughts about how she was going to go about having a kid, about seeing to it that her values were realized through her relationship to the kid and everything like that. Half the stuff she said was so nonnormative—she's out of the mainstream of our cultural notions about all this, and everybody thought she was off the wall and that she was crazy and everything like that. Well, you know, it worked.

She doesn't just pick up the kid when it cries, but she's extremely attentive in all ways. She said to herself, "Well, I'm not going to have a kid until I'm ready to be extremely attentive, for a couple of years." And the fact of the matter is that the kid is in large measure, I won't say docile—I mean, she's a willful child like most children, but she has an extremely sophisticated relationship with her mother in which, fairly early on, communication became possible, the sort of communication that makes it possible to have an ongoing relationship in which hostility doesn't build up to unmanageable proportions, where everybody knows as quickly as possible about the various elements of the social contract, about give-and-take within that kind of thing. Hostility gets expressed, but, for example, compared with me or compared with the standards that were established in my family—right?—there's extremely little violence in that relationship.

Here's an interchange between Laurie and me in which I learned something about parenthood and also made an assessment of the way in which she goes about it. The last time they were visiting, the kid was doing something—I can't remember exactly what it was—but she was right there, OK? And I said something to Laurie like, "Well, would Kali want to do this or do that, or do you think it's all right for Kali to do this?" I was essentially thinking of Kali as drawn small in the picture—a child, not fully competent, not really a social presence. And Laurie said to me, you know, "She's right here—why don't you ask her? If you're going to talk, why not include her in the conversation?"

Well, what's interesting to me about that is that it was clearly stated as a matter of principle. I mean, that's the kind of thing that she clearly has thought out and that has for her very strong social feelings associated with it. She also knew that Kali was listening to her advocacy, that Kali was paying attention to the fact that she, Laurie, was advocating something for her in that situation. I thought about it, you know, and I really had to rethink my whole attitude. I mean, I instantly knew what she was saying, and I agreed with her completely. It's that type of enlightenment that I assume would come from parenthood—discovering your own kinds of preconceptions. You can get that just from being around kids.

I certainly do wonder about the way in which having a kid or not having a kid affects my relationship with my parents. I have some real anxieties over my ability not to get completely hooked into a pathological kind of thing with my mother over the way I raise my kid. I mean, if I were to have a kid, of all of the things out there that interfere with my ability to be the ideal parent and to do it in the perfect way, one of those things coming between me and that goal would be my own parents, specifically my mother, who I think would make an issue of it just as a matter of form, because her mother did too, and that's what you do, you know. One way or another, you find out the things that annoy your kid, that you can do to annoy your kid just to make it known to him what his obligations are to her.

I think that in my family my mother was the nurturer, and I see myself certainly as participating more than my father did in nurturing, and so my interests are more like my mother's. I don't resent my father for that particularly. My definition of the roles is very different from my parents'. What I'm really saying is that right now, in terms of my relationship with my parents, it's my mother who's the one who bitches about life-style issues, and that to the extent that child-rearing technique is a life-style issue, it would be my mother with whom there would be confrontation.

Furthermore, because it was my maternal grandparents who were my *only* grandparents, it was my mother's conflict with her mother that I got to witness over *me*. And furthermore I assume that my mother, being her mother's daughter in many ways, would in fact maneuver to produce the next generation's version of that same kind of thing, and *I* would bear the brunt of that because I am the one in that line.

But I have no commitment to their particular division of the pie: as far as I'm concerned, the family is just a bunch of things on a kinship chart, and you can put them together in a lot of different ways. I'm certainly not interested in being, you know, the Silent American Father.

Of course, my mother is a resource of information about how to raise kids. I mean, she's also a child psychologist. And we discuss child-rearing. For example, if you want to trace influences, you know, I've said things as simple as, "Oh, you should see the Holmes's kid, you know; she does this, she does that, you know, etcetera, and they do this, and they do that," and my mother says, "Well, of course she's going to be doing that; she's getting a lot of attention." That kind of thing, because she sees kids who get *no* attention, and she knows that from what I've told her about how Paul and Linda divide the labor. She's very open about that kind of shit. She's very open about other people's arrangements.

There are some things I know I won't be able to determine before making a decision to have a kid—things that will only become available as information when I stand in the specific parental relationship to a child, things that I can't know from watching other people's kids. Of course, I could run into a particularly unique type of coresidential arrangement.

To me, coresidentiality or whatever is—it's another way of going about setting up social arrangements that don't depend upon the stereotyped notions about what kinds of relations are possible between people. I'm attracted to it for the same reasons that I really get positive feelings out of watching Paul and Linda—because they don't seem to be trapped in stereotypes about sex roles. She's off doing work, in some sense or another, away from the house, but Paul is no more a housewife because of that than Linda is his husband or whatever, right? I mean, roles are for people who can't think; they're irrelevant to people in the ongoing relationship.

But getting back to the coresidentiality thing, living with other people would open up a lot of possibilities about dissolving stereotyped relationships. It would also resolve a lot of issues easily, especially issues about raising and sharing kids, right? I really think that kids are shareable. For how long, for how many years? I think that's something that's up for grabs, and it would have to come out of the understanding that people make with each other. I'd make a long-term commitment, saying that I would be financially responsible for certain elements. That's the level on which I would be willing to be involved. I would say, "Well, the four of us or the six of us are going to raise this kid, and that means that everybody has to see to it that they muster their resources in such a way that they can send the kid to college, if that's what they want to do." This would be a good arrangement, because it'd be more resources to pool, and that's one of the major impediments right now: the resource base. To me, you don't have a kid so you can go out and wash dishes.

Coresidentiality or a commune is good from the population angle, too, which is important to me. It's also important to Susan, very much a part of why she would be willing to consider adoption. But in relation to a coresidential deal, five people can get just as well informed from one kid about what kids are like as two people can, right? And it may be better for the kid. From the kid's point of view, it may be a lot easier to have five people, because then no single one of them will get bored with, you know, walking the kid all the time.

However, there are only a limited number of people that I would even conceive of sharing a kid with. I mean, there are only a limited number of people that I know well enough. If I say to myself about Susan, whom I have lived with for so many years, you know, "Well, there are still a few things that I think she might fuck up on as a parent, and I'm a little worried about it," then that means that there aren't a whole lot of people that I would want to make that commitment with. I wouldn't want to start it up with just a group that we met at a cocktail party.

One of the kinds of anxieties I have is that it's all Dr. Spock:

it's just really a phase; there's nothing absolute and true about my point of view; it's just what white liberals who are the offspring of Dr. Spock parents believe at this point in time.

I mean, there's nothing I find so disconcerting as the Dr. Spock idea that essentially you get cycles of child-rearing theories: "It's good to breast-feed" and all that kind of stuff, or "It isn't good to breast-feed"; "It's good to be removed from people who say it *is* good, and therefore it isn't good, you know." And so on. No matter what level you plug in to this kind of thing, you're still trying to second-guess what it's all about on the basis of some fairly narrowly defined intellectual position.

Getting Your Shit Together

Kids are interesting. I think they can tell you something about yourself, and you can also produce someone who is able to have a good time, and that's also fun. And I'm not entirely convinced that kids are necessarily a pain in the ass, right? I'm not sure if it's the actual behavior of the kid that's unpleasant or if it's the routinization that's unpleasant. I don't know if it's the kid or it's you. I mean, do kids zizz up their parents, or are the parents naturally zizzy? And I don't know if that's something I'd view as a defect in the parent or a defect in the kid or just inherent in the situation.

What is it that makes kids appear to be intrinsically interesting? I certainly wouldn't consider having a kid if I didn't think it was going to be interesting—emotionally, intellectually engaging. Not only stimulating but new and different and having implicit in it the possibility for various kinds of new levels of understanding—by *understanding* I don't mean purely, you know, ratiocinative, cognitive understanding, just self-development in some sense or another.

The kid becomes a resource for you. I mean, I think that's a fair trade: I'm a resource for the kid also. And I certainly wouldn't want to have it unbalanced. I'm not going to do it out of a sense of duty to society or whatever, right? I'm not going to have a kid for that. So that what I assume you're doing is kind of forcing a person into a relationship with yourself just by virtue of your being able to make that decision, and then, like all other relationships, you try to make it as interesting and as satisfying as you can, for whatever reasons and in whatever ways relationships are interesting and satisfying.

I think that there are indeed some biological things going on that I would imagine would be some of the stuff that I would find out about that I don't know about. It's one of those great unknowns. I imagine there are aspects of yourself and your own experience that you're cut off from because of limitations in memory and all kinds of things like that. I mean, I just don't know what it means to be a kid. I have a very, very poor memory of the growing-up aspects of my own existence. And I imagine that whether or not it would tell me anything specifically about what it was like for *me* at that point in time, it at least would tell me something about what it was like for *someone* to be at that point in time, and in more detail, and that would feed back into my attitude about life and myself and my place in all of that. And I think that I would view that as certainly information, something that I don't know anything about now that I would expect to know something more about later, and if nothing else, that in itself is one potential reward.

I think I've learned something about the extent to which and the rapidity with which kids can become obviously willfully manipulative in a fussy kind of way; and I would certainly want to avoid setting my kid up to do that, and I don't really think that it's impossible. I mean, I'd like to set it up so that one could express one's feelings—and I assume that there will be conflict of opinion and feelings and interests between a parent and a kid. I certainly feel myself to be unqualified without actually entering into that specific relationship to make a guess about how I would judge, how I would make corrections for the kid's weakness, how I would myself abdicate power.

What I'm really saying is: How much control do I want, and how much control do I really have, and what's the relationship between those two? I'm not sure how much I want, and in the absence of that kind of information, it's a knowably unknowable area which is knowably unresolvable without having a kid. It's really leaping off into dark water.

That's why I emphasize, you know, feeling good about yourself, because I think that it's feelings of that sort that make it possible for you to respond positively in the face of mystery. I mean, that open-endedness, the ability to handle open-ended situations, is what I think is necessary in order to be able to make a decision in the face of this kind of uncertainty.

To a large extent, career, mother, money—those kinds of hassles can be viewed as either personal problems or social problems. In different moods I can take them more or less on myself. I can say—I mean, I *can* say, "Shit, that's the way things are set up, and the real problem is to come to terms with the fact that things are set up that way and to produce somebody who can enjoy it in spite of all that or because of all of that or whatever," right? Or you can say, you know, "There are definite impediments in the way because I personally have negative feelings about them that are related at some level or another to intellectual things, political orientations, stuff of that sort." But in the face of that, what are the counterbalancing tendencies that make you still think that it might be interesting to have a kid? It's the personal satisfaction.

I've come to recognize my own ability, at any particular point in time, to put a positive construction on what's happening. That's what having your shit together is: rewriting history in such a way that you don't feel bad. And the reason that that's important for anyone, I would say, who's planning to have a kid, is that you just don't want to foist a miserable life off on somebody else. The major thing for me is somehow or another resolving my own feelings about the future, but that's all just part of getting your shit together. If you have your shit together, then there's no problem. It's just another, you know, fun relationship. I think I could probably pull it out of my ass. I mean, I'm getting more and more to the point of feeling like a completely socially competent individual. I mean, I just don't ever have to worry about the kind of inhibiting anxieties that made it hard for me to act in strange, new social circumstances.

I certainly don't want to find myself having been trapped into thinking of having a kid as being in some ways a solution to the life-style problem. You know: "Ah, if I only had a kid, this would all work itself out"; or "If I have a kid, I won't mind having a nine-to-five job"; or "If I have a kid, then my place in the world will have been defined for me." I mean, I don't want to force that onto a kid, and I certainly don't *believe* it. Plain and simple, I'm sure it doesn't work that way, so the other end of the scale is, "Well, maybe you should have your shit together before you have a kid."

I know that I can get my shit together in my head, but I don't know if I can take care of the external considerations—subsistence, a livelihood, that kind of thing. Having your shit together—I don't know: this isn't necessarily a pressure that most people subject themselves to.

In my case, I would say that when I get to feeling less and less concerned about the future, then I'll be able to make a decision, I mean, about what a positive decision would involve. Not *confident*, but—I guess . . . I know I'm not going to be a Ph.D. and a full professor in 11 years or 14 or whatever: I know that I'm not working my way up any particular career ladder at the moment. And that in itself takes a certain amount of rejuggling of my image, and what I'm saying is that up until now, kids have also been a part of that particular image.

We can certainly make it together, and we'll have to do some serious thinking to figure out how we can make it as a three-some. There are a couple of possible ways that it might work out. I mean, on the one hand, we might actually at some point or another decide that none of that's relevant to the decision to have a kid and we really want to have a kid anyway. Or we might get everything together, right? We might be doing something—changing and doing something that seems like it's going to lead in a direction that we're happy with.

Paul

Paul and Linda agreed to have a child only after long and involved discussion and disagreement. Throughout the nearly two years of their daughter Nicole's life, they have shared their child care responsibilities equally. Paul, now 30, is a writer.

Deciding

Our decision to have a child was long and involved; the story stretches over several years. When we got married, I, at least, had some pretty conventional ideas about being married and having a family and all that sort of stuff, but I hadn't really thought about it very carefully. Then Linda and I were both in graduate school, and that got stretched so far into the future (we were eventually involved in it for six years), and we were so busy with it, that there was just never any real thought about having a kid. We never talked about it at all.

After we'd both started on our dissertations, we moved to the place where Linda had gotten a job. She worked for that first year while I stayed home and worked on my thesis, and again we were both so busy doing what we were doing that the issue never really came up. At the end of that year, our close friend Janet became pregnant, and this was the first person that we really knew very well that was actually in the process of having a child. I think both Linda and I started watching Janet and her husband, Bruce, very carefully. Partly as a result of being pregnant, Janet left her job teaching at a private girls' school, and I then replaced her. I'd basically finished my dissertation by then, although I still had to edit it, get it typed, and get my adviser to read it and approve it. Meanwhile, Linda had finished her dissertation and gotten fairly settled into her job—she was doing college teaching. Sometime during her second year at her job, around the time that Janet and Bruce had their son, Daniel, and after I'd started working at Janet's old teaching job, Linda asked her department for a leave of absence for the second semester of the next academic year. And one of the things she said she had in mind for that leave of absence was that that would be a nice time to have a kid.

This posed a problem for me—to put it mildly. I had almost schizophrenic feelings about what I was doing. On the one hand, I was finishing up my dissertation—the last big thing in the whole graduate school/college teaching track. On the other hand, I was holding down a job teaching young kids and I was involved in the job enough to know that I probably wasn't going to go into the college teaching business. I liked my job a lot, but I wondered if I wasn't doing it because of a lack of self-confidence about my ability to do the stuff you have to do to stay in the college teaching business—you know, the whole thing about doing original research and publishing it—even though I knew my dissertation was original and good work and all that sort of thing. Also, my job didn't pay much. It was lower on the professional status hierarchy than college teaching, and I definitely had feelings about that which weren't helped any by the fact that one of the reasons I'd gotten hired was that I'd gone to a fancy-ass graduate school—really silly and meaningless, because the skills called upon and everything for teaching young kids are totally different from the ones you'd use in graduate school stuff. The other reason I'd gotten hired wasn't so bad—

that I was a man, and men are fairly rare in the elementary school teaching business.

Anyway, I had these funny feelings about my work life. I thought maybe I'd copped out, given up on "the life of the mind" and all that sort of stuff. But I also knew that I was doing really hard work, respectable work, and I was good at it. My students liked me and all that sort of thing, and they were actually learning something—although what they were learning was a little hard to say sometimes. It's interesting though—the sort of statusy part of my feelings *wasn't* made worse by the fact that Linda was doing the "life of the mind" stuff I partly felt I'd copped out on. We've never been competitive in that way. I've always felt that it just wouldn't be successful living with somebody who wasn't out doing what she wanted to do, or what he wanted to do, if it were a man—you know, thinking for him/herself and all of that. Besides, Linda was very supportive of my decision not to go on into college teaching. She had her own misgivings about that profession anyway.

So, because of all this, when Linda said that her leave of absence a year hence might be a nice time to have a child, I said basically, "No, not now. I don't know what I'm doing. I have the feeling that I'm *not* doing one thing, but I'm not at all sure that I'll be doing forever this other thing that I'm doing now instead of that thing." It was partly uncertainty about the future, but with the added dimension that my teaching job was extremely demanding emotionally. I looked at how much emotional energy I was putting into my students and stuff, and I thought, "My God, how am I ever going to be able to deal with my own child if I work this hard at this job?"

From this point on, the whole question of whether to have a kid or not got worse. We set ourselves up as the Interlocutor and Mr. Bones. She got into the partly comfortable and partly uncomfortable position of being the advocate of having a kid, and I got into the position of presenting the arguments against it. She wanted the experience of carrying the child and having it and raising it and everything, but I wasn't ready. A lot of the time our talk about it would resolve into Freudian versus existential philosophical discussions, in which I, as the existentialist, couldn't see any good reason why anybody would want to have a child. When I'd talk to Bruce about it, he would sometimes push the existentialist stuff to the limit and say, "Well, fuck, you know, you can always take a powder if the kid gets to be a drag. That *is* an option open to you." I wasn't a consistent existentialist, I guess, because I was appalled by that—I couldn't conceive of doing such a thing. What I was really thinking was that in having a kid, you're signing up for a long time, and I wasn't sure at that point that I wanted to sign myself up for *anything* for a long time. I guess Linda felt a lot more together about that part of it, plus she felt the pressure of getting older in the sense that the older you get, the more of a risk you run in bearing children.

Incidentally, watching Janet and Bruce, both during the pregnancy and after Daniel was born, didn't change the pattern of our thinking much. Linda looked at Janet and saw that she was having a pretty good time with the whole thing. I looked at Bruce and saw that he wasn't having much fun at all. Bruce would come home—this was during the pregnancy—put on his earphones, get wrecked, and listen to music. That made quite an impression on me. I didn't have to ask him why he was having such a hard time, because it didn't seem to me to be necessary. He was a lot happier after Daniel was born, but I guess I mostly discounted that. Bruce was working and making a lot of money while Janet was home pregnant, and one specific thing I started thinking from watching them was, "Well, shit, you know, if this happens and it's the standard scenario, I'm going to have to go out and make a lot of money, and how on earth am I going to do that? I'm not sure I can cope with that kind of onus being put on me." Linda said to that, "No problem. I'll go on teaching, and we'll get day care or something." I don't know why, but that rubbed me the wrong way. I felt, "Well, fuck, what's the point of having a kid if you're not going to take care of the kid?"

Our arguments just got tenser and tenser, and we had a really rotten year—I mean the year in which Linda took a leave of absence from her job the second semester. I was beginning to think, "Well, shit, you know, if we can't even agree on this and you don't see my point of view and I don't fully see yours either, then what's going to happen when we try to bring the kid up or do *anything?*" And I was beginning to be afraid that there would simply come a time when the choice would be between my going along with the gag of having a kid or, if not, that would be the end of Linda's and my living together. There was never any actual ultimatum, but it was in the air, and I certainly didn't want it to happen. I never could quite imagine not living with Linda. Partly that's because I've always been extremely reluctant to change my own living situation. I hate to move, for example. But, you know, you've been married to someone for six or seven years or whatever, and it's been by and large a good thing. It does get awfully comfortable even if it isn't a good thing. But our marriage was mostly positive. Linda and I had always complemented each other fairly well, and I didn't want it to end.

Things got worse and worse and worse, and then somehow we decided. At some point along in there, Linda went off the pill, ostensibly for health reasons. Janet had done this, too, and what happened as a result was that she and Bruce became extremely sloppy about their birth control. That's my view of how they reached their decision to have a kid. You know, "We're going off the pill, and let's say it's for health reasons, and of course we don't want to have a kid, certainly not an unplanned one, but let's use something that amounts to astrology, practically, for birth control." They were using foam, apparently, and it was no great surprise when Janet became pregnant.

The other thing that happened was that we decided to go to Mexico with Janet and Bruce during my two-week vacation from school and during Linda's leave of absence. We had a really great time on that trip—I think it was the most fantastic two weeks I've ever had. And when I look back on it, I feel about going to Mexico the way some people seem to feel about dropping acid. They say, "Gee, after I did that, things were just never the same." You know, travel broadens your horizons or something. It was really a shock to get completely away from the rotten life we'd been living, just go someplace totally different—different language, different climate—and really have fun. So when I got back, I decided that things were simply going to have to change. I wasn't specifically thinking that I was going to have a kid, but just that generally things were going to change.

The first change I made was I decided I wouldn't go back and teach at that school the next year. I was going to write a book instead. I'd been teaching a foreign language—my Ph.D. was in linguistics—and I'd found that there just wasn't much good material around for language teachers that was usable in the classroom. So this was going to be a book about ways of making the learning of languages more fun. In dropping a steady job with an assured income—even though a meager one—and getting into a chancy thing like writing a book, I was saying to myself, "I'll just try winging it and see what happens. It can't be any worse than what's been going on." The Mexico thing helped there because it had been the same kind of thing in a way. There's nothing like being in a place that different from what you're familiar with to throw you totally on your own resources. I mean, you just have to follow your nose. We'd had some trepidation about that part of it before we went, but we'd had a lot of fun—like I said, the most fantastic two weeks I've ever had. So I guess I thought it might be the same with quitting my job and writing this book.

So first I threw out the whole career thing and the job situation, threw caution to the winds about that. And then the whole kid thing seemed to follow. I'd been writing the book for about three months, and it was going very well, and one night when we were in the sack we just didn't take any precautions, and we continued not to from then on. I think Linda was kind of surprised when we started balling there with no "Why don't you get up and put in your diaphragm?" kind of stuff, but that's what happened. I didn't feel I had capitulated—it just seemed there was a certain inevitability about the whole thing. My feeling was, "I'm pushing the rock up the hill, and I'm not going to have it fall down on me so that I have to push it up again; I'm pushing it over the top, and now I'm going down the hill and I'm going somewhere else."

We didn't talk about it at all, and it was a pretty weird and fearsome time. We went on this camping trip about a month later, assuming that Linda was pregnant, but then in the middle of the trip she got her period, and we had to come home early because she didn't have any Tampax or anything. We were both a little disappointed by that somehow, but it was good in a way because it gave us a chance to make our commitment explicit. We talked only briefly about it, and it was clear that Linda was still all for it. I still said, "OK, what the hell. It's certainly made our whole situation better, not battling about this any more." Than Linda became pregnant almost immediately, and that was that.

Deciding to have a kid was terrific for our sex life. There's nothing more erotic than that kind of screwing, as far as I'm concerned, partly because of the danger of it, I suppose. You know, "Gee, she might get pregnant!" But it's mainly because when you're balling to have a kid, you've really made quite a commitment to the other person. You're really putting your relationship on the line and saying, "Yeah, I'm not only going to stay here under the same roof with you, but we're obviously really tuned in to each other. We must be if we're even considering bringing a third party in on this deal."

Pregnancy

We didn't tell many people about the pregnancy for quite a while after it was definitely confirmed. Our feeling was partly that you're not really in the soup yet until somebody else says, "All right, this is it." *I* especially felt that I just needed time to square it away with myself, decide that "Yes, this *is* happening." Maybe I had that feeling more than Linda because I was on the outside—I wasn't experiencing the physiological things. We also kept quiet about it because of the fear that in the first trimester anything could happen. Linda's mother had once had a miscarriage, so miscarriage was a real part of the universe of discourse to Linda. We didn't want to get people's hopes up and then have it be really heavy for them if something went wrong. Plus, I suppose, it was my feeling that it was none of anybody's business. I mean, if you tell another person that you're going to have a child, you've told that person something quite significant, admitted him or her somehow into the inner sanctum.

I didn't enjoy the pregnancy at all, especially from the time that Linda started to show. I felt like I was in limbo—you know something's going to happen, like getting a shot of penicillin or getting your finger pricked before giving blood—it's going to happen, and you know it's going to happen, but it hasn't happened yet. There's just this horrible period of anticipation. I remember thinking at the time, "They give you nine months to be pregnant so that you can get your shit together and resolve yourself to the whole thing. But that's much too long for my money." You're just sitting there on the edge of your chair during all that time.

Prepared childbirth classes didn't help with this feeling at all. I hated them. I felt very different from all the other people in the class. The men would show up in their neckties and good clothes and stuff—it was obviously a honky thing. Only upper middle-class or middle-class people were doing it. I think that's true of the whole natural childbirth thing—all the books I've seen written about it are by Joe and Jane Smith who are honks and stuff. I'd go to those classes and I'd think, "Shit, here are all these people who know what they're doing." Actually, they were probably just as tense as I was, but they didn't seem so.

Another thing—our kid started kicking very early in the game, and I don't think that helped our sex life at all. I felt that if the kid's in there kicking around, I just really couldn't deal with that. You know, you don't want to poke the kid or anything. That's a silly, unsophisticated view of physiology, but still the fact that there was somebody in there definitely moving around felt like an invasion of the privacy of our sex life.

What happened between Linda and me was that we picked up on our earlier roles of her being the advocate of having a kid and my being the one who said what a terrible idea it was. I really don't believe in remorse—I try not to have anything to do with it—but if there were anything in my life that I would redo, it would be that I would tone down the way I presented my anxieties during the pregnancy. It was very unfair for me to keep saying, "Gee, this is a wretched idea, and I wish we'd never gotten into it," because it put her in the position of not being able to express her own anxieties. What the fuck, you know, she was the one to whom there would have been any physical danger. Fortunately, the reason I can be an existentialist is that Linda can hold her own and has always been able to. When I'd be making all this noise, she would say, "Look, this really sucks; you're not giving me a chance to express my own anxieties." So we had these difficulties, but I think I did manage to work it out to an extent. I figured, "Fuck, I got myself into this, and I knew what I was doing at the time, as far as you ever know what you're doing when you do anything." Not only that, but I thought about the question of "What if I have to be the sole parent of the kid? Is this something that I would be prepared to handle?" Because that is a possibility. And I decided that I could deal with that somehow.

Households

When we moved to where Linda got her first job, we lived with Linda's sister and her husband. There were some problems with the arrangement, but we got along OK for four years. Then, when Linda got pregnant, it was clear that something had to give because there wouldn't be enough room for the four of us and the baby. I hoped we could work something out with the people we were already with because of that impulse of mine I mentioned before—I don't like to move or change whatever the situation is now without some really great reasons. But I'll also sometimes just say after a while, "Well, what the fuck, let's try it. It may be totally foolhardy and turn out to be a disaster, but . . . " And that's what I did in this case because we really did have to move. What we did was move into a new house with Carl and his kid, Nathan, and with a couple we were friendly with, Peter and Barbara. Carl and Peter had taught in the same department as Linda for several years, and we'd all gotten pretty close. Carl was just separating from his wife, and Nathan was going to be staying with him a good part of the time. We set up house together about a month after Nicole was born, so we had five adults and two children. Nathan was three then.

We didn't move in with a group like this primarily because of

Nicole, although she was a consideration. My feeling has always been—I think Linda feels the same way—that if you live with a group of people, the emotional weight is spread around a little better. It just makes life easier for everybody. Perhaps more demands are made on you ultimately, but at least they don't all come from the same person. As far as the kid went, I think both of us saw the kid as being a potential source of emotional strain, and neither of us wanted to put that strain all on one other person or receive it all from one other person. And maybe if other people were involved with the kid, the kid wouldn't make so many demands on you. Not that we were trying to shirk any sort of responsibility as parents, but we just figured it would be a better thing for everybody—better for both of us, and better for the kid, too. It was for our own sanity—not so much sanity, maybe, but as a kind of insurance for our own spiritual well-being and that of the kid. There would be more people paying attention to the kid and more people paying attention to Linda and more people paying attention to me—more outside interests for all of us, more stuff for everybody.

One of the questions about living with other people in a group is this: How do you feel about sharing yourself or your spouse; what sorts of risks do you expose yourself to in that situation, and how does your child tie into that? I never worried about any of it all that much, partly because Linda and I have always been able to assume a kind of loyalty. I think we both have, to some extent, the sort of romantic view of being married to the same person and not getting involved with other people—well, no, get involved with them certainly, love them and all of that, but don't get involved with them on the level of intimacy for which sex is a signpost or something. You can't get involved on that level with somebody else without something going haywire. I think everybody else in the group felt the same way, and it's been a sort of given of the household. Of course, there's always some sort of sexual interest in your friends of the opposite sex. I certainly find Barbara attractive, and I imagine Peter finds Linda attractive, too. There's always a little extra fillip or something in those relationships, but it's probably never, or rarely, expressed, except maybe in various kinds of muted flirtatiousness. It's all part of the game, and it's fun, but I'd be appalled if anybody ever tried to follow through on it.

How this all works with children, I think, is a lot fuzzier—that is, how it works between an adult in the group and a kid whose parent is somebody else in the group. I don't know—my feeling has been that you treat such children the way you treat any other friends or any other people in the group outside your nuclear unit. In a way it's a little skewed because the kid isn't involved in the decision to live with the other people to the extent that the adults are—but that's still my feeling. Also, the way it's worked in this house has been that we've always been clear about which family was which and which kid went with which parents. If we had decided we were all "married" to each other and committed for the duration, then maybe the kids might have different perceptions of the distinction between their parents and the other adults they live with. But we didn't decide to do that. So my feeling has been that we had these family units pretty firmly and that whatever happened across those units would be just so much the better.

But it's more complicated than that. At one point, I talked with my friend David about the possibility of our living with him and Susan, and he said, "What happens if we move in and we're part of the family and then we have to leave? How's the kid going to feel?" He was worried about betraying his responsibility to this kid that's both his own and not his own. My feeling at the time was that this wasn't a big issue, you know. "The kid's always got his own parents, and nobody's leaving under a cloud, and what the hell, everybody will always have good feelings." Now, though, having been in that position with Nathan, I'm not so sure. I mean, Nathan knows I'm not his parent, and I don't think he'd think I was a bad guy if we weren't living under the same roof any more, but I'm not sure what my feelings of responsibility would be in that case. It's a tricky one. I mean, obviously you don't say to yourself, "I'm always going to maintain a certain kind of distance between myself and this kid, lest I should become too involved." I do know that when there was a question of Carl and Nathan having to move out of our house, I thought about it a lot and was pretty upset by the prospect. It wasn't so much "How is Nathan going to feel?" as "How am I going to feel?"

It's a little early to say because Nicole's only a year old, but she's obviously a very happy kid, and I'd certainly ascribe some of that to her living with five adults instead of two. As for Nathan, having him around was a lot more strain at first than I would have anticipated. A lot of stuff was up in the air for him when we all moved in together. I mean, he was moving, and he wasn't going to have his Mommy around all the time, and he probably had mixed feelings about the fact that Linda and I and Peter and Barbara were in some sense being substituted arbitrarily, without his permission, for Deborah, his mother. It was sad to see him not immediately accepting us the way we accepted him, but it was perfectly understandable. But I think that's changed a lot now. He's become a lot more confident and a lot more accepting of everybody.

Paul and Linda

Linda and I have always had not just different ways of looking at things, but fundamentally different ways of going about things—different styles. But that's always been more a good thing than a bad thing. I guess I said before that we've always complemented each other pretty well. Part of our arrangement, I guess, is that we have an instinct for what the differences are. For instance, I've never read her dissertation, and she's never read mine. When we were in college, I'd show her books and things that I really liked, you know—"Hey, this is great stuff; I would like to share it with you." She either wouldn't read it or wouldn't enjoy it, and I'd be very pissed off. When she passed stuff on to me that she thought was great, I usually *would* read it fairly compulsively and I'd usually enjoy it, although I probably liked it for different reasons than she did. If there was some author that we both liked, we characteristically liked different things the person had written. Eventually we just laid off and assumed, "Well, shit, if it's good stuff, the person will discover it sooner or later." It was some sort of competition thing, I think, but we got out of it.

One of the things that amazes me about David and Susan is that they can spend as much time as they do with each other and still manage to stand each other. I don't care how fond of the other person you are, if you're living in the other person's lap and there are no doors in the house that close—well, I just wouldn't feel comfortable living like that. The whole "room of one's own" thing has always been important to Linda and me. Ever since our first year of marriage we've deliberately set it up so that each one of us had a room that he or she could go into and shut the door and just be alone. This has been so important. However else our personal styles may differ in dealing with people or with the world at large, we're at least agreed on that.

I suppose, though, that we're so well agreed on that *because* our personal styles are otherwise so different. It would be extremely difficult for us to share a working space, for example. It's hard enough for us to share the same bedroom, given that the bedroom has more than just a bed in it. We've got two bookcases in our room now. They're side by side, and one of them is sort of Linda's, at least as far as the surface on top goes, and one of them is sort of mine. Our housekeeping habits are just so different; you can tell it at a glance by looking at these two bookcases. I'm forever shoveling all the crap that she's put on my bookcase back onto hers. So mine's relatively neat, and hers is just this mountain of debris.

We've got all these differences, but there's something else that's also true—I don't like leaning on people or being leaned on, but I think that sort of thing is one of the prerogatives of marriage. Mostly I try to work stuff out myself and not give other people a hard time. But when it's really just too much to resolve by myself and I need to unburden myself, it's mostly Linda that gets to hear what I have to say. It works the other way, too, I think—there are damn few people I would allow to lean on me to the extent that I would allow Linda to. She doesn't do it that much, but it would certainly be her due.

We divide up the labor of raising the kid 50-50—that is, we have a schedule. The day is divided up into three slots—from when the kid wakes you up in the morning until noon, from noon till about five o'clock, and the evening. The period from about five to seven o'clock is sort of a no-man's-land, largely depending on who's cooking supper or washing the dishes and stuff. Seven days a week times 3 makes 21 slots; one of us does 11 of them and the other 10. We both do all times of day, although partly because of Linda's teaching schedule, and partly because I like to do my writing work early in the morning, I've tended to take the kid more in the afternoon, and she more in the morning. The middle of the night stuff has been something of a bone of contention. I guess Linda tends to get up more often than I do when the kid's howling at two in the morning or something, but, on the other hand, I very often get the kid up in the morning and let Linda sleep.

We have some differences about raising the kid, but I don't think they're serious ones. On safety stuff I think I tend to keep a sharper eye out than Linda does. She'll say, "Gee, the kid was halfway up the third flight of stairs before I even noticed it." I don't see myself ever doing that. But I think we agree at some important level about what the kid can be trusted to do by herself and what she can't.

As I've been saying, Linda and I do have different world views, but I think that by and large this'll be good for the kid. We're not really each of us putting the kid in different worlds, but to the extent that we are, you know, my feeling is the more varied experiences and the more faces and views the kid can get to see and enjoy, the more of all of that the better. Our differences haven't led to serious conflicts about raising Nicole because there aren't any aspects of Linda's Freudian world view that I find really repugnant or silly, and I think she feels the same way about my existential approach to things. I suppose people who go to different churches have this problem when they go to bring up their kid, and I suspect a lot of people resolve it in this same way—namely, the two churches or views of the world aren't all that different anyway, or, if they are, they say to the kid, "Fine; go to both churches."

One thing that I do sometimes find annoying is that often when we're both there with the kid and it's a question of playing with her or something, Linda tends to volunteer for it faster than I do, and I tend to let her go ahead and do whatever it is.

Maybe this is the old race consciousness thing or something. Maybe Linda feels a little bit guilty about being a working mother. I find that a little hard to believe, but a lot of these old sex-stereotype things die pretty hard—and I imagine they die just as hard in women who have a lot to gain from their dying. So part of my reaction to this sort of incident is, "You want to volunteer for some work? Fine. I'll sit on my ass and sip my mint julep." But what's annoying is the implication—not intended by Linda, but still there, I think—that somehow she as a woman is better able to minister to the kid's needs than I am. I don't believe that.

One more thing on this. It's not directly about me and Linda, but something happened the other night about this sex-role stuff that really made an impression on me. I went to a meeting—a bunch of parents of one-year-olds were getting together to see about starting a play group—and there was one couple there that was really offensive. The woman kept talking about how we needed to get "surrogate mothers" for our kids—"the mother this" and "the mother that," you know—and that annoyed me a lot because obviously there were men there, too, and they were playing with the kids as much as the women were and getting as big a kick out of it. All except her husband, of course—he never touched one of the kids except his own, and then it was just to hand the kid to its mother. The same thing comes up all the time when I'm out walking with Nicole. People will look at us, and I can tell they're thinking, "Who is that strange man, and why is that child crying? Why isn't he at work? Where's her mother?" That stuff doesn't bother me, except to the extent that it implies I as a man have no right to be there.

Work

Sex and gender have certainly been dimensions of my working life. As I said, I taught for two years in a girls' school. I was one of two men teaching there the first year and the only man the second year. All the other faculty members were women, and all of the students were girls—or women, if you prefer. It could not exactly escape your attention if you were working in a situation like that that you were one sex and the other people were the other sex. Furthermore, the kids were by and large upper middle-class, if not aristocratic, children, and they had some fairly conservative ideas about how the world goes. Not only were they being taught by a man—unusual in itself—but by a man that didn't look like any men they knew. I mean, I had a beard and long hair, and their fathers weren't like that. So there was all this consciousness of gender in that job, and I thought that was a good thing.

Since I quit that job I've been writing—and not doing that badly at it, either, in terms of getting stuff published. Remember, I said that after we came back from Mexico I sort of decided to follow my nose and not worry so much about pursuing a career and making a whole lot of money. Of course, when you do that you have to figure out how to pay the rent, and what I've been doing leaves something to be desired as a test case because I happen to be married to someone who can pay the rent. I have mixed feelings about that. I mean, I don't think that because I'm a man I should pull all of the financial weight in the family, but I do have enough of those traditional feelings to think that I should be contributing something closer to an equal share to the family income. And my reaction to the prospect of putting Nicole in some kind of day-care situation is bound up with those feelings. I mean, as it is now, I have a "job" that doesn't pay very well and I take care of my child. If I weren't spending as much time taking care of my child, I would wonder if I were justified in having this job that doesn't pay anything.

I look at it the opposite way, too, though. Having a kid and taking care of her a lot exempts me from really getting out there and hustling in the way that I probably would if I were pursuing a writing career full time. In other words, having a kid has been good for my mental health. I haven't had to beat my head against certain professional walls at all, or not very much. I really hate that hustling and selling yourself. On the other hand, the kid sometimes interferes with the substantive part of my work. Linda and I recently shifted our schedule around so that we each get two full days a week without the kid. Sometimes I have to set aside those days for work in the library—or one of them anyway because the other one always gets used up doing something else—and I'll go to the library and find all the books I need are out or something. So, because of having to take care of the kid I've not only blown the whole damn day, I'm also screwed for the whole week. And that's really a piss-off.

I've sort of had a series of one-year appointments in this particular "career" as a writer. Originally I was going to spend just one year writing the language games book. Then the kid came along, and I figured, "Well, all right, why don't I keep doing this, because I can do this and take care of the kid." Also by that time publishers had committed themselves to two of my projects.

So it seems to be sailing along OK. I hesitate to call what I'm doing a career—partly because of the amount of time I spend with the kid—but I'd be perfectly happy to let my present arrangement go on. My hope is that after one or two years more I'll have enough of a backlog so that it'll be a self-sustaining thing. I mean, I hope to get to the point where the *publisher* knows me well enough to come around and say, "Here, write a book about this or that and we'll give you some money." I'll never get rich that way, but I would have a financially respectable job.

I'm sort of in limbo in my thinking about having a career. If Linda wanted to take time off from her job—for whatever reasons—I'd say, "Fine; you've certainly earned it." I'd be prepared to go out and look for a job with a real income. But I'm afraid that if I stay out of the job market much longer, employers are going to say, "What have you been doing all this time?" And when I say, "I've been having fun writing and raising my kid," they're going to laugh in my face and say, "Look, we don't hire people like you." And they'd be right.

I mean by that that they'd be demanding a sort of total loyalty and commitment from me, and I wouldn't be prepared to give it. Now, I don't accept that idea at all. I mean, what sort of schmucks are you going to have working for you who are willing to say, "My life is so fucked up that I'm willing to put everything into this job?" I've felt the absurdity of that stuff more strongly since I've had my own kid. If you have a family already, you can't possibly commit yourself like that unless there's something wrong with the picture. Even though people have to make money to survive, and even though lots of people like their work, nobody should ask you to wear yourself out at your work so that you have nothing left for your family.

You can't escape feelings in the other direction, though—that's why I said I was in limbo about all this. I was looking at my alumni magazine the other day; you know—"Here's Joe Schmoe who's head of pediatrics at a big hospital," or "So-and-so just got tenure," or "So-and-so has just been promoted to executive vice-president." And I thought, "Gee, if I didn't know those people were exactly the same age as I am, I would think they were older, somehow," because they're established, on a particular rung of the success ladder. When I mentioned this to Linda, she said, "We're just not on the success ladder, and that's all there is to it."

I think, or at least I hope, that my feeling is getting to be, "I don't know what I'm going to be doing next year or the year after, but I know I'll be doing *something*—probably something interesting. If it's not interesting, I won't be doing it for very long." In a way, the blessing and the curse of my middle-class upbringing was a feeling of noblesse oblige—"I don't have to be doing this: I'm doing this because I'm good at it and I like it, but certainly not because I have to do it."

Raising a Kid

The ideal father—well, the ideal father is demonstrative. He doesn't throw up smoke when it's a question of how he feels about his kid. My own father had a great deal of trouble expressing his affection for anybody, or any of his feelings about anything, for that matter. But I never doubted that he liked me, because I figured I'd cracked the code. I knew what he was talking about, that he felt pretty good about me, so I never for an instant worried about it. My younger brother, Ethan, didn't make out so well. I think maybe Ethan and my father didn't know how to speak the same language, and so Ethan was unsure whether my father liked him or not. Maybe that was because very early in the game the myth got started that I resembled my father in many respects, and that Ethan resembled my mother. I do get this thing about being demonstrative from my experiences in my own family, I guess. Even though my father wasn't especially demonstrative, there was an atmosphere of feelings being expressed—especially anger. A parent may make a lot of noise and jump up and down and all of that, and it may be slightly terrifying or something for the kid, but there it is— it's right out there, and everybody can see what's going on, and it's straightforward. For a kid, I think this is a terrific thing. My mother and father used to fight a lot. My father would yell and my mother would cry, but it would all be out there and it would get resolved, whatever it was. I feel really good about my relationship with Carl's kid, Nathan, now because the same thing happens—when he pisses me off, I tell him he's pissing me off, just like I used to do with my students.

One thing that a lot of people do that goes against being demonstrative and open is they talk about really heavy stuff in front of the kid as though the kid weren't there. This is a wrong thing from the word go. I mean, even if the kid doesn't understand what you're talking about, the kid picks up the vibes and the intonation very fast. Kids will know what you're talking about even before they can talk themselves. You're just throwing stuff at the kid that the kid's not ready for—the sort of stuff that it takes *years* to work out at best. I don't know if there's ever an age when the kid's so young that you can do that kind of thing. Doing that is like balling in front of your kid.

Another thing about the ideal father is that he's accessible. But I have to qualify that immediately by saying that in some respects, for me, Nicole's feelings and education and whatnot don't come first. I mean, you have to preserve your own sanity. It'll be best for her in the long run if things are set up so that I take time for myself and my own needs. If I do that, I'll save energy, some of which will then get expended on the kid. And the kid will be less likely to get the feeling that I'm spending time with her grudgingly. I've already learned from experience that the most frustrating times with Nicole are when I make the mistake of thinking I really ought to be doing something else. The best policy is: Don't attempt to do anything else that involves an attention span or serious thinking or anything. Because the kid won't let you do it, and you'll feel, "Shit, I want to do this other thing, but you're stopping me." The best way around that is simply to say, "OK, for better or for worse, I got my work done or I didn't, but now it's time to be with you and that's it." If I have the kid and my first loyalty isn't keeping her entertained, that just spells trouble almost inevitably.

You don't have to give the kid your undivided attention, perhaps, but if it's obvious that you're becoming engrossed in something that the kid's not a party to, she picks up on that, I think. For example, she's discovered this harmonica we have, and she likes to hold it up and blow in it. The other day, after she'd done this a few times I took the harmonica and started actually to play something on it, and Nicole got really pissed because I was obviously having a good time doing this and she wasn't in on it. The same thing happens with the recorder. She thinks it's amusing to make it go "toot toot," but when I try to play some music, she gets very pissed and won't have any.

Generally, I think children should be encouraged to use people as their resources for entertainment as much as books and toys and that stuff. So if the kid wants to be entertained and I'm the person she wants to be entertained by, or I'm the handiest or something, I'll often elect to go along with the gag—partly because I know full well that sometimes I won't. If I'm too damn tired, I won't do it because I can't. Of course, that's a little tricky because Nicole can't talk yet. I look forward fondly to the day when I can say, "Look, I'm tired. I'm not so tired that I wouldn't have picked you up and played with you if you couldn't talk, but now that you can, you can understand that I'm tired, so stop asking me to play with you." But I don't hold out any great hopes that it'll work that way.

I already mentioned one of the frustrating times. Another is when the kid's upset and I can't figure out why. There are boring times, too. When the kid's taking a nap is a boring time— you can't really start anything of your own because the kid'll probably wake up when you're in the middle of it. You know damn well it's like washing your car just before it rains. One of the most enjoyable things is taking the kid out for a walk, either in the backpack or the stroller. Nicole seems to really like it. She looks around, talks to herself and stuff. I enjoy it, too, because I can just walk along and think my thoughts—you know, not frivolous thoughts exactly, but anything you think about is on borrowed time, and that's very refreshing. I find I have a lot more time, walking with the kid, just to look at things and listen to things and be a lot more aware of the whole environment—I guess partly because the kid's looking at everything, and I have nothing better to do.

One thing I really look forward to is when the kid learns to talk. I can hardly wait. It's partly a business interest of mine, being a linguist. I watched Daniel's learning to talk with a great deal of pleasure, and it's been the same way over this past year living with Nathan and watching him master language a lot better. Nathan's just turned four. He could say stuff before, but now he can carry on a conversation, which is what talking is all about as far as I'm concerned. I think kids definitely become full-fledged people when they learn to talk.

Although I have some mixed feelings about this, I also look forward to the time when the baby can amuse herself without calling on me so much. My feelings are mixed because . . . well, I hesitate to say that I want to *control* her development, but I would like to set it up so that I could eventually say to her, "Aha! We think alike!" I don't know if "autocratic" is the right word, but I'm a positive thinker, somebody with fairly strong opinions on how the world should go. And I'm a very competitive person. I play monopoly to win—I couldn't conceive of playing it just to fart around. I think I have a fairly strong personality. So maybe I'm going to impose all that on my kid.

But I don't really think so. Basically, I would encourage everybody to be independent. When I say I'm an existentialist, I mean that I find it hard to really like somebody who's totally dependent on somebody else. That's the existential man of bad faith. I said before that I've always felt very strongly that remorse is a waste of time. That's part of my existentialism, too—I try very consciously not to regret things. You have to start from right where you are, always. So I don't want people to be dependent, and I specifically don't want them to be dependent on me. Maybe that's partly because I have tendencies toward complete irresponsibility. That's why I went out and married somebody who also has a strong personality. I couldn't conceive of living with anybody that was my shadow or underling—it would be so boring and frustrating and uninteresting. All of this goes for Nicole as much as for Linda or anybody else. I would not find it a satisfactory arrangement at all to live with a bunch of assistant people, and I certainly don't want my daughter to grow up to be an assistant person.

Carl

Carl, 32, has been separated from his wife, Deborah, for nearly a year, during which time he has been unemployed and has had primary responsibility for caring for their three-year-old son, Nathan.

Marriage

Ever since I went to college, really, I had the *idea* that I wanted to get married and have children. Getting married meant having children—that to me was inherent in the whole thing. What was behind this, I think, was the notion that once I had a family I wouldn't be lonely anymore. I'd felt lonely, cut off from people, for long stretches of my life, and I'd never been able to quite figure out why. At this time I'm talking about—when I was in college—I thought I'd grown up in a fairly "unfamily-like" family, where the tone was always that we were all pretty good friends who often enjoyed each other's company, but where there was also some unwritten rule never to try to get really close.

Anyway, I built up this ideology of family life partly in

reaction to my childhood and to my sense of loneliness. About a year before I got involved with Deborah—I was in graduate school then—I read *Anna Karenina* for the first time, and that novel really crystallized for me these feelings about what a family should be. The part of the book that interested me the most was the part about this guy Levin and the woman he eventually marries, Kitty. I interpreted their marriage as really getting into the stream of things, the flow of life, and I saw their having a kid—which is emphasized a lot in the last part of the novel—as being the logical fruit, so to speak, of moving in that whole direction. It's all set up as a pretty definite contrast, because Anna and her lover, Vronsky, don't get married, and they basically don't love the child they have together. So what it all meant to me was that if you just have a passionate love affair, you're isolating yourself from the real world, the world at large, whereas if you get married and have children, you've found a way into this deep kind of connection with everything and everybody. You're opened up to the world around you and committed to life flowing on into the future. These ideas were very important to me for a long time. They still are, although not in such a pure, dogmatic form. When I started teaching at the university up here, I used to make sure to set up at least one course every year that would have *Anna Karenina* on the reading list.

When Deborah and I got married, which was the summer before my last year in graduate school and right after she graduated from college, these ideas of mine were pretty well developed. I think now that they probably were a problem for her, although that wasn't at all clear at the time. I mean, I don't think she had developed any particular perspective on the whole question of marriage and children, and so there was nothing stopping her from just sort of swallowing my ideas. During my first two years on the job up here, she used to come to my classes and be a shill for me to help get discussion going and so on, especially to the classes in which I was pushing these family ideas a lot. I think she worked very hard intellectually to agree with all this stuff of mine. But that was the problem—they were *my* ideas.

There were other things about our situation that made it look like we were living in a world that was basically mine—a world with me at the center and with her revolving around me as my satellite. For example, she got a job right after we were married, so that was the old pattern of wife supporting hubby through school. She didn't like the job much and quit about halfway through the year. She felt guilty about that, but I think what she was doing was rebelling against that subordinate role. Then after I got hired at the university, she spent the summer before we moved worrying about finding a job up here. She ended up applying for some clerical jobs at my university, but that was the same thing—*my* university. So during our first year up here, she didn't have a job of her own and she didn't have many friends of her own either.

So there were all these undercurrents already in our marriage that we weren't confronting, and one night when we were in bed we decided to stop using birth control and start trying to have a kid. I don't regret that decision at all, but it probably would be true to say that we plunged into it without really trying to imagine what problems would be created for us by having a child. What happened was that Cambodia was invaded by U.S. forces a couple of months after we made this decision, and we both got heavily involved in the protest activities at my university. That ended up lasting the whole summer, and our marriage practically broke up over the stresses and strains of that whole situation. At first we were both just going helter-skelter on all these political projects, and we joked about how we never had time to sleep together. Then we just drifted apart more and more and got more and more tense with each other. Things just got very unpleasant as the summer went on, and at some point in there Deborah went back on the pill. She told me afterward that part of the reason for all the tension was that she'd been very disappointed when she got her period—that is, when she found out that our decision to have a child, which had been a beautiful moment for both of us, hadn't yet resulted in her getting pregnant. This is just my speculation, but I think maybe the fact that she didn't get pregnant soon after we decided to try to have a kid—maybe that sort of called my whole vision into question for her. Or maybe she was saying to me subconsciously, "Well, OK, when we have this child, it's not going to be such a perfect fulfillment of *your* ideals."

In any case, almost immediately after we talked about what had been going on over the summer we renewed our attempts to have a child, and she got pregnant almost immediately. We told everybody about it right away. Again, I don't regret Nathan's existence, but in retrospect it's clear that we didn't think hard enough about what was happening in our marriage and whether this was a good time to have a child. I enjoyed the time when Deborah was pregnant—except the early part, and the reasons I didn't like that had nothing to do with her being pregnant—and Nathan's birth was just a big high for me for about two weeks. We did prepared childbirth, and we had an arrangement while Deborah and Nathan were still at the hospital where I could be there almost all the time. So I was participating in the whole process, and I just remember that it was a lot of fun being the center of attention and being congratulated on this great achievement. Another part of it, after we all came home from the hospital, was a sort of pleasurable disorientation from all the old routines.

But it was a really hot summer, and we were living in this really cramped apartment, and our problems hadn't gone away. First it hit home that there was just a shitload of new chores to do—tons of laundry and stuff like that—which was made worse by the fact that Nathan was colicky and cried a whole lot. Deborah felt like this kid never left her breast. Something happened in the middle of that summer that Deborah always remembered. You know, you can't have sex for about six weeks after childbirth, and for us that moratorium had been a lot longer because Deborah had had some complications with her pregnancy about two months before Nathan was born. So the day when it was OK for us to have sex again was a really hot day. I'd started teaching summer school by then, and after my classes were over I went out and bought Nathan's crib. Up to that time he'd been in a bassinet some relative had given us. For some reason all I was interested in when I got home that day was assembling that damn crib. Deborah always remembered that, that I wasn't that eager to make love with her then, and it was indicative of our problems. For one thing, our sex life was generally worse after Nathan was born. It hurt Deborah physically for a long time, and of course it just is true that having a kid to take care of saps all kinds of energy, including sexual energy. We'd tell ourselves we were too tired to make love. It was partly true, but it was also an excuse we used to avoid our anxieties about our marital problems.

Another thing that didn't help was the deep depressions I kept getting into about my work, where I felt I was just totally incapable of being any kind of effective teacher. I got into this state during the fall semester in each of my first three years of teaching, and it was just very hard and frustrating for Deborah—especially the last two times, first when she was pregnant, and then starting when Nathan was about four months old. During that last time I had a lot of trouble summoning up the energy to deal with anything. I certainly had almost no energy for taking care of a child, and it seemed to Deborah a lot of the time as though she were all alone with this screaming baby. Starting when Nathan was about eight months old, I began to get more of a handle on my working life, started to see ways of not getting so overwhelmed and panicky about it, and that's really been a process that's continued on up to now. But I think that too wasn't ultimately so great for our marriage. I suppose what I thought was, "Wow, this work is going better; everything must be better," which meant taking the marriage for granted and neglecting the problems. And of course the problems got worse. When it became clear that our marriage was in serious trouble, what I did was throw myself even more intensely into my work.

What began to happen more and more was that she would get annoyed with me about something, I would get irritated and defend myself, she would take back her anger and apologize, and we'd patch it up. I've always had trouble expressing anger, and I believe it's important to do it, but there was something about the way we did it that was frustrating and self-defeating because we'd repeat this same pattern over and over again. I think we both felt each time, "Here we go again." I don't really understand how all this stuff works, but somehow or other we weren't really confronting our bad feelings and going on from there. Instead we were letting those bad feelings seep out and then papering them over. Often it would start when I'd be reading or watching TV. She would interrupt me, often with a demand for affection, and my response to that would be to get really pissed off. I didn't like her intruding on what I was doing, and I thought it made everything false to demand love in that way. What she was picking up on was my tendency to choose to read or whatever rather than acknowledge her presence and pay attention to her. So it was a vicious circle.

Some of these fights were about Nathan, and the issue that I remember most was safety. I felt that she was overprotective, and I think she felt that if it were left up to me it wouldn't be long before Nathan suffered some serious injury. I know that's a pattern that gets culturally reinforced in this society, but the opposition is not always as sharp as it was in our case. It got so that I didn't look forward at all to excursions or outings that the three of us might make together, even just to a playground, because I knew that we'd immediately get into these bitter disputes about what Nathan should or shouldn't be allowed to do. We pushed each other to extremes of what our natural inclinations were. You know, I had some reason for thinking that Deborah wanted Nathan never to go anywhere or explore anything, and she had equally good reason for thinking I was utterly indifferent to Nathan's physical safety.

We did this pushing-to-extremes thing in a lot of areas, each setting the other person up as this hostile, opposed being, and to some extent making that other person actually *be* that opposite. It came to be symbolized in my mind whenever friends that were primarily hers were around and I just felt like going someplace else. I think she may have felt the same way about my friends, though not as strongly.

Anyway, we separated after being married for five years, and frankly, I'll be a little surprised if we manage to get back together again. I think the thing I contributed the most to our marriage not working out was my unwillingness to help bring to the surface the things that annoyed and dissatisfied me. Instead,

I stuck with my ideals about marriage and the family. I'd say to myself, "Wow, I'm married now, I have a kid now, so I'm in this richer context than I used to be in." Petty frustrations and annoyances would build up in day-to-day living—as they do for everybody—and I would never connect them with the state of being married. They were over on one side in my mind, and on the other side I was willfully continuing along on this ideal track about this deep bond between Deborah and me and how that was the source of this deep bond with the life of the world. The mundane little details had to beat me over the head quite a few times and say to me, "Pay attention to us because we aren't really so little," before I was forced to recognize that I wasn't living the way I thought I was living.

Carl and Nathan

When we separated, Deborah got a job and found an apartment by herself. I moved in with Paul and Linda and their new baby, Nicole, and with Peter and Barbara. We agreed that my situation would be better for Nathan and also that Deborah had enough to cope with trying to support herself and be independent for basically the first time in her life. Also, I was going to be unemployed. I hadn't gotten tenure at the university, and I hadn't been able to find another teaching job. So I became, for a while anyway, Nathan's primary parent. He was three when we separated. He lived mainly with me, and even though the reasons we did it that way were good reasons, it was very hard for Deborah. I mean, when families break up, the expectation is that the children stay with their mother in this society. Now after almost a year we're moving back toward a situation where Nathan will be with me half the time and half the time with Deborah. But it sure hasn't been easy for Deborah. I'm trying to sympathize with what she's going through.

My being the main parent wasn't really a sudden change from the way we'd been doing things. From the time Nathan was born, I was involved in changing diapers, feeding him, giving him his bath, and putting him to bed. In fact after a while it fell out that I almost always bathed him and put him to bed. For the last year and a half or so before we separated, I had the main

responsibility for Nathan one full day a week, two other after-
noons a week, and then every day in the morning before I went
to work and in the evenings after I came home from work. This
year he's slept here at my house every night, and I'm with him
in the early mornings and from 2:30 in the afternoon on weekdays when I pick him up from his nursery school. He's been with
Deborah all day on Saturday and Sunday; that's changed now so
that he sleeps at her house Friday and Saturday nights, too.
We'll probably change it again pretty soon so that he spends
three nights a week with her.

I have all these ideals, so what's my idea of the ideal father?
Well, I remember distinctly when Nathan was born that I didn't
have any big rush of love toward my child. What I did think and
feel really clearly was, "Here's this new person, this stranger
that's come along, and it's weird, because unlike any other new
person that I've met, I know I'm going to get to know this person
really well, and he and I are going to be very important to each
other." I was glad I felt that way because I thought it was an
indication I wasn't feeling any possessive love. Here was this
separate, independent person that I would be connected with. I
would be an important person in the world for him because I
would be introducing him to other parts of the world—other
people and other things.

So a big part of my ideal about being a parent was—is—
paying attention to my kid and loving him in a way that
encourages autonomy and independence. I was reacting—
somewhat unfairly, I now think—against my own father. He had
always been very scrupulous about not pushing me and my
brothers into being like him or doing things that were important
to him, but I'd come to feel that he hadn't been close enough to
us. I would say to myself, "When I have a kid, I'm not going to
sit around and ignore my kid like my father did or pay attention
to the kid only under a certain amount of prodding. I'm going to
open the kid up to more different kinds of activities than my
father did." I have these hang-ups about my lack of manual
skills and interests, and I wasn't going to pass that kind of thing
on to my child.

But I haven't done all that differently from my father, and

since I think I'm not that bad a parent, I guess I'm coming to the conclusion that my father wasn't so bad either. I mean, my older brother Andrew is good at carpentry and gardening and photography and all that kind of thing, and he includes his kids in those activities. But I just can't do it. To me, developing those skills has come to mean becoming a completely different, a better person than I am, and I can't just totally transform myself for the sake of my child.

There was a period when I would try to get Nathan to go off and do something that wouldn't require me to pay attention to him so I could read or do a crossword puzzle or something. I'd feel guilty while I was doing this, you know—"Shit, I'm doing just what I didn't like about my own father," especially after a few minutes when Nathan would come and demand attention from me and I would give it grudgingly. In fact, later on when Nathan was resisting books and reading, I thought maybe this stuff had something to do with it, that reading was mixed up in his mind with my not paying good enough attention to him.

I've certainly done my share of things that conflict with my ideal of helping my kid become autonomous and independent and an eager explorer of reality. One of the rituals we have now at bedtime is building with blocks a house that supposedly looks like Nathan's grandparents' house. Grandparents means Deborah's parents, because my father died a couple of years ago, and my mother lives too far away to see Nathan that often. We go through this thing where he asks me to build the house and I say, "Why don't *you* build it?" and he still insists that I build it. So I get started on it, and I'll be happily building away, and then he'll get interested and start to participate. But he'll stick blocks on in a way that's totally unstable or that messes up the design I've worked out, and I'll almost always get irritated and correct him. Every time I do this I know that I shouldn't, that I'm getting in the way of his learning. But I still step in and stop him and fix the house up the way I want it. For some reason I just can't restrain myself from imposing my house on him.

I'm not at all happy about interactions like these, but on the other hand it would be way off to say that I'm unhappy about the relationship between Nathan and me. I've been there from the beginning, helping to provide for his emotional and other needs, so that there's a rich history of emotional stuff between us. It's that history that has made him so attached to me now. I can't see any other possible explanation for it. As far as I can see, day after day, week after week, month after month, year after year—so far anyway—no matter how often I make what I consider to be mistakes or no matter how often I fail to respond to him as much as maybe I should or as much as he wants at that moment, despite all that he still seems to enjoy my company, and he still seems to love me. He seems to think I'm OK as a parent, so I must be providing him with the sustenance and support that he needs and takes pleasure in.

The part of Nathan's life that was the easiest and the most fun for me was between eight or nine months old and two or two-and-a-half years old. That period was also the happiest time of our marriage. I found the different stages of his learning to talk extremely fascinating. First he learned words and he would put them into baby-talk sentences; then he learned sentences and put them into baby-talk paragraphs; and so on. But also, just generally during that time, he didn't give much trouble about bedtime or anything, and he just seemed fairly happy with himself and his world. The hardest time was the first few months after Deborah and I separated and he and I moved in here with our extended family, or whatever you want to call it. I mean, for a while there he was just careening around and being "hyperactive," as they say. Bedtime became a real struggle. I had a lot of trouble coping with that, partly because it seemed like such a dramatic change from the way he'd been before, and partly because I just have a lot of trouble dealing with the kinds of aggressive, angry feelings he was expressing.

But what the hell, the kid was hit with a shitload of stuff all at once—his parents separated; he moved; he had to deal with all these new people; he stopped taking his daily nap; he started going to his nursery school a lot more hours than he had been; and he switched from a crib to a regular bed. Who wouldn't go a little wild? We worked that stuff out OK, I think, at least the immediate zizzing around and being out of control, but he *has* lived his life among complicated relationships and people coming and going—not just his parents and their problems, but also living with five adults instead of just two. I think it will have a lasting effect on his personality because he's much more tuned into relationships—plays a lot of games to find out what relationships are about—than he is into skills and activities and things like that.

I worried about that for a long time—and I still do a little bit—but I'm coming around to seeing that his awareness of relationships can be a real strength. One of the things about my own childhood that wasn't so hot was that I grew up not just having trouble expressing my emotions, but really being ignorant about what my emotions were. Nathan, on the other hand, is becoming an emotionally bolder person than I am. He still acts out what he's feeling a lot, but he's also learning to talk about what he's feeling. I'm very glad to see that, and it's a process that I try to help along. When we have a fight, I'll say, "You're pretty angry, aren't you? You're certainly making me angry. Let's talk about it." And we do. It's getting to the point where he'll come up to someone and start a conversation by saying, "You know, I was feeling a little upset before, but now actually I feel better!" The person he's talking to sometimes finds that a little startling, but I think it's wonderful.

As far as I can see, when a kid has two parents, all that means is that the kid has two parents. One of them is a man and one is a woman, but I don't see any different ways of being a parent that are inherent in the fact that one is a man and one is a woman. In fact, I've always prided myself a little on not being sexist, probably more than I have a right to. When we went to the prepared childbirth classes, all the other men there looked to me as though they were very nervous and uncomfortable about being there. I'd say to myself, "Aha! Look at me; I think this is great, and they don't." I used to do the same secret boasting whenever I'd take Nathan by myself to a playground on a weekday and I'd be the only father there. I had an especially clear set of feelings of that sort at the place we lived from when Nathan was ten months until he was three. It was a working-class neighborhood, and all the neighbors had pretty large families. Because my teaching job gave me pretty flexible hours,

I was home regularly on various weekdays and I was also visible, because there was this grassy area right across from our apartment where the neighborhood kids used to congregate. I would take Nathan over there, and all the other kids would gather around. They were all quite a bit older than Nathan, so they made quite a pet of him. Anyway, I figured Nathan and I were probably pretty mysterious to the neighbors—Nathan because, "Why doesn't he have any brothers and sisters?" and me because, "Who is this strange kind of man who plays around with kids in the afternoon instead of going to work?" I got a big kick out of that.

Academia

Part of my anxieties about myself as a teacher had to do with conditions peculiar to college teaching—namely, the fact that my classes didn't meet all that frequently; some of them met only once a week. I would come into the class and teach the class, and if that class wasn't a real masterpiece, I would feel awful afterward. My attitude was, "Once a week, zowee, socko, two hours of superlative entertainment and learning, and, if not, I'm a total failure." I was hung up on the idea of the teacher as this big performer. It's sort of analogous to the predicament of the "weekend father" in conventional divorce situations—take the kid to the circus, and you'd better have a good time because this is the only chance you've got.

I think this performance view of teaching is basically unsound, as far as real learning is concerned. It makes the students into a passive audience. They come at regular but separated times to be turned on by this great show, after which they go home and wait for the next show. It's true students expect this sort of thing, but there are various ways to break down those expectations. One way is just to work on them during class time—run things so that people are forced to see that you the teacher are not the center and focus of everything that goes on. Another way is something that Linda always did a lot better than I did—figure out how to encourage people to come in and see you a lot. Probably more than anything else that gives a day-to-day quality to the whole educational process.

Now if somebody had asked me, before I had Nathan, about the theory and practice of teaching, I would probably have come up with something resembling what I've just been saying—that the more you can make teaching and learning like a day-to-day experience, the better it is. Not just between the teacher and the students, but between the different students, too—between all the people that are involved in the situation. I would have said that, but it was only living with Nathan for a while that helped me to know what that kind of educational setup was like in practice. What I mean is that this better kind of teaching—more resilient, more flexible, more information flowing back and forth—happened pretty much inevitably between me and Nathan, and that experience helped me to deal with my anxieties about college teaching. Because of being a father, I don't care so much about being a great performer in my classes and I've become more adept at making the courses I teach have a day-in and day-out quality.

These different conceptions of what good teaching is are related, in my mind, to a whole set of objections I have to the way the academic study and teaching of literature are set up in this country. Most of the professors of literature I've had experience with look upon literature and the teaching of literature as this cozy little compartment that's complete unto itself. What this means when it comes to writing a book about literature is that such a book should isolate its subject—poems, plays, novels—as much as possible from what these people often call ordinary life, so that a novel, or whatever, is made to appear as though it had almost no connection with petty things like raising children. And of course these same academic types also think that anyone who's interested in spending time with his or her kids and being involved with his or her kids is likely to be an unprofessional sort of person. They see time spent with children as time taken away from reading and writing books.

My negative and hostile attitudes toward this sort of professionalism existed before I had Nathan, but a lot of the same thinking that went into those attitudes of mine also went into my conception of what it meant to have a kid. My sense that I wanted to be the kind of father who spends a lot of time with his

kid and has an equal role with the mother in the nurturing of
the child—that approach to being a parent was derived from the
same inclinations as those that led me to object to what life was
like in the English department where I worked. Having a child
helped me to understand, not that I wanted to stop teaching and
stop reading and writing books, but that I could teach in a
different, more humane way and that I could write books that
wouldn't be so arid and professional. That means writing a book
that puts whatever piece or pieces of literature you're talking
about deep within that flow of life I got so excited about when I
sensed its presence in *Anna Karenina*. And it means being
aware of the obvious parallels between teaching and raising a
child. What you're trying to do in both cases is help bring the
child or the student to the point where she or he is your equal.
You begin with the assumption, which I think is a true one, that
the parent has a greater array of skills than the child, has more
resources than the child, is more familiar with the world in
general than the child is. Similarly, the teacher, at least within
the confines of whatever it is that he or she teaches, begins with
a greater knowledge and a greater familiarity with that particular thing than the students have. The goal in both situations is to
bring the child or the student to the point, not where they've
acquired the knowledge that you have, but where they're
equipped to acquire it with the same ease or with even greater
ease than you. You'll totally defeat this purpose, as a parent and
as a teacher, if you're mainly interested in displaying yourself
and insisting on the initial inequality.

That's the way I've come to view the academic world and how
I might function within it, and my thinking's been influenced a
whole lot by my life with Nathan. Dealing with him was one of
the main things that helped me to see that my psychological
difficulties about my professional life were a way of expressing
valid political dissent from the way things are set up. I suppose
the spot I'm in now shouldn't surprise me—my teaching became
more and more "unprofessional," and I wrote a book that wasn't
too far off from my idea of what academic books should be like,
and here I am without tenure and without another job that
carries the possibility of tenure. My search for another job has

been quite unprofessional, too. I haven't followed up on job possibilities that were likely to separate me from Nathan. I doubt that I'll stay in this line of work and I'm not at all happy about that.

Families

I have this general ideal of openness to the world and to experience, but it's not that easy for me to live up to that ideal because in a lot of ways I'm very shy. One of my tendencies is to get into small groups of people that I feel comfortable with and then to feel annoyed and threatened when new people come along to visit or enter my group. My first impulse is to see those new people as intruders. But my idea of the family conflicts with this impulse of mine because I like to think of it as a group that develops as many ties as possible to other groups and other areas of life and experience. This means, among other things, that it always has other people coming and going, entering into the life that's being lived in that family. Maybe that's just a fancy way of saying that the family should always be looking to make new friends and explore new territory. It should be in the middle of the flow of life, to use the phrase I've picked up from reading Tolstoy. The family is the primary unit of human relationships, the center from which its members venture forth into relationships with the world beyond the family.

The people within the family unit are also open to each other, just as the family as a whole is open to the larger life beyond itself. Part of what that means is that no member of the family demands love and affection from any other member. As I indicated in speaking about my life with Deborah, I think that love is falsified by the very fact of being demanded. On the other hand, people do show what they're feeling in this ideal family of mine. They show it spontaneously because if they're truly connected with each other, they're committed to the entire flow of emotions between people. They trust each other enough to be constantly showing both good and bad feelings. This is the part of it that I didn't do very well when I was with Deborah.

Another way of putting this is that the members of the ideal family are interconnected with each other. They love each other dearly, and they feel close to each other, yet they feel so close to each other that they don't think much about the fact that they're close to each other. An instance of that last part would be that when Deborah was giving birth to Nathan and I was there with her, I was feeling really high, but I wasn't thinking about the fact that I was feeling high; I was concentrating on helping Deborah push Nathan on out into the world. Anyway, because of this kind of closeness the members of the ideal family don't have to make emotional demands on each other, and they don't require each other to have friends of a certain kind or to be this or that type of person or to pursue this or that activity or occupation. In other words, the members of the ideal family are close, but they're not possessive.

It may sound like I'm talking about free love, or an "alternative life-style," as they used to say in the sixties. The family is this community of adults and children who are so good at being close to each other without being possessive of each other that they don't bother with traditional relationships like husband-wife or parent-child. But I don't mean that sort of thing at all—I just think it would be too complicated and intricate. But not only that. In some way that I can't rationally account for or fully define, the structuring and limiting of relationships of the sort that the conventional nuclear family exists to accomplish—that kind of restraint is what makes openness possible between people. What I'm saying—and I could refer to *Anna Karenina* in this connection too—is that I think things like being married to one other person, being faithful to that person, and being, as a parent, more important to your child than any other adult is—things like that aren't just arbitrary and restrictive social conventions. They're social conventions, sure, but they exist because there are good and substantial reasons for their existence.

My ideal family can be the conventional nuclear unit or it can take another form. I'm living right now in a nonnuclear, communal family. I don't know how long this arrangement will last, so in that sense it's not a family because we haven't all made a commitment to each other for the duration. But in some respects we are a family—according to my ideas about what a family is. That is, we're living together and we care about each other, but we've preserved the smaller family units within the larger family. The couples are still couples, and the kids make a distinction between their parents and the other adults.

I think maintaining those defined, conventional relationships is an especially good thing as far as child rearing is concerned. I mean, I'm living in this house with all these other people and I'm Nathan's father. I look upon myself as the primary opening for Nathan to the world at large, but to some extent the world at large is right here for him within these four walls every day in his dealings with the other people here. He gets to be confronted with more diverse kinds of things, both to cope with and to be turned on by, than he would be if he were living just with me and Mommy and baby brother or sister. Although it's sometimes mystifying for him, I think that he benefits from the fact that his daily world includes both his "family life" with me and this other thing with the other people, which is some combination of both a richer family life than he would have just with me and also a constant exposure to the larger life beyond the family.

Of course, life in this house isn't free of conflict and funny feelings—for me or for him or for anybody. During that time right after we all started living together when Nathan was sort of out of control, I used to feel that everyone else was thinking, "God, why doesn't he get this kid under control? Why did we let him in here with this kid?" I felt I was on trial as a parent and that it was my responsibility to step in when Nathan did something that irritated or pissed off one of the other adults. And I sometimes resented the other adult getting irritated because *I* wouldn't have been irritated by whatever it was that Nathan was doing—making noise, for example. I sometimes thought some of the other adults would perceive only the yelling and banging around and not the good time Nathan was having, and because of this feeling I had of being on trial, I would step in and stop Nathan from making so much noise, all the time thinking, "Boy, I don't like this. Nathan's being disciplined for something he wouldn't be disciplined for if these other people weren't around." Or if I didn't step in I would say mentally to the other adult, "Whoa, leave my kid alone."

My feeling of being on trial in these situations was almost entirely a projection of my own anxieties. The other people here didn't do anything to indicate that they wanted Nathan to be my sole and exclusive responsibility. It was a hard thing to get over, but what helped me was this sense I developed that what our household here should be is this network of sort of hierarchical, yet flexible, relationships. I got to be able to say to myself when it seemed to me that Nathan wasn't getting a fair shake from somebody else in the house, "OK, in dealing with these people here, Nathan's out there operating in the big, wide world, and he's old enough to deal by himself with at least some of what he encounters out there. It's between him and whoever's interacting with him at the moment." Or, as I developed more of a sense that the other people in the house were part of Nathan's family, I came to recognize that not only would it be harmful to him for me to interfere with his dealings with other people, but that it would be breaking the ground rules of the family situation for me to do that. I would be making my little subfamily too exclusive and possessive, not open enough to the larger family.

Whatever form of family life Nathan grows up in, I hope his life has been and will be a process whereby, as he lives day to day, he becomes more and more competent to take care of himself and to respond to the world around him and to enter actively into it. I want him to grow up to be an equal, interdependent human being among other equal, interdependent human beings. That's quite an idealistic goal, I know. I've thought a fair amount about some of the stubborn human facts that stand in its way, some of which are just built into everybody's life situation. I mean, when a kid is little, the kid just doesn't have the skills to take care of herself or himself, and I think that from that physical dependence flow other kinds of dependence which build up and become extremely difficult to break down. It happens all the time with me and Nathan—falling into this thing where he says, "You do it for me, because I can't do it for myself," and implicitly, "Why should I bother to do it when you're so far above me and can do it so much more easily and quickly than I can?"

That's not the whole story, of course. I suspect one reason why kids always get into this distinct stage of constructing fantasies is precisely that they feel very acutely how subordinate they are in the real world, this mysterious place they've been thrust into. They make this other world in which a kid can be "the boss all the time," as Nathan says. Nathan's been into these fantasies for the last several months now—getting out these little toy people of his and not just telling them to do this or that, but insisting that I get into his fantasy world and follow his orders too, like he owns the company and I'm his foreman or something. It's an obvious and clear reversal of the situation in real life—I'm not telling him what to do now, he's telling me. Because there's no doubt about it—I do tell him what to do. No matter how enlightened I may think my guidance and nurturing of him are, there's still a basic sense in which I'm always telling him what to do, always coercing him into participating in this world he didn't make.

Every person experiences inequality. Every person experiences first the fact that he or she is subordinate to and dependent upon some big people for satisfaction of her or his needs of all kinds. I think that fact has a lot to do with why it's so hard to set up social arrangements that are truly equal and just. Everyone has this history of being the slave, and everyone naturally tries to get back at the masters, like Nathan does when he makes me his henchman in relation to his toy people. If people have been the slaves of masters—parents—who didn't try to give up their power, then they'll want to get their licks in when they have children themselves, and the whole thing gets perpetuated. It's far from easy for parents to give up their power—I find myself waging a constant battle with myself about that—just as it's far from easy to build a world in which nobody has power over anybody else. It's far from easy, but it's not impossible. It's just a long, continuous struggle.

Jim

Jim enlisted in the army at the height of the Vietnam War in an effort to change the direction of his life. He is now a construction worker, married, and with two children.

The Army

I'm 28 years old, and I've been married seven years. I have two kids—a daughter, Kathy, who's four now, and a son, Tim, who's one and a half. I enlisted in the Army when I was 18—right in the middle of the Vietnam War. I'd gone to the state university for about three months. Then I'd flunked out and started working on a construction job. But what I was mainly doing was drinking a lot and getting into trouble with the police. I had nothing better to do, I guess. I knew I couldn't keep on doing that, because that's a dead-end road. So I went into the military just to get out of that environment. I had no feelings about the Army either way, I just wanted to get out from where I was. I did think it would be good to enlist instead of being drafted, because I didn't want to go to Vietnam. But I didn't

149

think that part out very much—didn't think of the Navy instead
of the Army or something—I just went in. I was really hung
over the day I went to the recruiting office—it was that kind of
routine. I just went. I was kind of naive about it. The guy at the
recruiting office told me that if I enlisted I would be guaranteed
not to go to Vietnam. And once I was in, I found out I had
signed up for a guaranteed trip to Vietnam.

I did this all on my own, nobody said I should do it. In fact,
my parents and everybody else were shocked when I enlisted. I
can't say being in the Army exactly "straightened me out," but it
did keep me out of that dead-end environment I'd been in. I
know of lots of the friends I used to hang around with that are
still stuck in that drinking and getting into trouble stuff. They
didn't manage to make any changes. So being in the Army did
something for me, obviously. Maybe it was a hard way to do it,
but lots of people do things the hard way, right?

I went to Vietnam after a year in the Army, just after the Tet
offensive in '68. I was an E–5 specialist—the equivalent of a
sergeant—and my job was to direct artillery strikes. I flew
around in this small plane and told them where to shoot. After a
while, I gradually developed antiwar feelings. People talked
about democracy and all that kind of stuff, but it didn't quite sit
right with what I was doing. I could tell, particularly from the
kind of job I had, that the Vietnamese people supported the
other side. And I was directing artillery against villages and
things like that. There were particular instances that just struck
it home to me. So after a while I just stopped flying—just
refused to do my job. It was a combination of political and
survival reasons—people were beginning to risk my life in ways
that I didn't feel were justified by what we were doing.

In the Army, any duty that involves flying is voluntary. So you
can refuse to do it without directly disobeying orders, but I
didn't know that. I didn't know whether it was legal or not to
stop. They did try to keep me flying by giving me some real bad
harassment—giving me the worst jobs and generally doing
anything they could to make life miserable for me. But they
couldn't make me go back up in the air. What happened was
that the small unit I was in got incorporated into a larger unit

and got sent back from an advanced post to a rear post. At the advanced post, there'd been nobody higher ranking than we were, or if there were, we'd been able to live with them. They were OK because they were right in the thick of it with us. But it was different back at the rear post, and almost all of us from the smaller unit were in trouble all the time. There were all these career Army people back there who weren't taking any of the risks, and they wanted to have all this regular army stuff which we didn't have to bother with before—you know, clean uniforms and saluting and that kind of stuff. It was like being stationed back in the United States.

After a year over there, I did get sent back to this country. I got married to Karen then, and the two of us went to live at my new post in Arizona. I'd known her for a long time, and we'd almost gotten married before I went to Vietnam. We had no money, and we lived in a little trailer that was about 20 feet long and 8 feet wide. But it wasn't too bad. I had a lot of friends there; I'd gone through training with most of the guys and been in Vietnam with them. A couple of my friends were living with women, so Karen wasn't totally isolated either. The Army part of it was kind of slow—we were supposed to be training people, but it turned out that we didn't have anybody to train, so we mostly did nothing. We'd go horseback riding, ride around in the desert and do target practice, get stoned, and go home. You'd have to work three or four hours a day, but that was just sitting around reading a book. There was nothing to it. There was very little military discipline, although guys would sometimes end up in the stockade after a real stream of infractions. But it was hard for the Army to control people who had come back from Vietnam, so mostly they left us alone.

College and Work

The Army had this deal that they would let you out three months early if you were going back to school, so I took advantage of that and went back to the school I'd flunked out of before. That was probably the only place that would have accepted me. It's practically a rule that they'll take you in with no questions asked if you're a little bit older, if you've been out working or in the military or whatever, and you want to go back to school. I stayed in college for two years, then left and went to work for a while, and then I went back for another year and a half. Karen had gone to this same school back when I went the first time, but this time she didn't go. She worked to support me through school. We didn't realize it at the time, but we were in the typical male-female roles and stuff like that. I still had some illusions about that stuff when I came out of the Army. I think all of those are gone, or at least most of them.

I quit college once and for all when I only had about a semester to go. I was just getting fed up with exams and all that stuff. I couldn't see the point. Most of the people I know who did graduate still don't have jobs. I went back to construction work, which is what I've mostly always done except for one period of working in a factory. Karen has done secretarial work, and she worked in an electronics place for a little while when I had a broken leg.

There's a lot of sexism at my job—as there usually is in an all-male situation like that—and kids don't come up very much as a topic of conversation, maybe because most of the guys are single. There are two guys that are married with kids, and the two owners of the company have kids, too. That's interesting, because they're both divorced and they both have custody of their kids. One of the ex-wives is an artist, and the other's in theater or something, and both of them didn't want to have anything to do with the kids. So the men are raising the kids. But one of them isn't doing too good a job. He's up-and-coming and rich, you know, and he basically ignores the needs of the kids. It's because of the pursuit of money—if it's a choice between going to a meeting at the bank and the needs of the kids, he'll definitely override the kids' needs. Anyway, I guess the only time that kids figure into my job is when something has to be done that might be a little bit risky. People will say, "Let somebody who's not married do it."

My kids've both been to where I work, and Kathy's old enough to understand what I do. I think it's important that they know what work is. I encourage her to help with the housework and stuff like that. I think it's important for her to participate in that—cleaning the house and washing the dishes. It doesn't matter if she can only do one or two or three dishes as long as she's participating in that kind of work. It's not "women's work" I'm talking about—she knows she can use a hammer or a saw if she wants to. There's no problem with that. There's nothing except society's definition that says that only a man can do such and such a job. There might be some limitations because of physical strength and stuff like that, but I don't even know about that; I know some women who are stronger than I am.

If my kids wanted to build houses like I do, it wouldn't bother me. They can do whatever they want to do. I think there's all kinds of work. There's intellectual work, there's digging a ditch, and so on. It doesn't matter what kind of work people do. You work with your head, you work with your hands—they're not quite the same thing, but I don't think there's any real division or hierarchy. One isn't better than the other. I think those two kinds of work—head and hands—should be integrated, because if they're not, there'll be problems.

Jim's Father and Mother and Their Divorce

My parents got divorced when I was about 15—I was the oldest of five kids. My father's family was really wealthy—an old California family that was one of the first to go out there. Their ranch was in the place that became the downtown of one of the bigger cities in California, so they had to have money, right? My mother's family was just the opposite—like my grandmother on my mother's side did laundry for a living. They had no money at all. They were Irish Catholic, while my father's family was Protestant. My father went to college and all that, and then he was in the Navy during World War II. That's when he met my mother. And when he married my mother, he got kicked out of the family, basically. To them, marrying an Irish Catholic was like marrying a black person. They kicked him out and disinherited him.

We survived all the time I was a kid by odds and ends of jobs that my father did. I remember he sharpened scissors for a while, and he worked for the Boy Scouts. He'd run one or two of their camps in the summertime and do other stuff for them in the winter. When my grandfather died—I mean my father's father—he put it in his will that my father could never have any money unless he got rid of "that woman." Meanwhile, there was this other woman that my father had known since childhood, and he'd always seen her every couple of years. So he started up this big relationship with her, and then we moved to California. I didn't know it at the time, but the reason we moved to California was so he could get a divorce—California divorce laws are real easy and liberal. He planned the whole thing without telling any of us kids.

After the divorce, we never saw him for seven years. My mother supported all of us by giving us lots of spaghetti. My father didn't send any alimony; he was supposed to, but that sort of thing's hard to enforce across state lines. My mother's family helped us out a lot, and my mother worked. She also went to school at the same time—a state teachers college—and now she's an administrator in a public school system.

After seven years, like I said, he wanted to see us all again. He came for Christmas for three years in a row before he died of a heart attack. Each time he stayed for about two weeks. Before the first time, everybody was a little nervous about it. We didn't want to talk about it, partly because my sister was extremely upset. She'd had a lot of emotional problems for a number of years. Our attitude was, "Whatever happens, happens." Of course, when he came, it was difficult seeing somebody you hadn't seen for so long and who'd left in such bad circumstances. Our reception of him was pretty cool. I think what my father was trying to do . . . well, things hadn't worked out too well for him. He never married the woman he took up with, and he never got the money from his family. He got an allowance, but he never got that big inheritance. So he was trying to reestablish contact because he was beginning to realize what he gave up in exchange for money. But it was weird, because when he came back he never talked about what happened. It was like he was trying to deny the whole thing or pretend it never happened. You know, "Here I am again. What's new?"

When I was a kid, my relationship with him wasn't bad—actually it was pretty good. He wasn't a bad guy. There were hard periods every few years, when he'd be between jobs or something, but nothing ever seemed out of the ordinary. We did things together and stuff like that. But it was hard for me to understand when he got the divorce. For about two months there, my mother and father were fighting fiercely—he was throwing things at her and stuff—and that was a real hard time all the way around. So sure, I didn't particularly care for it; I resented it, sure. I guess you could say I sided with my mother. I mean, after the divorce all of us immediately moved back East, and he stayed in California. And like I told you, I didn't see him for seven years.

I didn't hate him, though. The only time I thought much about what he did was when it looked like Karen and I might have to get a divorce. I knew a lot of situations where divorce was a positive thing, but basically my view of divorce came from the way my father had done it—you know, he just abandoned all his responsibilities and said, "To hell with it." I was afraid I'd end up not having any contact with my kids, which was the way it worked with him, and I didn't want to condemn myself to that kind of thing.

Otherwise, I felt sorry for him. I think my younger brothers and sisters were all a little bit more hostile in their reactions to him, but I mostly felt sorry for him, and I think my mother did, too. I could see that what he was doing was selling himself, basically, and that would have to be psychologically a very destructive thing for him. He was missing out on an awful lot in not seeing his kids. I don't know. My mother says I have a lot of his personality. Maybe that's why I went easy on him. But I'm sure that my father was crazy. Of course he was. Otherwise, he wouldn't have done what he did. Nobody but a crazy person gives up kids for money.

Having Kathy and Tim

Our decision to have our first child was simple. We'd been married for three or four years and we just decided it was time to have a kid. I'd always assumed we'd have kids, but for a while we just put it off and were just sort of enjoying things a bit. It wasn't really a well thought-out process, but we did have to talk about it and make a decision, because Karen was on birth control and she had to quit that.

I was in school then, so we were in the conventional sex roles— she was supporting me through school. But partly because I was in school I knew I'd have a lot of free time, so I didn't expect that Karen would be the only parent or the main parent. In fact, only three months after Kathy was born, Karen went to Scotland for two weeks with her sister. She was really down emotionally after the pregnancy and after dealing with this newborn kid a lot, and she needed a vacation, so she went. I stayed and took care of Kathy. It was a lot of work, and it was in the middle of winter, so I felt kind of stuck there with the kid, but it was OK. My mother-in-law helped out some, especially when I had to go to classes.

Deciding about our second kid was much more of a big deal. Part of it was fairly simple. We weren't planning on having much more than two, and we didn't want Kathy to get too old before we had another. We didn't want to have one kid really young and one kid really old, because we wanted them to grow up together. We didn't want the growing-up period to be drawn out forever. Karen and I both come from large families, and it seems like it goes on forever.

But the main reason we decided to have another kid was that our relationship was going through a bad stage—insecurity feelings or something like that. Having a kid was sort of like something to do. We thought, "If we have another kid, that sort of is going to tide things over." But instead it made things worse. It did gloss things over for a while, but it didn't resolve the contradictions that were there. I mean, after Karen was pregnant and the new kid was going to be a fact any day now, both of us started getting on each other's nerves and stuff for a long period of time. Then, after Tim was born, we'd have struggles over who was going to be taking care of the kids, and things like that. I'd come home from work, and my energy for dealing with the kids would be really low, and we'd have these struggles. Things were pretty antagonistic—I mean, we came pretty close to splitting up. It's been a year and a half, and even now the stuff is still being resolved, but we're a lot better friends now and things like that.

Another thing that was going on in me was the feeling that the next kid would be a trap—it would seal my fate. You know, "This is your life now for a long time." The first kid didn't seem to do that. A lot of it had to do with our relationship—Karen and me—and how it was very strained. But I also just felt that with two kids to deal with there would just be a lot more work and a lot more expense and just a longer time for us as parents of being involved in the growing-up process. I would be working and dealing with my family so much that the time I would manage to have as an individual would get to be very closed down and limited. I know a lot of people feel that once you have one kid you're already in the soup. But that's just lukewarm soup. With the second kid the soup starts boiling. I don't think what I'm saying is any universal thing, necessarily. It was probably just the circumstances that Karen and I were in that made it particularly hard.

I can't really explain it, but I did really see the second kid as a seal on my fate. Before that, I could at least daydream that my situation might change, but the second kid for some reason represented making everything more definite and settled. We thought beforehand, "What's the difference, one or two?" But after Karen was pregnant, there was a definite difference that just grew and grew as the birth came closer and closer. You could just feel it between us, and it worked out for a very hard time. I think I had some desires not to be married anymore, not to have all these responsibilities and things like that. It had been all right up to that point—there had been these growing levels of responsibility, but I'd accepted them—but with the next kid, it just seemed like too much. I could never again just fool around and have a good time like I did when I was 18 or 19. Another reason I had this feeling, maybe, was that when Kathy was born I was alternating between work and school, so I still had some free time, but when Tim was on the way, and after he was born, I was doing nothing but working hard all day.

These feelings of mine really affected my relationship with Tim after he was born. I was hostile toward him in a way I never was toward Kathy. Karen was hostile to him, too, but her hostility never went to the levels that mine did. I'd be taking care of Tim after coming home tired from work, and I'd have a headache or something. Tim would be crying—wouldn't want to be quiet—and there would be nothing I could do to make him stop crying. And I'd just get really hostile toward him. Of course, this happened with Kathy when she was a baby, too, but it was just a lot easier to get to that point of hostility with Tim because of this whole thing of me seeing him as a symbol of my sealed fate. I've gotten over it now, though; I don't feel ambivalent about Tim anymore.

Raising Kathy and Tim

I had some experience dealing with kids before I had any of my own. I was the oldest of five kids, and after my parents got divorced I ended up being baby-sitter all the time while my mother worked. I cooked meals and stuff like that. Me and my brothers used to fight like hell, too, and if I was in charge I had to do the discipline, right?—swat 'em in the head, you know. All that experience—I don't know—it was rough, but it may have helped me later on to get out of the traditional sex roles Karen and I were in for a while.

Anyway, I do make an extra effort to spend some time with my kids. In the morning, before I go to work, I get Tim up with me and fix breakfast for him and me. I used to do this with Kathy, too, but now that she's older she sleeps later. She doesn't get up until just before I leave for work. I enjoy doing this, and I enjoy having only one of them to handle. Then I say good-bye to them, and I don't see them until eight or nine hours later. In the evening I make a point of not drinking, either on the way home from work or after I get home, because I want to be able to concentrate on being with the kids. Karen and I alternate putting the kids to bed, but it doesn't always work out right. Sometimes I have to put in a 12-hour day, and I don't get home until after the kids are in bed. Or sometimes I'll just have had a long hard day and I'll be too damn tired; there's no way I can put the kids to bed on a night like that. And then it becomes a struggle between Karen and me about who's going to do it, and that's really hard. Kids like you to play with them, of course, and I do play with my kids a lot. I try to take them to a park or playground at least once a week. On the weekends—Sundays especially—there's more time, and I go on trips with them—to the zoo or just out in the country for a walk in the fields. I just had a two-week vacation—the first one I'd had in a long time—and that was really helpful because I could spend a lot of time with the kids.

I think I enjoy Kathy more now—she's four—than I ever did before. She seems to be becoming a person, like she's developing a whole personality. For one thing, it seems like her body's taken on a much more even and proportioned development. For another, her vocabulary's increased a lot and she's able to analyze things a little bit. If she's done something wrong and gotten punished for it, she can talk about it later. She'll say, "Well, I didn't really mean to do that, and I was feeling this or that." I think in general she's beginning to recognize herself as separate from her parents. She's stopped being a baby at all now and gone on to being a kid. Next year she's going to be in school.

I don't mean that Tim's not a person. He's one and a half now, and he's just starting to talk. His vocabulary is probably up to about ten words, all dealing with things like eyes, ears, face, hands, up and down—stuff like that. He has distinct emotional reactions to different things, and he's definitely an aggressive kid. You can't tell sometimes whether he really means what he's doing or whether he's acting it out. But there's just a much fuller development when they get to be Kathy's age. When a *baby* grabs for something, sometimes it misses it, and after a while the baby learns how to grab things without missing. I think when a kid gets to be Kathy's age, her mind is finally beginning to grab things a lot better.

Like I say, Tim is pretty aggressive, more aggressive than Kathy ever was. Maybe this is because he's the second kid, or maybe it's because I was more hostile to him than I was to Kathy. I don't know; I'm not a psychoanalyst. Maybe it's because he's a boy and Kathy's a girl. I really don't know anything about it. I haven't studied early childhood. I think I've read some things that say there's no such thing as sex-related differences in children. If I were to say what my common sense tells me, I would say there's a definite difference between boys and girls. But some people tell me I'm crazy to think that or say it.

Karen and I pretty much agree about raising the kids—at least on the day-to-day stuff. For instance, we both encourage the kids to be outgoing, to *do* things. And we both agree that if they're doing something they shouldn't—having to do with safety or whatever—then we just stop them. That's it; there are no ifs, ands, or buts. On the safety thing, we mostly encourage the kids to take a few risks. Kathy can climb to the top of a jungle gym right now. That's pretty good for four. Tim goes down the slide by himself. He's a little bit afraid as he's coming down, but he goes back up and slides down again. I think that's good. Of course, you have to stand close and watch them carefully, but I think kids should be encouraged to learn to climb and do other things that are a little bit dangerous. I think if you stop them from doing that, or if you show them you're a little bit afraid for them when they're up there, that's not so good for the kids. Our kids have gotten their bruises and stuff like that, but neither of them has ever been seriously hurt. So I'm glad we've encouraged them. I've seen lots of children that are really afraid to do anything at all. They pick up on what's going on around them. If a kid is around two older people all day long, the kid is going to get the attitudes of the older people, just like Kathy and Tim use terms and have attitudes and generally reflect the things that Karen and I think and do. A kid living with older people won't necessarily be afraid, but that kid will get used to not doing anything because the older people he or she lives with are inactive. I think older people should participate in child rearing, but not in a way that makes kids passive and timid.

But getting back to Karen and me—how do we arrive at decisions about the kids? Well, usually they happen very gradually; it seems like a natural flow. For example, there won't even have to be a decision about what school Kathy's going to go to next year. She'll go right into the public school system because there's no other choice for us—we don't have the money to spend on anything else for her. If I were to think of the biggest decision we're making now about the kids, it would be whether they should get swine flu shots. They say swine flu is even riskier for children than for older people. It's a tricky one, and we're trying to decide it right now. We've been talking it over for a couple of weeks—we talk about it for a couple minutes at dinner; then we talk about it again another time. Somehow in the process a decision is being made in a mutually agreeable way. We both agree that this whole thing is probably a political hoax, but that still has to be translated into whether we and our kids get shots or not. Basically, I think we've decided against it.

If Karen and I disagree, all I can say is there's usually a lot of struggle about whatever it is. That's all; there's just a lot of struggle. Maybe it gets resolved in her direction, maybe it gets resolved in my direction, but sometimes we really do have to negotiate. I don't just let her make the decisions. There are some things she decides about by herself, though. And there's no doubt about it—she's the one who has primary responsibility for raising the kids. I mean, with me working so much, it almost has to be that way. If we're both sitting there in the same room, who will the kids ask for when they want something? They'll always ask for her, right? Because she's the one they've gotten used to being with all week long, eight hours a day and more.

That guy who said having kids is both good and bad for a marriage—he was right. In some ways the kids make it very hard for Karen and me to split up. We both love our kids, and raising them makes for further ties between us. But raising them also makes for a lot of strains and tensions, right? It seems like there's always those two aspects to anything. And how it works itself out is almost a matter of history or something, the history of the whole thing. But it works its way out. Some people end up getting divorced; *I* may end up getting divorced, maybe because of the kids, maybe because of all the circumstances. But maybe not, you know.

I was talking before about how I felt trapped by all the responsibilities of being a parent at the time we decided to have Tim. But there are a lot of positive things, too, about being a parent. I know the difference between myself and people my age that are still single, and I can't imagine being single and isolated and not having kids. It's just really nice to come home to kids that are happy—it's fulfilling. It's also stabilizing. I don't mean that having kids is the same as when I joined the Army to stop drinking and getting in trouble. I mean stabilizing in the sense of wanting life to be positive and seeing it as positive. I don't know if that makes sense. You just know better when you have kids that life is good, and that when you get older and the kids grow up, that'll be a good situation too. It's good for people to be in relationships with young children. It gives you a more positive and stabilizing outlook on yourself. You know that you have a lot of influence, so you think about the things that you do. You think, "How's this that I'm doing going to affect my children?" I don't know. Life just seems to take on a lot more positive aspects when you're a parent than it does when you're sort of roaring along as a youth, devil-may-care.

Communism

I'm a communist, and so my views are very definite about certain things. I think most of the problems in this society stem from the society and not from the individual families or other situations like that. How did I get to think that way? When I was in Vietnam was the beginning of a long process of change in myself. I saw what the Vietnamese people were doing, and I respected them. On our side, there were all these planes, and thousands of soldiers, and mammoth artillery, and everything. And here were these people that were basically fighting with nothing, and they were winning. That had to influence me. I realized the changes I was going through more when I came back here and worked with other guys that had seen the same things, worked to make this government stop what it was doing. And then I started to find out that the government was in the hands of the capitalists, and stuff like that. It's been a long process of change for me, and it's still going on.

I think parents can't be parents until the society changes. One parent has too much time with the kids, and the other has too little. The husbands or males or whatever usually end up working too much. You come home, and you're really tired from working, and it's really hard to be a parent. I can't be a father until I have the free time to be a father, right? But I don't have enough free time, basically. I have to work five days a week, sometimes six, in order to eat. So that leaves one day, Sunday, to cram it all into. And as for women—well, whoever's in the house (right now that's mostly women)—whoever's in the house can't be a parent, really a human being, unless she can get out of that house. If you're in the house all the time with—never mind two kids—three or four or five or six kids, it breaks your own development. And you in turn are going to take that out on your kids, and that's going to result in your kids' not having positive images and positive outlooks.

This whole struggle to survive is so consuming that at one time in this society people used to have to send their kids to work. In fact, people still do send their kids to work. You can find that a lot in big cities, or you can just walk into lots of little stores and see the whole family working there to survive. Also, you see lots of people that work two jobs, husbands that work two jobs. How much can you do with your family in that situation? Or you see both the husband and the wife out working full time. How much can they do with their kids? They come home and they're *both* tired. What the hell! And so you get alcoholism. Even if it's mild alcoholism, it affects people.

I've thought about having another kid, but I have a lot of questions about it. I'm not worried about that stuff about world population. That may become a serious problem, but it's not one right now. People aren't starving because of population; they're starving because of the economic system. The real question for me about having more kids is political. If I have a lot of kids, I'll be even more trapped in this struggle to survive and I won't do as good a job with those six or seven kids as I will if I have just two. Also, if I'm working so hard to survive and keep my family alive, I won't have any energy left to work to change this system, the rotten situation people are faced with.

So you shouldn't have to work all the time. And women should be able to get out of the house—they should be able to work and

go to school the same as men. But it's more than that. I think
that there has to be universal day care. Kids belong to society,
basically; they don't just belong to their parents. You don't own
your kid. That kid is a product of society, and if the kid is a
juvenile delinquent, that concerns everybody, not just the parents. Society has a responsibility toward children. I mean, the
amount of day care that's available in this country compared to
the amount that's needed is like one percent to a hundred
percent. In the first place, most people I know can't afford it. In
the second place, if they can afford it, it's only because the two
parents are both working at full-time jobs, which means they
still don't have enough time for their kids. And what day care
there is, particularly commercial day care, is organized just
functionally, just to keep the kids there in the room. It's not
organized toward the kids' development.

Kathy's in a day-care situation that's not as bad as these
commercial deals. We can afford it—at least it's not killing us.
It's a parent cooperative; we like that. And we like the teachers
and the way the classroom is set up. I think Kathy's learned
quite a bit there—the teachers discourage traditional sex roles
and so on. In fact, there's this one teacher, Sheila, that we
especially like and who's become a good friend of ours. She
never graduated from high school, but she's just really sharp—
knows what's going on politically and is great with children. The
part of this situation that's not so good is that some of the other
families in it are fairly well off, and some of their attitudes
reflect their position in society. Like we have these potluck
suppers to make policy and stuff, and we could never have one at
our house because it's right in the middle of a housing project
and it's very small. The suppers almost always happen at the
house of somebody who's pretty well off, and I usually feel pretty
uneasy at one of those places. So, like with everything else in
this society, there are contradictions in this setup; some of it's
good and some of it's bad.

What can't take place in this society as it is now is the kind of
day care I'd like to see, the kind they have in China. I've seen it
on TV, where very young children are encouraged to be ener-
getic and to be learning—learning even things like gymnastics,

which is an ability kids can develop rather rapidly even when they're very young. What that kind of day care means is that the whole society's taking a positive role in the development of all the children. It's not just the two parents storming along economically trying to survive, but it's everybody that's concerned about the development of those kids. Also, that kind of day care is a lot more integrated into people's lives. It's not just someplace you drop your kid off. Parents participate in it a lot, and it even gets integrated into the workplace, so that you can play with your kids at lunchtime or whatever. I'm not worried at all about parents no longer having close ties to their own kids, and stuff like that, in a socialist day-care setup. They'll still be the ones that have the most time with their kids, and they'll already have had strong influences on their children in the earliest stages of the kids' lives. The bond between parent and child is pretty strong in any society.

Having kids has affected my politics and my commitment to communism, sure. I mean, if the government decides to go to war again, it will probably come and try to arrest me. It's a risky proposition, believing what I believe. They've killed the Panthers, and they've killed people like King, and they've generally killed people in this country who were talking about revolution. So I'm conscious of taking risks, and I know that the risks are going to get greater. In fact, I may even be separated from my kids because of my politics, right? I might have to go to jail or something like that. Anything can happen.

But mainly, having kids has made me more committed. It's helped to give me a really positive outlook on life. Kids are the future, so things should be done for them. I mean, when I'm an old man, things are going to belong to the kids, and how I'm going to be treated as an old man is going to be dependent on how the kids have grown up. But beyond that, it seems that the more you give to children, the more things are going to get positive.

I think we make the world ourselves; we don't wait around for our kids to do it. The more educated they are and the more positive life is for them, the better everything will be in the long run. If kids have very positive situations, and they're looked to as being very important for society as a whole, that sort of reflects the society itself.

I have only one specific hope for my kids, and that's that they should grow up to become communists and revolutionaries. That's partly why I want them to go through the public schools—I want them to have to handle the stuff everybody else has to handle. I don't want them to be off in a private school or something where they might think they're set off from other people. I think about the world I hope my kids will live in in all sorts of funny ways. Like, I think I have a somewhat different attitude about dying than people who haven't been to Vietnam or something. I've seen a lot of people die, so it's a real-life thing to me. It's not theoretical. I mean, there could be a nuclear war— that's a real possibility. In fact, every time I hear a siren I think about that possibility. That's a reflection from being in Vietnam, too. When they used the sirens over there, that meant we were going to get hit with something. So I know that when they're blowing sirens—like at noontime, they blow sirens all the time— I know that they're practicing, practicing for the real thing. I don't think, "Ooh, it's going to happen—here come the bombs," although that used to cross my mind when I first came back from Vietnam. But every time it registers with me that they're practicing; every day they're practicing to make sure the whistles are working. And believe it or not, when I hear those sirens and that practice for war, it makes me feel really positive about kids—it really does. Because I hope that my kids live to take down the sirens. That's what I hope—that they live to take down the sirens.

Tom

Tom, 31 years old, the son of an auto mechanic, put himself through school to become an engineer. He and his wife, Elaine, have a two-year-old son, Adam, and are now deciding whether or not to have a second child.

Tom and His Father

I think one of the big things the men in my father's generation lacked was the ability to have close and affectionate relationships with their children. They got embarrassed about that sort of closeness, acted like they were betraying their manhood or something. My father was certainly that way; he never showed much appreciation for me or my brother. Instead of praising things that we did right or did well, he always criticized us for our faults. It was only the things that were done wrong or poorly that he noticed. I know my father did this consciously—I've talked to my mother about it since he died. He was very concerned that we not get a distorted opinion of our own worth and abilities. He didn't want us to be too self-congratulative and proud. It wasn't that he had some high standards that he wanted us to meet, he just wanted to keep us in our place.

I guess mothers have always been, in most cases, a little more sympathetic to their children than fathers have been—maybe just having borne them has something to do with that. So my mother was not always just criticizing us. She could see things that we did well and let us know, but she would never, never think of crossing my father in the criticism that he was dishing out. She just completely knuckled under to whatever he insisted on.

He would criticize me about projects that I would try to construct or work out, or about maintenance-type things around our house that I would try to take care of. There'd always be something wrong—I could never do it quite right. I didn't have the feeling that he thought I wasn't being masculine enough or anything like that. He was just criticizing me no matter what. Anything that we had contact over would provoke it. I worked it out by trying to have as little contact with him as possible as the years went on, and he was quite happy with that. He didn't view the role of a father as being any more than just making enough money to put food on the table. Other than that, he couldn't really see his role in child rearing. Child rearing was an annoyance to him, something getting in his way. I mean, he never really did things like changing diapers or putting us to bed or feeding us—he never participated in that at all. And he certainly hadn't had any particular desire to have children—he'd just had them. He and my mother were so uneducated and ignorant of choices that the idea that you could actually decide not to have children never occurred to them. It wasn't a valid question in their lives. They were Catholic and thought that there was nothing you should do against having children.

Consequently, I was born less than a year after my brother. As the elder child, I think the real burden of my father's criticism fell on my brother. I think my father expected more of him, looked to him to carry on my father's name and tradition, although I can't imagine why that would be a good thing. My brother accepted all the criticism, thought it was justified, and tried to prove himself worthy according to my father's standards. He was constantly trying to do things that he thought would please my father. He worked in my father's auto shop, tried to learn that type of work, which I was just turned off by completely. He was always very militaristic, from very early on. He loved rifles and guns and uniforms and marching. My father being very stern, my brother thought that would please him—military rigor and discipline and so forth. And in fact my brother went on to join the Air Force and is now in the Air Force professionally.

Being so close in age, my brother and I hated each other, always. We fought constantly. It was partly due to the comparison my father made between me and him—you know, my brother's being more able to live up to what my father wanted. So that really set us up for a wonderful relationship, and to this day we have very limited contact with each other. I don't feel the tension anymore when we do see each other—we just have very little in common, and I'm sorry about that. I really would like to have had a sibling who was close, whom I could share things with, but . . . we've been apart for so long.

Getting back to my father and me, we didn't fight a lot. That was really not an option. As I said before, I learned to just keep away from him. But I had a lot of bitterness and resentment toward him all the way through, growing up. I felt he was very unsympathetic and very disappointed in me—just couldn't wait till I was gone. I felt I was really ignored and tolerated more than accepted and loved. I only expressed this resentment after I'd left home.

He didn't have any ambitions for me and wasn't particularly pleased when I became an engineer. In fact, I think he probably would have been happier if I had become an electrician or something. He was always talking about how much money plumbers and electricians made. He himself was an auto mechanic, and I think my going to college was in a way a rebellion against his blue-collar background. He criticized me about going to college, of course. "You must be out of your mind!" He couldn't afford to help pay my way through college, but he did offer to let me live at home and pay rent. For him, that was a concession. But I chose to leave home. I just didn't want to stay there anymore. I got some scholarships, but basically I worked my way through college. I made it on my own, and I felt like I got no help from him. In a way, it was a triumph over him to have done it in spite of his rejection, criticism, and lack of support.

The Good Father

Because of this bad relationship with my own father, I've tended to look to friends of my own generation for models of the good father. And that's kind of funny, because Elaine and I knew several people with children before we had Adam, and in most cases the children were "difficult" children—extremely dependent, unable to adjust to their parents' normal comings and goings, and also high-strung, just turning to tears at the least thing. We tended to put this sort of behavior down to parental deficiency or inadequacy—you know, "If those were my kids . . . " But I still thought these fathers were good as models for me, that the men were trying to cope with difficult situations. They shared in the work of raising their children, including just the physical work. I feel very strongly about that. I think that in itself is a major relief valve in reducing tensions that could arise between parents over the upbringing of the child, and just between themselves. But beyond that, I saw these fathers giving their time and participating in the developmental aspects of child rearing, having a sympathetic approach to the child and seeing his difficulties, instead of all the time just trying to figure out how to get him out of your life, stopping him from interfering with your pursuits.

Most of all, though, Elaine has been very helpful to me in making me aware of what she thinks a good father is. She's done a lot to change my attitudes. Obviously, from my background I didn't have much of a feeling of what women might think a father's role should be, other than the traditional thing of fathers having no role at all. I hadn't really worked out an attitude on it myself, but Elaine had some very definite ideas about it before ever entering into marriage, much less motherhood. She was very sure she didn't want to have happen to her what happened to her mother and her mother's friends. I think women are the ones who have to be much more careful, or they suddenly find themselves married and with kids, before you know it. And if they haven't really worked out who's going to help with them, they find all of a sudden that "Gee, well, we're the only ones that are even interested." There they are again in the traditional role.

So Elaine was very careful about not getting caught in that situation, and our talking about it, even before we got married, helped me to get clearer on what I thought fathers should contribute to child rearing. I don't feel that I've been forced into it unwillingly, because I really agree with the philosophy of shared responsibility, but it took someone like her to bring that out. If I had married a woman who was very traditionally oriented and didn't care whether I participated or not, I probably would have fallen into not participating, because it's just the easiest way out. It really takes a much bigger effort to try to share the responsibility. I get to share the rewards too, of course. I really have a feeling that Adam is a product not only of Elaine and her care, but that he's a combination of both of our cares. Whatever rewards we feel from raising him are partly due to me.

Tom and Elaine: Having Kids

There never was a point where we had ultimately reached a decision to have a child—where, you know, one day we didn't know one way or the other, and the next day we did. The decision really just developed over a number of years. We'd been married almost three years before we had Adam, and we had talked about having kids or not even before we got married. We didn't get married assuming that sooner or later we'd have children, but we didn't shut the door on it either. It was an open topic. We knew that we wouldn't begin to try having one until we had been married a couple of years at least, and had had a time to adjust to each other. After that point, I guess we started feeling that our relationship was able to withstand the on-slaughts of a child.

The thing that made having a child attractive was not the

great joy that a child would bring into our lives. I guess we did it out of curiosity more than anything else. You really don't know enough, before you've ever had one, to say, "We're doing it for the things that a child is going to bring into our lives," especially since neither of us had had that much experience with other children. I mentioned before that we knew several people with difficult children, but we tended to discount that information and let our curiosity be the major factor.

We were both in our late twenties when we got married, but we didn't feel pressured by that fact in making our decision to have Adam. We weren't that worried about producing a child with birth defects. But right now, we're trying to decide whether or not to have a second child, and how old we are is definitely a factor. We're both pushing the age limit, so we're going to have to resolve it one way or the other fairly soon. Thinking about having a second child is quite different from thinking about having the first one. I mean, now we know what we're in for. With the first child, there's no way you can really know what you're getting into. You do it much more cautiously the second time. We haven't definitely decided yes or no, but at this point I would say it's more yes than no.

I think it would be good to have a second child for Adam's sake, but I certainly don't want to do it for that reason alone. You can't depend on their ever liking each other, as my own life shows. In fact, usually siblings don't. But I think we're wise enough not to fan the fires of competition between two siblings like that. We've both seen that and suffered from it so much ourselves. But on the other hand, I don't want to set myself up for expectations that they will immediately love each other and never have any disagreements. We know that's not likely. I just hope that they can stand each other enough while they're growing up so that when they're adults, they'll see that they have enough in common to be friends.

I realize that every additional child does add more stress to the family—there's no doubt about it. But I feel we've gotten to the point where we can accommodate that additional stress. I couldn't have said that a year ago, but the way Adam is developing independence and needing us for attention less makes me confident that we could assume the additional stress and responsibility of a second child, probably within a year.

Certainly so far, having Adam and raising him has had a very good effect on our marriage. We have much less time to worry about trivialities than we had before. I guess the common achievement, the common goal of raising Adam, is something that really binds us together. It just obviously gives us a lot more in common than we had before. We had a good marriage before Adam, but I'm sure our marriage has been strengthened. I can see how having a kid might work terrible hardships on a couple who aren't getting along, and I think we feel fortunate that it's worked the other way for us.

We were really together on the decision to have Adam, had virtually no conflict at all. And I think it's been the same with his upbringing—no patterns of significant disagreement. There've been some minor things—like at one point I felt Elaine was pushing food on Adam too much. I thought it was unwise to force-feed him, but . . . I don't know, we worked that out to the point where it's not a problem anymore. Adam is a voracious eater anyway, so it's kind of solved itself.

There are some differences between Elaine and me that probably come from cultural patterns, maybe from sex roles. For instance, if we're at the playground, Elaine is just a lot more hesitant than I am to let Adam do certain things that might endanger him physically. I guess I'm of the opinion that he should get as much exposure as he can, short of putting his life in danger. I know there are families where it's the father who's the more protective of the two parents, but still, I think culturally men have a feeling that it's better to have more exposure and more experience, even if that does mean a few skinned knees and dirty overalls.

There's another area that shows itself when Adam is being really demanding. When he's been that way for hours and there hasn't been one socially redeeming aspect to his personality, when there's just not a speck of charm left in him, I just have less patience with him than Elaine does. She seems to have a much higher tolerance for his negative behavior than I do. I'll get mad and swat his fanny or slap his hand if it seems appropriate, much sooner than she ever will. This is a personality difference between Elaine and me, but I think it's culturally backed too. It was the same pattern in my own family. I can't say that I've rejected all of my father's traits, but I feel like I've controlled them and limited them to appropriate situations. Adam prefers Elaine to me at this point, I think, partly because of this stuff. She is just more patient and lenient with him. He knows that he can go to her and get something that he might not get from me. He's very, very quick to pick up these differences.

Also he prefers her because he spends more time with her, since I'm the full-time worker in the family. So there's another cultural, sex-role thing. On the other side of that one, I used to have exotic value to him, as the one who went away and came back. Up until he was about 16 months or so, he used to ask for me during the day. Elaine would tell me how he'd always be saying "Dada, Dada" all day long, especially around the time I usually came home. Then he would get very excited when I came in, and I'd pick him up and hug him. Elaine would come over, and I'd hug her, and Adam would be very jealous of that. He would push Elaine away. He wouldn't let me hug her, because he had to have me to himself for those few minutes. And you know, in a way I liked that. I felt special to him. But since then I seem to have developed less importance, or maybe it's just that he's more interested in other things now. He can really involve himself in play for much longer periods, and has more complex play. So when I come home in the evening, he won't come running, even though he hears the door and everything. I'll spend five minutes taking off my jacket and whatnot, and he'll know I'm there, but he'll go on playing somewhere. He'll be off in the pantry or in the kitchen on the floor playing with pots and pans. I'll come in and I'll say, "Hi, Adam," and he won't even recognize my presence. He just continues playing. "Hi, Dad. You're here, huh? So what."

But Adam does spend quite a lot of time with me, although not as much as he spends with Elaine, so maybe that's another reason I'm not all that exotic to him. I guess he sees her about 75 percent of the time and me 25 percent of the time. On working days, I get home at 5:00 and he goes to bed around 9:30, so we have four-and-a-half hours together. In order for him to have more time with me and less with Elaine, we've adjusted his schedule so that he goes to bed late and gets up late. That evens out the child care a little and gives him exposure to both of us.

A lot of this time in the evening, Elaine is there too, but I generally have the main responsibility. She can do what she wants. Sometimes she goes out for modern dance classes, sometimes she'll just go in the bedroom and read, which Adam accepts, but only after putting up a fight. Sometimes we have to lock the bedroom door, and then after a while of banging on the door, Adam realizes he can't get in and submits.

On the weekends, I generally do more of the physical care things. For instance, I usually do all the diaper changing. Every night I put him to bed, and I always give him his bath—Elaine never does that. On the weekends this continues, plus the diapers and other things I don't get a chance to do during the week, like feeding him breakfast or lunch. I'll also take him out on my own. If Elaine wants time to herself, I'll take him to a playground or a park, or we'll go shopping. I probably assume more than 50 percent of the care on weekends.

It's not something that we've worked out very formally—we don't usually set definite hours where one of us is responsible totally and the other is nowhere around or is inaccessible. I guess we haven't had to do that yet. I can see it happening, though, if we have another child or if Adam gets especially demanding. We just may have to divide it up more formally and say, "Well, this is your day off. This is my day off." And we won't see each other the whole day.

Recently I had Adam all to myself for a week, when Elaine took a trip to California. The first couple of days, he asked for Elaine around the time that I put him down for his midday nap. He missed her at that point because that's something she normally does with him. I just said, "She's gone away, and she'll be back," and he said, "All gone!" It's amazing how they can dispense with you. This happened over that first weekend. She left on a Saturday, so I had two full days with him to sort of ease the transition, and except for naptime, he didn't miss her terribly much. We kept occupied, you know, I took him places.

But it started to get sticky on Monday when I went back to work and had to drop him off really early at his baby-sitter's and pick him up late—much later than he was used to. He was fine at the sitter's, took his nap. He didn't eat much, but he made it through the day. But when we got home, he just burst into tears. He just buried his head in my chest and wouldn't let me go. He just cried and cried, and I knew he really missed Elaine. He couldn't express it, but I knew what it was. Then for the rest of that evening, he would not let me out of his sight. Even if I just went around the corner into another room or something, he just came running and screaming after me. I guess he figured if one can disappear that easily, so can the other. But that only lasted that evening. For the rest of that week, I only worked five hours a day. I could pick him up from the sitter's closer to his usual time, and that helped a lot. I could let him run around the yard for a while before it was time for supper. That seemed to give him enough contact with me so that he didn't demand my total presence all evening long. All in all, I thought he adjusted rather well to Elaine's absence.

The day that Elaine was returning, I said to him, "Momma's coming back tonight." He didn't really understand and kept saying, "Debby, Debby." He thought Debby was coming back— the little girl next door who plays with him a lot—because at that point Debby was a more immediate presence to him than his mother. He knew something was happening, but he wasn't quite sure what or who was involved. Then at the airport, when Elaine walked through the door, he seemed to recognize her at first, but there were so many other people around and so much commotion and greeting that he was kind of caught up in that atmosphere and just kept running around. He didn't especially focus on Elaine, but just kept frolicking around and mingling in among those people. As we were walking to the baggage claim area, he was obviously very elated, running down the hall, jumping all the way, really very happy, unusually so. But he still wasn't clinging to Elaine or anything. At the place where you pick up your baggage, I stayed with Adam while she went to get her suitcase. But when Elaine disappeared into that crowd, Adam let out a yell. He would not let her out of his sight, not now, not after all of this. So she stayed with him while I got her suitcase.

For the next few days, he was much, much more demanding than usual. He probably felt some anger or frustration at her not having been there all the time, and he was going to let Elaine know it, get back at her in some way. His feelings have evened out since then fairly well, although in my darker moments I look at him and think he's undergone a complete change in personality, gone from being a relatively happy child to being somebody with a really foul disposition. He only behaves this way at home, of course. When you take him out, he's fine, and everybody says, "Gee, what a great kid! You don't know how lucky you are." But at home when he's only got us around, I guess he feels like we have to take him, no matter what. We can't very well kick him out, and he knows that in some way—and God, if things don't go just right, if he doesn't get everything he wants at certain times, he just breaks up completely, and we're just battling constantly. Both Elaine and I are cognizant of the fact that we can't just roll over and give in to all these demands, because they're continuous—they just keep escalating. If we did give in, things would come to the point where I don't think I would want to live with him any more.

It's partly growing pains, I think. I believe he thinks it's *our* phase, because a lot of times he'll come up to me and say, "Mad! Mad!" He'll come up and tell me I'm angry even when I haven't been and when he hasn't been doing anything to make me angry. He just assumes that's my whole personality now. I guess it works both ways—I look at him as having had a real change in his personality, and I'm sure he sees the same in me.

I really do want a second child, but sometimes I'm not sure I want to go through the first couple of years. It's definitely gotten easier as Adam's gotten older. So with the second one, I'd like to sort of jump over those first stages and get right into raising a more mature child. You have to like them at every stage in their development, of course, but some people are better suited to dealing with some ages than others.

For some reason, the rewards of being a parent seem much more nebulous than the drawbacks. The negative aspects always seem much more concrete. But what are the rewards? One of them, surely, is just being able to sit back every now and then and watch your child opening up to the world, observe the child's reactions to reality at different stages. At every stage along the line, those reactions change. It's a very fresh way of viewing the world—and I mean doing it yourself, as well as appreciating it in your child.

I guess I began to see Adam more distinctly as a person like the rest of us when he started to learn language. It seemed then as though he started to take off and left babyhood behind forever. Communicating with language seems like a quantum difference from just communicating with physical signs. Of course, I had a sense of Adam's unique character and personality long before that, from about the time when he was four or five months old. I don't know why I started sensing it then. I guess I've blocked a lot of that early period out. But they really do start developing character traits by then—maybe it's connected to the fact that they start sitting up around that time. In any case, that's when you start to be able to filter out the demands for food and other physical satisfactions and see particular styles of demanding attention, affection, and so forth. Those are the things that really separate children from each other.

One thing I try to guard against is making Adam dependent on me, looking up to me and idolizing me. Of course, it happens every day. Adam would be absolutely desolate if Elaine and I weren't around. What would he do? But I've tried to de-emphasize that sort of hero worship for fear that I might look on it as too much of the reward of being a parent. Then I'd want him to continue, and that would be a bad thing for both him and me in the end. If he doesn't develop enough independence and have enough of a life of his own, he won't be able to cut the cord when the time comes. He'll be hanging around at home, depending on me for financial and other types of support. I really think that's a disservice to children. I know many people who are dependent on their parents like that, and I think they've really been shortchanged.

But I'm not really very worried about it. All in all, I like the way Adam's developing so far, and I don't foresee any great problems like this, other than the to-be-expected rebellions in teenage. They can always get screwed up somewhere along the line.

Working

I think one of the factors that was unresolved before we had Adam was the issue of working and careers, for both of us. One of the reasons Elaine was hesitant about having a child was that she wasn't sure how she could maintain a professional life and also be a mother. Work is important to her, and she didn't want going into motherhood to mean giving that up completely. But there didn't seem to be any alternatives available to us. I mean, we both want ideally to be able to share the child rearing and the breadwinning, but it just hasn't worked out that way.

When Adam was about six months old, Elaine went looking for part-time work. She wasn't necessarily looking for a job connected to her career; I think she mainly wanted to get out of the house and away from Adam for a part of every day, although she didn't want to wait tables or anything like that. She's in social work, and she did run into a number of possibilities in that field. But they all seemed to have major drawbacks— they involved really difficult commuting way across town, and they were community-type projects in really tough neighborhoods. She was afraid she might not have enough energy to do that hassling with both work and travel and then come home and still have anything left to give Adam. Also, I guess the danger of working in a tough neighborhood was a factor. We're just a lot more security-conscious now than we were before we had Adam. I don't mean that we're constantly worrying about economic security and comfort for our child, just that we know how devastating it would be for either one of us to lose the other as a partner, much less for Adam to lose a parent.

Elaine's pretty much satisfied with taking care of Adam most of the time until maybe he's in school, or at least old enough not to require so much attention. At that point she fully expects to go back to work, at least on a part-time basis. I think she's overcome the grave misgivings she had about the housewife syndrome and routine, misgivings that were based in her experience. In her neighborhood when she was growing up, all the mothers stayed home. They were all undeveloped intellectually and professionally, particularly her own mother. So the role of a housewife was one that really frightened her and continued to frighten her after Adam was born. But now she's found friends who are in the same boat as her, who are not just undeveloped stay-at-homes, and who don't want to let themselves get limited that way for the rest of their lives. It's really helped her a lot. Some of these friends have already done what she's planning—gone back to work after their children were in school—so that's also helpful to her. I'm just very appreciative that she's willing to postpone her career like this. Working it out this way fits in pretty well with her particular line of work, too. Social work is emotionally very draining. She might find it hard to attend to both a social work job and Adam at the same time. But when Adam's older and doesn't need as much attention, she'll probably feel she doesn't need to conserve as much energy for him and that she'd be cheating herself at that point if she didn't go back to work for her own self-fulfillment.

Having a child has given me a somewhat different sense of my own work as an engineer, made me more appreciative of the job I have, and made it a lot less likely that I'd ever quit and go looking for work elsewhere. My employer has treated me quite well, done a lot for me, and I would really think very seriously before giving that up. Also, I'd have to think hard about how I would provide otherwise for Adam now that Elaine can't really bring in any money. It's sobering to realize that you are now the one and only support of two other people besides yourself.

Before we had Adam, I would tend to fantasize a lot about other jobs I could have been doing or other careers I could have had, had I not gone into engineering. And at times I would feel like I had cheated myself in not taking up a field that I had more inborn interest in. I don't feel a natural inclination to the type of work I'm doing, particularly to the people that I work with. I have never found people at my job whom I've had much in common with. I've never made my friends there. So in many ways engineering probably wasn't the best choice for me.

I'm really in it now because of what I chose to major in at college. That decision was based a lot on parental pressure. Even though my parents couldn't keep me away from college, they at least wanted to see that I was doing something practical, something in which I could conceivably earn an income and a living, as opposed to these rather unspecific, non-career-oriented fields like humanities. But you know, as it's turned out, and as the years have gone by, I really feel like my own personality was more attuned to the humanities as a major in college and maybe as a career. Of course, I might not know where my next meal was coming from if I had gone into humanities. And I'm sure one of the main reasons I stayed in engineering is that my parents were always struggling financially. One of the main goals I set out for myself in life as a child was not to have to struggle like they did. It was just such a hassle for them, and I just didn't want to have to worry about that too. And I can say that I haven't had to. I mean, I haven't accumulated any great wealth—hardly—but money has been one thing I haven't had to worry constantly about, and I'm very grateful for that.

I've told Elaine that I'm willing to share the child rearing as much as I'm able, even to the point of completely quitting my own job and doing the child care full time, if she were to want to or to have to go back to work for reasons of her own. But the thing is that it never has really seemed possible for her to get into that position of taking a full-time job. One of the drawbacks to it is also that if she were to be working full time rather than I, we would be living on much less money. For some reason, social work does not command as high a salary as the engineering profession does—not that it shouldn't, but it's traditionally been a woman's field, and women's work is paid less because they're not usually the sole support of the family.

I do have some misgivings about doing child care full time. I wasn't thinking of a really long period of time, like ten years or something, but more like one or two years, until we got to the point where Adam would be in school and we could both be working. But even for that one- or two-year interim, I still have misgivings—not so much economic ones (although we would be living on much less), but mainly from the standpoint of not having really many people around like me, men who are doing the same sort of thing. I know very few fathers who have been able to break away from work entirely and really step into child care full time. I know several who have done it, but they're quite unusual and very exceptional. I just think there's much less of a support group around for men who do that.

I think at my office they would look upon my doing such a thing as kind of strange. Nobody else I know at work, or whom I've ever worked with, has ever done it. Engineering is really a very conservative profession and attracts conservative people into it. Even so, I wouldn't worry about getting my job back again if I left for a couple of years to do child care. I feel secure there, and I know they appreciate my work. I say this even though it's generally true that when you're applying for a job in engineering, if you have a gap in your work history, it's regarded as a black mark. They're always more interested in that blank space than in the time you were working.

A friend of mine from the Peace Corps did quit his job to do child care so that his wife could finish her doctorate. He was working for one of the big corporations, and he asked them for a one-year leave of absence. Those are routinely granted for things like military leave, educational leave, and so forth, but when he told them that he wanted a leave to devote a year to raising his kid, they just couldn't believe it. They started laughing at him, wondered how he could possibly be in his right mind and want to do such a thing. So he had to quit instead of taking a leave of absence, got no benefits or unemployment—nothing—and they had to live out of the bank for a whole year. He got another job after that year, but not with his old company. He didn't want to work there any more after the attitude they'd taken.

Values

The biggest problem in our marriage, all the way through until recently, was disagreement about where we would live. Elaine was from the East, and I'd spent most of my life in California. When we got married, she moved out there, but there was no particular reason for our choosing to live out there for good just because I happened to be there to start with. So we had agreed that we would stay a couple of years there, and then, if we still weren't sure, or if we knew we didn't like it there, we would try the East for a couple of years and then decide which was better—or less bad. Elaine consented to live in California at all only with grave reservations, but she felt OK about it with the reassurance that, after a couple of years, we would come back East. As it worked out, I remained more committed to carrying out that agreement than she was. Two years or so after we were married, I came East and found a job and we moved, planning to make a final decision about where to live after about two years more.

After those two years had passed, when Adam was about 16 months old, we thought very seriously about going back to California. I had gone out there and gotten a job offer, so we really had to decide. Our original positions had gotten reversed—Elaine was the one who wanted to move back to California, while I was not at all enthusiastic about it. She felt it was just too difficult to raise a small child in the East because of the climate—the illness that it produced, and the isolation and confinement for six months of every year. All of that made her think that she absolutely had to get away from the East, that she just couldn't stand her life that way. But when it came down to it, we both decided we wanted to stay in the East. And that decision had mainly to do with other aspects of having a child.

The feeling that finally prevailed on us was a fear of the life-style in California and what effect that would have on Adam in growing up. California seems to us a place where people don't really develop deep attachments to one another, where there's more emphasis on personal development and seeking one's own fulfillment and pleasure, and less of a sense of responsibility to families and children and society in general. There's a more hedonistic tone to life there, a feeling of immediate satisfaction of wants. So the values that are held more strongly in the East are ones that we would like Adam to be exposed to more than the values that are most accepted in the West.

It's partly that people out there are less likely to take the time to pay attention to their kids. There are so many things to do.

People are living outdoors a great deal of the time, and they're constantly on the move. Even though children are included in the outdoor stuff, there's just so much actual motion in getting to the sites of pleasure or recreation—people do spend a good deal of their time on the road in California. I don't like that feeling of never being satisfied where you are, that feeling of "something else somewhere where we're not at now has to be better, so we have to get there."

Also, we worried about Adam's associating with kids who've been through a lot of family turmoil or whose parents don't pay the right kind of attention to them. I really feel there are a lot of people in California who have very little confidence in their parenting abilities, and it's manifest in a lot of the really almost religious espousal of new techniques and methods. People just embrace each new technique that comes out, and when that one doesn't work, they throw it out and move on to the next one. I've seen my cousin go through this, and she has produced just really messed-up children. She's just constantly putting them in one school and taking them out and putting them in another school, with these different theories attached to each one. She doesn't really have a theory of her own, so she's constantly looking for other people's. She has no confidence in her own ability to decide what's right for her children. Part of it is not having your own family and elders around. There's no support for your views, if you happen to have any to begin with. Whereas in the East, people do have their families around. People do have very definite views on child rearing, and they don't rely that much on the latest fad. This isn't to say that the old way is totally the best, but I think some of the old-fashioned parents did a better job than the ones who are depending on books and fads. So it just gives me a greater feeling of security to raise a child in the East than out there.

Of course, there are problems everywhere. We've lived in a lower middle-class town ever since we came East, and we've liked it pretty well. We haven't had that much in common with the neighbors, but they're certainly very pleasant people. They're mostly first-generation European immigrants who own their homes and are really settled there. Then there are young transients like us. But in some ways it's a limiting environment. For instance, Adam spends two mornings a week with a baby-sitter, a local woman who takes care of five or six other kids too, of various ages from four months to five years. Adam likes it pretty well—he likes watching the other kids or grabbing things away from them. And the woman is very competent and calm— she just never gets ruffled about anything, even though she's got three of four toddlers running around, some of them for ten hours a day. I'm amazed that anyone can stay calm in the midst of all that. But she leaves her TV on all the time. Adam doesn't sit glued in front of it because he's not focused enough yet to sit down and look at a TV program; but the older kids there do watch it constantly, and I think Adam would fall into that pattern too when he got older. So I wouldn't want Adam to continue going to this baby-sitter much after he's three years old or so. She and I just have different views about what should be provided for the intellectual development of children.

Actually, we've bought a house farther out in the suburbs, and we'll be moving there in a few months. We did that for reasons similar to those that would eventually make Adam's baby-sitter a problem—the poor quality of the schools in the town where we are now. It's a long-term consideration. The local high school lost its accreditation this year, and if that sort of thing continues, people are going to move into the town who don't have much concern for education. That really wouldn't be the best thing for Adam. Obviously we think education is important.

But the suburbs are no picnic either. They're the locale for the sort of stuff I see among the men in my office all the time. They work day and night, and they say to me, "What's wrong with you? You're not staying late." They pretend that staying late is a badge of your dedication to the profession, but it's really a dedication to more profits for the company and more income for themselves. I don't know if it's that they dislike going home, but I think many of these men do show a lack of consideration for the work that their wives are doing at home raising their families. Of course, in many cases the wives don't expect anything more. Both man and wife may be really hung up about money. I mean, the man works himself to the bone to make absolutely every penny he can, and he does quite well, because three or four hours of overtime a night can really add up. And the wife doesn't mind for her husband to be away all the time. She doesn't care for him that much anyway, and she likes him to be off producing the bucks. But I don't see the Eastern suburban atmosphere as being as threatening as what goes on in California. I can avoid a materialistic compulsion about work much easier than I can avoid a compulsion about leisure.

I was in the Peace Corps during the late sixties, and I really went into it for political reasons. I had been an undergraduate at Berkeley during the beginnings of the Free Speech Movement, and I guess that kind of opened my eyes to what was going on. By the time I finished school, I was pretty turned off to what I saw as available to me in working society, and pretty turned off to this country generally. I wanted to get away, and the Peace Corps was a very good way of doing it because I could not only get out, but I could also do something beneficial.

When I came back I was even more discouraged and disappointed in this country. I wanted to turn around and leave immediately. But after a while, I started getting a little more realistic about it. I realized that there was really no life for me or any other American in a country like the one I'd been in. I realized that this really is home and that it deserves another try, trying to make it work. I also came to feel that I owed a certain amount of loyalty to this country, that it was my responsibility to do something about the things I didn't like.

I certainly think my sense of responsibility to change things I don't like has gotten stronger since Adam was born. Changing attitudes about something like child rearing is the most important thing an individual like myself can do. And what I mean by that is working to get across the idea that raising children should be a dual effort on the part of the parents, and that society has a responsibility to make it possible for that to occur. Who goes into what careers and how much money goes along with which careers should not be so rigorously delineated by sex. Nor should the working day and the working life be set up so that one parent has to go away for up to ten hours a day, making it impossible for both parents to share both work and child care.

These are very serious flaws in our system, but I can't wait to have my kids until the whole system changes. That might take a hundred years. My role is to try to change attitudes as a step in bringing these broad changes about.

I can't say that I've had that much of an impact, though. Other men at the office don't envy me for taking up more work with my child. To the extent that there's been any reaction at all to my being committed to child rearing in a different way than they are, it's been mostly surprise and curiosity. But there's certainly been no great desire to follow suit. There are a few who do take an interest in their children, mostly younger men with kids around the same age as Adam. It surprised me to find anyone at all. But even those guys aren't at all sympathetic to the idea of working half time and letting their wives work half time. There's still no question in their minds as to who's going to work full time. Engineering's probably the last profession that will change.

Allen

Allen, 38, has been an empathetic activist, social worker, and teacher of English and basic skills to both prison inmates and college students. He lives with his wife, Sarah, their 12-year-old son Jason, and their 10-year-old twins, Mike and Leah.

Allen and His Fathers

My relation with my father was complicated because when I was three years old, he came down with TB, and he was in a sanitarium for somewhere between six and seven years. So I really didn't have a relationship with him from the time I was three until I was about nine or nine and a half.

There was some continuity. I got to visit him irregularly at the state sanitarium in Ohio; I knew that I had a father, that my father was in a sanitarium, and that he was responsive to me. He made things for me—they didn't know what to do with themselves, basically, so they got into leatherworking and woodworking, and there was a fairly steady stream of wallets and belts. The thing I remember treasuring was a faun that he had fashioned out of wood.

189

The funny thing about TB is that, on the face of it, you look fine. During that time, all I knew was that he was sick, that he couldn't do much, that he had to take it real easy. Visiting him was like visiting someone in jail—the patients were guarded just like prisoners. (In those times, TB was dreaded and those who had it couldn't wander around if the state could help it.) We actually drove past a jail on the way to the sanitarium, and I remember waving to the prisoners in the jail and they waving back. That became for me the sense of it: my father is being *held* in this place. People in my family felt about it that way too: he was being held in confinement.

My mother tried to keep this little family intact—I am an only child—and did so for about three years, till the time I was about six and a half. But then, when I was six and a half, for reasons that I still don't really know, I got sent to this orphanage for Jewish kids who were either orphaned or out of wedlock or broken homes—I was a broken home–type kid—and we all got tossed in together in this place. (Eventually, the family got back together again—I got out of there when I was eight and a half— and my father was going to get out of the sanitarium.)

During that time, I got to know a *bad* father. My cottage father at the institution was someone who was a "bad" father because he was clearly dominated by the woman. They were a German immigrant couple, German Jewish, and they must have gotten out before the war. But the woman ran the show, and the man, to my mind, was a bad father because he was so weak— and the woman was so *abusive*. I mean, she beat us up—she would hit us. There was a lot of physical abuse, and there was no *protection*—he was entirely passive. He didn't do any hitting, but she did, and there was no appeal to him.

Well, I'd worked it out (kids are very clever about that): "You've got to figure out ways around her: she's not going to get *you.*" I remember that for me it was, if she ever got me—I certainly wasn't singled out for beatings, but I got my share—if she got me, I was very rigid about not crying. I wouldn't break down in front of her. That was my way of handling the situation. So the sense in which her husband was an inadequate father was that he just wasn't available; there was injustice that he was not responsive to. I think that that stayed with me.

Now my father, from stories about when he was young, was quite a fighter, an aggressive guy, a street battler. And I can remember when he came out of the sanitarium, I was physically afraid of him. He had a real flash point, a real temper. I would do things that would bother him, and he would say, "You're the dumbest white man I ever saw." We really didn't have an easy relationship. It wasn't easy for him to resume being a father. I was very strange to him; I wasn't a kid in his own image. I was much *softer* as a child than he had been. See, he was *hard;* he was first generation—not an immigrant, but his parents were.

So in that period there was a lot of stress and there was quite a reverse; that is, my mother was the person who was giving me the protection from a lot of stress between me and my father, as I experienced it. And I can remember being physically afraid of my father. He never hit me, but there was a lot of anger in him, and it was at the threshold of becoming physical. That was something that went on for three or four years—from the time I was 9 to about the time I was 13.

But at the same time he was really trying to be a father. He would do things for me; there were things he wanted *me* to be: a good athlete, a real street kid. I think partly because it was so important to *him,* I became a good football player, though never a good *athlete*—I was always clumsy, ill-coordinated. But for him, his way of fathering was to get involved in sports, to be very supportive. One of the things which he did when he first got out of the sanitarium was to organize a little sandlot baseball team, and really he did it to be sure that I would be part of the team. And also, he didn't have anything else to do, since he couldn't work for about a year after he got out of the san. He just sort of had to hang around.

And it was always, "Fight your own fights when you're out on the street; know how to take care of yourself; don't let anybody give you any shit; if anybody gives you any shit, you go back out there." I remember coming home crying—over and over again—and my father saying, "Don't let anybody give you any shit; get back out there on the street, kid." And he would never intervene—he had a real code about that.

But kids have always loved my father. He's really been a magnet. Our house really was a neighborhood center; kids were drawn to our house from all over the place—it was a very comfortable place to be. This was true from the time that I was about nine right through high school. Our house became a kind of hangout place, and my parents were real models for most of my peers, things that they didn't have in their relationship with *their* parents. That, oddly, didn't take into account what my real relationship with my father was. There's a real paradox there. My father was looking for a different son—I think that's part of it.

An uncle of mine, my mother's brother, came closest to being a father for me. He was very remote and romanticized because he was in the war—Coast Guard cutter chasing submarines. I would see him occasionally in uniform, and he had war stories, so I was drawn to him as a little kid. There was always sort of a recognition—it's very instinctive, knowing that you're accepted by an adult or knowing that you're being rejected—and with him I was really accepted. There was a long relationship, really. I started a correspondence with him when I was about ten years old, and that went right through college. And I visited him quite regularly. I think there was some combination of his being a *heroic* figure to me, and also his being the guy in the family of whom everyone said, "He's the smart one—he's the only one who has a college education, the guy who's really striving." Those were the lines of identification.

He was always a guy filled with jokes and humor, and everyone loved him because he was really *alive*, entertaining, quick with people, but not *mean*, at least as I saw him. His humor was right on the edge, but mainly he would do crazy things. Whenever he would visit, he'd do all kinds of things in public that were outrageous. Like, if you were riding through the street in two cars, he would pull up behind you and hit your bumper, and he'd jump out of the car, and he'd start screaming—and everyone would stop. He'd pull all these shticks, and I always thought that was pretty terrific. He was the wild man. And I related to him.

Eking It Out

I'd started graduate school and had quit during the first year, feeling that was quite wrong for me. I couldn't resolve the fundamental conflict I felt between what I wanted to become— a writer—and what I was in graduate school—a student of literature. So I quit.

Then I went through a period when I was in the Army, and then I came out of the Army and was hacking it alone. About eight or ten months after I got out of the Army, I met Sarah and we were married, but then it was still really a period of hacking it. I worked for the Welfare Department for a little while and then quit that to really write full time.

But at that point Sarah became pregnant. She and I had been quite clear that we would have children. But we hadn't really come to a point where we said, "Well, we now want to have a child," and in that sense our first child wasn't willed. With Sarah still in school and me writing, it wasn't a time where we would have chosen to have a child. When we knew that Sarah was pregnant, then I also knew that I had to go to work. If the child had come to us that day, we couldn't have sustained it, so we had to make changes.

For me it was a period of stress, not great stress, but one where I felt responsible, and I had to make certain moves. Sarah was terrifically happy, and I was pleased, but I think it was more stressful for me than for her. It wasn't a feeling of panic: "What am I going to do? I've got to take care of this young child." I was quite acceptant of those changes, but I also knew that I was giving up something—my writing—that was important to me. I never thought that I was giving it up completely, and I still don't have that feeling about writing fiction. But I did have to recognize that there was a trade-off that had to be made at this point in our lives, and that was one of the things that had to give. I couldn't see simply continuing as a writer when there was no income in sight.

I thought I would pick up what in my mind was a minimal sort of job. For a time I worked at this bookstore, but that turned out to be miserable. So I went back to the Welfare Department as a caseworker, welfare worker, and that also became really dreadful because you couldn't be effective in that job, and you saw what was happening to the people that you wanted to help or tried to help. So I knew that I was able to exclude a couple of things, and it was at that point that I really thought seriously about going back to graduate school, and thought about teaching.

The decision to go back to graduate school was a tough one, because we knew that it meant also a fairly long period where we were already a family and still eking it out. I got accepted at all the places I applied to, but I couldn't get any support because I had given up a fellowship when I quit graduate school before. That was a blight—that was really a black mark. What I did was go back to the school where I'd finished up as an undergraduate. I did know people there, and I thought there would be more of a chance for me to figure out some way of surviving. That turned out to be right, because they hired me as a reader for a course, and that really was my main source of income that year.

After one year I finished an M.A., and I could have stayed on there—I also had a fellowship at that point—but I decided to change schools. I'm the kind of person, if things seem too easy for me, I kind of get resistant. Things seemed very easy for me there—I was doing well, I had a kind of mentor and sponsor, and it all looked very nice. But I decided I didn't want that. I wanted to make things harder for myself, so I went to a different place. I did have a fellowship there, though—one of those NDEA fellowships. That helped a great deal, because it gave me about $3,500 by the time you added in your dependents, and it also paid tuition. So that eased my situation a whole lot.

But it was still definitely a case of eking it out, financially. I had to take out three loans in the course of getting my Ph.D. That's pretty grim, in fact, because I'm still very much in the process of paying for going back to school. Each year I chip away at it. It really has been costly, because here I am, I'm 38 years old, and I'm still paying off for going back to school.

Sarah wasn't working all this time either. She was full time with the kids. Our first child, Jason, was about six months old when we moved after my first year of graduate school. We went to my old school with one child, and we left there with one child—and none in sight. The second case was very funny, really. I think Sarah became pregnant just at the end of December, right around there, and at that point we were trying, I think quite consciously, not to have any children. But we talked about, "Wouldn't it be nice to have another child? Wouldn't it be nice to have another child with Jason?" And we both agreed as to how that would be really a nice thing. And the next thing I know . . . I have no idea how that happened. But really pregnant this time. Sarah was very serious—she had two.

I got a teaching job in '68, when the twins were one year old or one and a half. That was my first real job. It was a meager thing, but it was a real job, and I had an income starting in '68. But up until that time I'd never had a job with an income, and the combination of struggling economically and trying to make a start in a career in which I had a lot of anxiety and insecurity about myself as a teacher of literature—that was a very draining combination for me and really wiped me out as a writer, I think. The problem was that I stopped imagining. I had had not just a rich fantasy life—I think most writers do have that—but I also had a sort of narrative . . . a lot of my mental life involved the conceiving of scenes and stories, and during this whole period I lost that capacity. I couldn't sustain any kind of writing except the academic stuff, which I didn't really see as primary. I could do it, but it was not what I wanted to do. Recently I've felt sort of on an upswing. Having changed jobs, having reached a certain kind of stability, I think, in what's going on in my family life, married life, I'm really much more optimistic about myself as a writer now than I was three or four years ago.

Allen and Sarah

From the start, there was never a sharp division between Sarah and me in terms of caring for the children. I did all the things she did, except, of course, for breast-feeding. In terms of actually caring for the kids, right from infancy, I did all the same kind of caring that she did. That was very shared.

It fell out, I think, in a fairly typical way: that is, most of the care during the daytime was Sarah's and I would pick up when I came home and in the evening. And that's a pattern which we've really kept pretty much right through; and more and

more so for Sarah, the time to be free has been in the evenings—
either before dinner or after dinner, she's been able to do the
things she wanted to do. She's been very systematic about
freeing herself so that she can do the work that's important to
her, primarily her art. And that's worked out very well, I think.

When the twins were born, that was just a very hard period.
Child rearing became more nearly *work*, especially in the early
months. It was just overwhelming. We shared a whole lot of
what was involved in the first six months, and that was very
hard. I mean, I got almost nothing done in school. I really
became absorbed in that early nurture business.

The twins' arrival also made things hard for Jason. I mean,
it's classically difficult for an older child to have twins come in.
(Sarah's a twin herself, though in her case the twins were the
first children.) The literature, the psychological literature, is
filled with cases of how difficult it is for a child who has to take
in twins. And it was hard for Jason. He was very much threatened by them, resented them, and was hard on them, and
therefore we were hard on *him*, and he was hard on *us*. That
part of it was really demanding. We knew that it was hard for
Jason, and either Sarah or I would try to do things with him to
give him some relief. There was a period when I think I tended
to do that more than Sarah, and one of the issues we had to work
through was, "Why should Jason get special treatment?" I mean,
for six months or so that was clear; but after a point it seemed
that Jason was getting some privileged-character treatment, and
it was really Sarah's sense of the need to be just and the need to
share with the older kids that led her to insist, "You'd better
stop that. If you do it for him, you've got to do it for this one and
for this one." And that became difficult.

On the things that Sarah and I mutually recognize as being
the important issues, there's a very strong and consistent line of
agreement. On things *domestic* we have some fairly sharp
disagreements, and they almost always concern some variation
of the extent to which the children should be able to take care of
themselves and to do things for themselves, which is Sarah's
position. *My* position is that they need parenting in *x* situation—
they need help in learning how to make their beds; they don't
just get up and make their beds without learning how to do that,

without being helped to do that. And then the further question: Who's going to help them? There we have, I think, a fair amount of disagreement and conflict. I guess that there are two basic ways of looking at it, namely, either it's a relatively unimportant thing and just a place where some conflict gets expressed, or it's really symptomatic of some very deep difference between Sarah and me. I tend to think that it's relatively minor and under control, but it's been very persistent. Since the kids have been infants, practically, my sense has been that Sarah has been expecting more of them than they are capable of. And I have the further expectation that she ought to be "mothering" them, rather than that I ought to be "fathering" them, in many of those situations. It gets played out in her refusal to "mother" them and my experience of not "fathering" them but "mothering" them.

There you get certain role expectations—I'm getting you dressed in the morning, washing your face or washing your hands—I mean, those would be "mothering." Now, I *do* those things, but in my mind the real "mothering" things are a set of nurturing and sustenance and supportive things. I think basically I don't have sharp categorical distinctions of that kind, but if pressed, I have the idea that basically what goes on *inside* the house is the mother's domain and what goes on outside the house is . . . now I really don't *believe* that; it's the traditional mothering-fathering distinction, and it forces me . . . that kind of thing is the area of difference that Sarah and I have about what her role is.

What would she say *my* role is? In many cases it would be expressed in terms of "Why don't you support me more when I'm disciplining the kids and making them do these things for themselves? Why are you always undercutting me and saying that I, Sarah, should do these things for the children, rather than supporting me? And why aren't you coming in there as a good secondary discipline kind of force that reinforces the point I'm making?" We've had a long history of conflict, where I'm looking for her to be more supportive with the kids, and she's looking for basically more autonomy in the kids and implicitly, I think, more freedom for herself. That's been a very consistent sort of unresolved area.

I feel as though *I* was mothered, and I want my children to be mothered. I resent it when I feel they're being denied that, and I further resent it when I have to do those things myself, when I have to move in. That's the way I react to it. I don't resent it because I'm a man—I think that's important to say—I don't feel emasculated or degraded in doing that at all. There's none of that stuff. It's more that I'm able to find what to me is the problem area in my marriage in terms of "It's a mothering problem." OK, well, that's sexist. When the conflict comes up, she experiences it that way because to her it's all about herself being able to grow as a person, and she can't as long as she's forced to do these menial things, and the children can't become autonomous, and I keep maintaining their dependency. I'm really an obstacle to her growth, forcing her to do those things. But I think, partly because the kids are growing and partly because *we're* growing, that this is becoming less of a problem.

At some place that I haven't thought of yet or I can't account for, these things get resolved, and in terms of how we look at the world, I think the kids are getting very consistent messages from Sarah and me. But I don't know, maybe at some more fundamental level, or maybe just a different level, they'll get a different set of messages with a good deal more conflict. We both agree that the kids should be unharnassed to the maximum extent—we agree on that as a goal. But we have very different ways of going about that. I have a *process* view of how that sort of thing comes about, and I think she has an *absolute* view: she wills it, and she expects it to be there. That's *my* view of what's going on. Now, she would say something quite different. But we're consistent in our view of what are the reasonable risks and where we've tried to be protective of the kids as they've gone out into the world. I can't think of a single instance where we've had a serious conflict on that.

I'm always the deviant—I mean, in a very controlled way—I'm always leading the kids astray to do this or that, and Sarah's always bringing them back. We play that game a lot. Now, it's entirely understood that it's a game; the kids understand it as a game, and we all enjoy it. I clown a whole lot with the kids, and I am familiar with them in a way that Sarah is not—not that she's distant or remote. The games I play are all spontaneous games—I hate to play board games or card games or that kind of stuff. To me, that's one of the nicest parts of being a father, the play. We get beat up, we play kind of wild, and Sarah's always, I feel, a little disapproving—less so as they get older, of course; that stuff sort of passes.

Basically I regard myself as a fairly high risk-taker. I don't protect myself. Sarah's more cautious. When we're out doing things, I'm the one. who's taking risks and encouraging the kids to take risks. But I think what's important is that there's a difference and yet it's not a problem because Sarah trusts me and knows that I'm not reckless.

There's probably a class thing there—she was raised upper middle class; she was very sheltered as a child and also had no sense of physical wants. At the same time, she had a terrible sense of emotional want. She felt comfortable, had a protected childhood, yet it was filled with all kinds of emotional anxieties and a whole set of unfulfilled needs, partly as a result of her being a twin, partly as a result of what she's described as a very inadequate relation with her father.

And I pose myself there as quite the opposite. I mean, in spite of all the things about my own childhood, I feel that my emotional needs were somehow well met and my physical needs weren't. I think part of it was that I was a poor kid who, in spite of having sort of a tough childhood and being working class, still was soft in some way—I think that that was part of what Sarah *liked* about me. I don't have a very good relationship with her parents, with my in-laws. I have a lot of hostility about her own earlier experience, so instead of being supportive of some of those things, I tend to bring out her anxieties about her own earlier experience, rather than help her to overcome them.

I think we share and we sort of meet on that point of wanting to do things differently, though I think Sarah—partly because she came up in an analytic family (her mother's a psychoanalyst), and partly because she herself went through some analysis—seeing the kids, she's more tuned in to emotional problems that they're experiencing than I am. I tend to minimize the problems in their emotional life and treat them casually. And at this point, I think, again, that Sarah is with me on that and she will trust me to recognize the difference between what is a serious problem and what really is something that in the course of things will work itself out—quite contrary to her mother, who's indicating that all our children should be in analysis. Each time her mother comes she looks upon us aghast and sees all kinds of terrible problems in all of our children.

I think that's a good indicator that we're doing differently from our parents. On the one hand, I think that I'm a good deal more consciously tuned in to my kids' emotional life than my parents were tuned in to mine. I think in a deep way my mother was very much tuned in to my life, my father not so. But not in a conscious way. I am more conscious. Now, Sarah, on the other hand, is willing to be a little less conscious about that than her own parents were. And in that sense, I think we've both departed from the patterns which we ourselves experienced.

Fostering Autonomy

I always felt like there were very strong communications from the kids right from earliest infancy. It wasn't just me communicating, but I was getting it back. It's just a long continuum of communication, and I can't say when I felt like saying to any of the kids, "Come, let us reason together." My most vivid memory is that if we became upset, the kids became upset. And if they became upset and we became upset, it was bad news. The one thing that was always clear was that *contrast* was the effective thing—defining yourself as other than what the child is. It works. If you define yourself as the same as the child, you're of no help to the child. I feel that that's true in adult relationships also. It's not to deny the meaning of empathic life. I mean, that's very much a part of being able to define yourself as *other*.

It was really only having children that allowed me to experience the boundaries between people in a way that I could understand. I went on some bad trips with Jason when he was an infant. Jason was my first child, and I didn't know what to do with his infant anger—or what I took to be his infant anger—and I reacted with the same. What I took to be his rage evoked rage in me—that is, the same feeling—and that's a bad trip.

I'm talking about really early infancy, that is, up to six or eight months—certainly within the first year of life, but more like the first six months, when you can't know what the hell is going on inside—or at least so I felt. I'd say to myself, "Well, he's angry," and if I found myself becoming angry, all that did was intensify what he was experiencing. I knew that that was happening, and that's where it began to be clear to me that to be helpful to him, I had to differentiate myself from my own feelings of anger. Whether I really understood what he was feeling didn't matter, but I had to be able to differentiate. Now, it clearly works both ways. That is, the infant can pick up what you're feeling and give it back to you, or you can pick up what the infant is feeling. As long as there isn't a differentiation, if these are troublesome feelings—if they're getting people upset— then you've got a problem. If they're good feelings, clearly it's no problem. But it's necessary to differentiate selves at the point where you want to be helpful to your child. When I'm able to differentiate and be *another*, then it's dramatic. It really is helpful, does the job, and it's very satisfying.

What's involved is sort of building up an ability to recognize what this particular dynamic is all about—knowing, "Here it is; I know how to deal with this now; I know my role." And that's one of the really nice experiences of being a father, I should say—knowing in a very clear way that you have helped your child who has experienced a difficulty, knowing that you've been able to be supportive. What pleases me most is being able to get a kid unstuck. A kid is stuck somewhere, and because I'm his father or her father, I can work with the child. No one else can work with the child on the same basis. It's an organic thing— that is, a relationship that's very deep and that has a history.

I've had a harder time helping Mike get unstuck than I've had with our other two kids. Mike is one of our twins—the other's a girl, Leah. He's like our middle child—he's the one who's slowest in development, and he gets the short end of most everything. It seems to happen all the time: Jason gets to go somewhere on his own or with me, and Mike's left out. Leah has different ways of dealing with that. She'll react like, "I'll go next door and play with Joanie," and Mike will react like, "I'm being left out." And he has no way of coping with Jason—he gets wiped out and destroyed very easily. But it's not just Jason. I mean, it could be me, or it could be other kids in school. He doesn't have a good defense system. And *I* was like that as a child, so that I know exactly what he's experiencing as a kid because *I* experienced it—though that doesn't make me any more supportive of him. In fact, I find myself behaving, when I catch myself, like my own father behaved toward me. If the issue is, he's having a hard time finding his shoes, or he's having a hard time getting his belt through the loops, it's, you know, "What's the *matter* with you? Why can't you do that? *I* can do that. I can even do it for you, but why can't you do it yourself?" And that's a very bad interaction, because I know that it's destructive. When I catch myself, I try to stop myself, but I can see that it's all a sense of "I've lived through this before, and I ought to know better," and there are certain points where I really have to make the effort not to reproduce what I felt was a bad father-son pattern.

Still, the thing that gives me most satisfaction is being able to help the kids when they experience difficulty. That plus gaming, again, the way in which children experience the world—being able to share in that and have that kind of openness about myself as a person. I guess those are the most satisfying things. Instead of experiencing parenthood as, oh, a tremendous set of responsibilities and burdens that I as a parent always have to be worried about, must control this and that. I don't tend to experience my children and my family life that way. It's rather that this is a way of remaining open, not closing down my own life.

I try to encourage openness in the kids, but let me just say the other side of that. Rarely, like once or twice, they have interacted with kids that I didn't like. It really bothered me that there was a kid that I didn't like, but I did have that reaction: "Oh, you're making friends with this kid, and this kid is going to screw you up." I really can think of only one case where it happened. It was a kid that Mike had met, and it was a real gut thing with me. I was really upset with myself, because I pride myself on that not happening. I said to Mike, "There's something wrong here," and he was hurt, and he didn't want to hear what I was saying. I didn't feel as though I did anything decisive, except express the way I felt. I never said to him, "Don't see him any more," or "He can't come here any more," but relations did end up being broken off. I can't quite account for it, except that I expressed what I felt. The kid was a sneak, a real underminer. I felt that he was really a troubled kid, and I know that that was much more significant than the level at which I was reacting. But I felt like his troubles would become my kids' troubles. You know, I felt very badly about that whole thing. It was the only time that I can remember something like that happening.

Leah is more like Sarah as a personality, and Mike is much more like me. And the only way we can account for this is innately, not any molding that any of us have done. But Jason is anomalous. He's not like Sarah or me, as far as I can see. The innate thing doesn't work with him—we don't know *who* he is. We can't identify him as a personality type. The only thing we're sure about with him is that he's very smart. He's smarter than Sarah, and he's smarter than I am. As he gets older, I feel that there's more distance growing up between us, but I don't have anxiety or a sense of needing to control the direction of his growth or his behavior. There are a whole lot of things that I react *against*—don't do this, don't do that. It expresses itself mainly as a set of negatives, and it's almost all at the level of his interaction with the twins that that gets expressed.

I guess I always felt that I was a traveler. As a child, my way of growing was really to be on the move. I wandered a lot as a kid—I really ranged. I don't mean to say a lot of aimless wandering—I was usually going somewhere or other, but I was really on the move as a kid. To me, one of the awful parts of suburban life is that the children can act very homebound. They have a kind of attachment to the home and a kind of passivity about their being able to meet their own needs, and they're very dependent on parents to take them here, there, and do this, that with them. So it's a great pleasure to see Jason starting to relate much more with other kids, going out—and his interests there will be very different from mine. I mean, he'll want to go to the science museum. As a kid, that isn't something that I would have done. He'll get interested in something like rocketry, model rockets, and very quickly he's out of my ability to help him. He certainly knows much more about rockets than I do, so I can't be a guide figure or lead him anywhere—I can support him and say, "That's great; go and do it." He knows that I can't help him in that direction, but I try to be, just in a very low-key way, supportive of his doing these things.

Taking Risks

I think that both Sarah and I felt quite strongly that we would do the political things that we thought were important and right, even though they involved personal risks, put us in jeopardy. I have been in jail a couple of times, and that became a very real thing to our kids. We told them about it, what it was about, and that was a problem. I shouldn't say it was a problem—it was basically very good, but it was something that we had to *deal* with. We couldn't just say, "Well, these are our politics, and we'll protect the kids from their consequences; they won't know about them." When Sarah took Jason with her to Washington for an antiwar demonstration, it was a mixture for him—I think it would be for most kids—of "what an exciting adventure, what a great outing" and, beyond that, some sense of what the purpose of the demonstration was.

I anticipate Jason's developing moral and political inclinations that are opposed to mine. It's sort of a problem for kids. It's easier to have conservative parents—that's easier to deal with than to have parents who think of themselves as more radical. But I expect something like that to show up at some point. It would be a matter of concern, but I kind of look forward to the point where there are those kinds of disagreements arising and we can talk about them. That's my projection of the thing—that there'd be those differences and that we'd be able to talk about them.

I look at my own children as evidence, almost, that reinforces things that I care about in the larger world. The moral dimension, the dimension of conscience, is the most important; and within that, or in relation to that, are the political and social drives that I have, which I would say have been strengthened rather than weakened by having children. I see myself in contrast to what is often put as the typical adult—that is, "You'll be very bold and you'll do all these things and you'll be an idealist until you have children, and then, when you have children, you'll become more careful, you'll worry about their security." Now, my own development doesn't confirm that pattern. I've taken considerable risks, I think, in terms of my work and beyond my work—by work I mean my job, not my writing— and in doing so, I've tried to carry forward the things which I feel are really important. If I step back and say, "What kind of model do I want to be, what do I want my children to know about me?"—it's that I care, that there are things that I care about and that I include them in that care. I want them to understand that in caring about things larger than our own domestic life, I'm caring for them. And that they can extend their range of concerns to include these things also.

I remember last fall Jason said, "Well, they have all those problems in the city with school and all—the black people are really creating a lot of problems. But we're out here, and we just don't have to worry about it, do we?" That really shocked me. My instinct was to come down on him and sort of shake him and say, "What's the matter with you, you selfish . . ." But I'm ashamed of that reaction, and instead we had quite a discussion back and forth. I tried to find out more about why he felt so threatened by that situation, what it looked like to him—because clearly it looked very different to the two of us. I felt by the time we had finished talking that he had started to look at the thing somewhat differently and had sort of picked up something in himself, that he had come to understand the way I was looking at the situation and how I felt a different level of concern.

That's the way I expect to keep moving, and the things that I feel need to be done will continue, as far as I can see, to involve considerable risks—making myself vulnerable personally and making the family vulnerable, I suppose, too. But I just think that it's possible to keep those risks in a positive perspective and that the children can share in the whole process. My own world view *hasn't* changed basically as a result of being a parent; it's been deepened and extended.

There was a time when our children were very young—it was right in '67 or '68—when my own consciousness was changing, and I was moving from being a more inward-looking person to being a more outward-looking and more involved person—during this time I was moving much faster than Sarah, and there was a great distance between us in terms of political awareness and political involvement. But that's really changed in the last three or four years and is now certainly equalized. I was doing things that people would say were kind of strange, given that I was a family personality with responsibilities. I was taking risks that were "out of proportion" and "excessive." I still have those commitments, and I think that Sarah and I have learned to relate to one another within those commitments. I think there's been a real strengthening of our relationship.

There was a point when an extended time in prison—not just a one-night stand in jail—was a fairly distinct possibility. As I look back on it now, I don't sense a basic difference in myself. I don't recoil from having been able to accept that—insofar as I could anticipate it as a real possibility—and to accept the cost that we might all have had to bear, without being able to see through to the other side of it all. What you hope is that you're not, in fact, locking your children in with you. You just know that those are very serious risks, that you're making your family vulnerable to a whole set of possible things, and that you've chosen to do so. You have to think very carefully before you make that choice.

Sam

Sam, in his sixties and twice married, ran a grocery store with his older brother for 30 years. He is happy with his large family.

Marriages

The first time I got married was in 1933, right after I finished high school. My first wife was from a prominent local family—her father was an industrialist, owned about half of a printing firm here in town. We had our first child—our son, Dwight—14 months later, and when Dwight was still very little he got pneumonia. He was a real sick kid, and it cost a lot of money to make him well—they had to tap his lungs. When he got out of the hospital, the bill was $1,900. You can run that in a week now, but I'll tell you what that was then—back then I'd gotten a raise from the $25 a week I'd started out at in the grocery business, and I was making $40 a week. So when we got Dwight out of the hospital, we made arrangements with the hospital that I would pay them $5 a week. And I paid them $5 a week for six or seven years, and after that was all paid off was when we had

207

our next child—that's the reason for the big difference in their ages. Actually, we had twin daughters—Patricia and Paula. And would you believe it, the delivery charge was $35—that was for the home care before the birth and everything. Two years later, we had another daughter, Carol, and that brings us up to roughly '42. In '43 I went in the service.

I was in the Navy, stationed in this country. After a while, my friends began sending me letters filled with hints that things weren't good back home. One weekend we were taking a draft of men to Florida, and we stopped over at a place not far from where I lived. My company commander said, "You don't live far from here, do you?" And I said, "Ninety miles." He said, "You haven't got leave papers, but do you want to go home? We'll pick you up at the pier at 0800 Monday morning." I said, "You'd better believe it!" I had a feeling that things weren't so good at home, and my parents wanted me to come and see for myself, so I got off the train and hitched over to my town—I believe that's the only time in my life I ever did that. When I was let off at the edge of town, there was a police cruiser there. I knew the fellow that was in it, and he offered me a ride to my house. I got in the car, and he said, "Don't be surprised when you get home. They're having a big party over there, and there's been some complaints, so we had to stop over there tonight. They're drinking some." My wife wasn't an alcoholic, but she did drink too much. Anyway, the officer let me off, I walked into the house, and I walked into a situation that wasn't the greatest. There were some people there that I knew—from that moment, they became former friends—and I asked them where my wife was. She was upstairs, apparently in bed with somebody. My son, Dwight, was coming down the stairs as I started up. He gave a big leap, and I said, "Where's mother?" He said, "Well, she's ... " Just then a guy came out of the bedroom. I'm not a fighter, but I was wearing a big U.S. Navy ring, and I pummeled the hell out of him. The police realized that something like this was going to happen, so they were right there to take the guy to the hospital. He was going to prefer charges, but they said he hadn't better—it was a two-way street. I guess I had no reason to really pummel him, but I paid a hundred and some dollars to get his teeth fixed, and I took my son, my oldest child, out of the house that night, and that was that. I'd just had it. I'm not violent, but I don't share in that way. Nobody's going to be in bed with my wife. No way.

Maybe I made a mistake. I mean, I probably could've forgotten what happened. I'm sure it wasn't any fun for my wife while I was away in the Navy. She was a nice lady, a nice mother—I mean it. And she did a fantastic job with my children. I think she just needed to be taken care of by a man and had a rough time when I wasn't there. Before I went into the service, we had no problems—we had a lot of friends, but I don't think she ever looked at anybody else—not in that sense. We were very happy. She didn't like the fact that we didn't have much of a social life, because I had to work the kind of hours in my grocery store that I did—seven days a week and seven nights a week. But she came from a family that was well-to-do, and there wasn't that kind of money around in those days during the Depression unless you worked all the time like that. But she and I got along. Outside of my oldest boy, my children never saw hardly a harsh word.

Anyway, I took my oldest boy to my parents. They knew all about it already—it's a small town. When I got back to the base, I talked to the chaplain. He felt I had to go home, so he started right that day making papers out, and within 30 days I was out of the service. This was in 1946, so the war was over, but it would have been a year before I got out otherwise. My wife decided she wanted a divorce, but I said, "No way," and that was that, because she had no grounds. I got an apartment to live in with my son, and she and I both got lawyers, and we drew up a separation agreement—this was all without going to court. She would have the children for six months, and then I would have them. But she was still running around and drinking and whatnot, so I ended up having all the children all the time. My apartment wasn't big enough for my whole family, so I bought a piece of land up at this lake outside of town and built a cottage there. I had it built by a contractor, and it was a beautiful place. We lived there year-round. The other reason I built that cottage was just to get away. I was very upset with life at this time. I had hoped that everything would be the same as it was before I went into the service. I wasn't a flag-waver, but things were great before I went into the service. I mean, I was a happy man. I had my family, and I was reasonably prosperous. I'm not a gambler, so I had saved, bought $21,000 in war bonds. But instead, here were all these problems. So I built this cottage for an outlet for me and my children.

It was four or five years before my wife and I got divorced. We were unbelievably friendly during all this time, and she just ran around and did her thing. The reason we got divorced was that she had two illegitimate children that had to be put up for adoption. I began to feel I'd done the wrong thing—if she'd been divorced, she could have gotten remarried and kept those children. It was wrong of me, I agree. She should have had a divorce, because she's been an unbelievable lady and a fantastic mother. So then I did give her the divorce.

Meanwhile, I'd gotten acquainted with Bernice, and we got married along about 1950. Bernice had a son, George, by a previous marriage who was right in between Dwight and the twins in age. It was partly a situation where George needed a father and my children needed a mother that would do things that they wanted to do. Bernice would get up and water-ski with them and swim with them and whatnot. But don't get me wrong—my kids thought an awful lot of their mother, and they still do. George never knew his father, so he lived with us, and my kids did too. The thing was, my first wife wasn't remarried, and the kids were maybe up to an age when they wouldn't have minded if she was remarried. They didn't like seeing a guy for maybe four months and somebody different after that, you know what I mean? I gathered this; I never talked to her, but I gathered that this might be. But when they came to our house, it was always the same thing—it was always Bernice and me.

When Bernice and I were married, I sold my cottage up at the lake—sold it for $40,000; it's for sale now for $130,000—because we needed a really big house. There were going to be the five kids, plus any that we had together. And my parents were going to live with us too. They were both very old, and my father'd had a stroke, so I asked my aunt, who was living in California, to come and help take care of them and I'd give her a home for the rest of her life. And I did too. She still lives with us. She's 80 years old now; she walks with a walker, and she does all right. One of my older brothers was gonna be with us too. He'd been working in the store one of my other brothers and I owned, and he'd been living with my parents. He was alcoholic and needed to be taken care of. He also still lives with us. So we had Bernice and me, the five kids—and maybe some more later on—my father and mother, my aunt, and my brother. We bought this house in town with 15 or 16 rooms and moved in there.

Within a couple of years, Bernice and I had our son, Rick, my father died, and my mother died a year to the day after my father. Bernice had gone back to work when Rick was six months old—she had her own beauty shop—and our home was just too big for her to take care of and still run her business. So we sold it, bought this big piece of land, and built this house that we're in now. We built it 20 years ago—the whole kit and caboodle was roughly $30,000. We haven't had a mortgage on it for I don't know how long. We paid the mortgage off. Today the house is assessed for $90,000.

When Rick was born, Dwight was already in college, George was in high school, and the girls were all in grade school. The girls basically spoiled their baby brother rotten. We had a woman come in and take care of Rick—she worked for us 12 years. She was unbelievable. All the kids got along just great together. I never heard a hassle between them. They were from three different families, but if you could see them all together, in no way would you ever know that it wasn't all one family. We made a rule that they were all brothers and sisters—there weren't any half brothers and sisters, never. If George would come in, and Dwight or Rick were here, and he had a friend with him, he'd say, "This is my brother." And George'd always introduce me as his father. We've been very fortunate, unbelievably so. If I didn't tell you that these children didn't all have the same mother and father, you wouldn't believe it.

Working

People in my family have always been workers. My grandfather was a master plumber, and he had this big shop. My father was mostly a newspaperman—he worked for different papers in the area, and he was managing editor for the paper in town here for 26 years. He also worked for a couple of U.S. senators—wrote speeches for them and things like that—and he was a "revenooer" for the IRS during Prohibition.

I started working in the grocery business when I was 12 years old. Because of my father's political connections, I could have got into West Point, except that the year I graduated from high school was the one year during the Depression that West Point didn't take any applicants. So I didn't go. Besides, hey, I was already making big money then—$25 a week. I'd gone to work for the same man my older brother worked for. He owned a little chain of grocery stores, and my brother was managing some of them. By the time I got out of high school, I was running the store this guy owned right here in town and making that big money—so why wait a year to go to West Point? I was married by this time—we had a nice apartment, and I bought a car and paid for it without financing. In fact, from the time I first went to work, I bought all my clothes and things with my own money. About the only thing my parents didn't allow me to buy on my own was my shoes, because they didn't think I'd pick out good ones.

After a few years, my brother and I bought out the man we were working for and ran the store here in town on our own. It was a corner store, a neighborhood store. At first, we each took home $70 a week, and before long we were doing a tremendous business—we really did for a small store. The store was only 28 feet wide and 57 feet long, and we took in three quarters of a million a year. Bernice worked too—like I said. She made about $12,000 a year from her beauty shop. She'd still be in business today if she hadn't had a bad accident a few years ago—she still works now and then, does funeral jobs and things like that. I'm not a Woman's Libber, but I don't mind telling you that Bernice was a better business person than I was.

A couple of years ago, when Rick was in the middle of college, my brother had some personal problems and had to retire, so, much to my dismay, I had to buy him out. I didn't want to do

She says, "I want a house," and her husband says, "Well, that's great. We've got two children, so I'll just work longer hours." He started working so hard that they didn't have so much fun together any more. So when I went out there, I talked to Dick and said, "Is it imperative that you work this kind of hours? How about going halfway in between. Don't put that kind of hours in, but work enough so you still have a little bit of money to spend." It was the same situation as me and my first wife, except that I helped my daughter and her husband work it out.

Most of my advice was just common sense. One time George borrowed money from a loan company or something. I saw the notices and asked him about it, and he told me right away that he'd borrowed money from a loan company. I said, "Come with me. We'll go down and pay it off." We went to the bank, and I said to the loan manager, "This is my son George. He's working, and he's making such and such, and he's worked there so many years. I think he's a good credit risk, and I will sign for him. I don't want him borrowing from loan sharks." The manager said OK and wrote out a check, and George paid the loan company off. George wasn't upset with me at all—since that time he's bought three or four cars, and I don't think he's ever borrowed from loan companies to pay for them. Just common sense: "George, you're paying a lot of money that way. They'll get you over a barrel, and you'll be hooked."

Maybe I was wrong, but I did want my children to do what I thought they should do. I don't mean that if I was a doctor, they had to be doctors. But I do want them to work. I always had to work long and hard for whatever I got—nobody ever gave me anything—so I don't care how much money my kids make, but I do want them to work. I want them to be productive. On weekends we'd play golf or swim until we dropped, but the kids goddamn better be to work at eight o'clock. When George was still living with us and working here in town, I'd say in the morning, "Hey, George, get out of here, you've got to get to work." He'd say, "Well, I can get there ten minutes late," and I'd say, "Good thing you're not working for me." But I also said to my kids, "Working is bad enough, but you've gotta work, so whatever you take up for a vocation, if you take it up, you like it.

Like what you do." My children can work at whatever they want, but I want them to be happy in what they're doing—happy in life.

I'd hate to have children today—I really would. When my children were young, you never had to worry about vandalism like you do today. We didn't have the problem of civil disobedience like they do today. And you had to be 21 to drink—you were almost an adult before you started drinking. I'm against 18-year-olds drinking. Dope and that stuff was taboo, of course— I mean, most of my children, if you'd said "marijuana" or "opium" or something to them, they'd think of an old Chinaman sitting on the floor. I say I'd hate to have children today, but my grandchildren are making out all right. They're all involved in athletics—football, hockey, baseball. I wouldn't be surprised if one of them ends up as a pro hockey player—he's really good. Another one, he's real sharp—he read up on how to raise bees, and he's going to do it. My grandchildren won't get into marijuana and all that because their parents know where they are and who they're with. We knew where our children were and who they were with, because basically they were here at home. They liked it here.

All my kids are workers, producers—even the girls. Maybe I was a little stricter with the boys than with the girls—I guess my daughters just automatically became productive. The twins both learned how to do keypunch accounting, and they worked in banks, running those bookkeeping machines. Carol worked in computers. The girls are all married—the twins both married young, at 19 or 20 years old. Their husbands all have good jobs— they're all prosperous, they all own their own homes. They did it on their own.

I had some problems with my oldest boy, Dwight. I thought, and he thought, that education was his thing. And it would have been, except that he's very short in stature, like his mother. He got his degree, and he was working as a teacher. He'd married a Spanish girl from Ecuador, and he had to move down South because his wife didn't like the weather up here. But he decided to give up teaching and go into business, and I got terribly upset with him about it. I guess he didn't think he could take care of the disciplinary stuff of teaching—small people sometimes have an attitude that they're little runts. But I was very, very upset— I mean, the rest of the family, including his brothers and sisters, gave up some things so that he could be educated to that extent. And here he was giving it up. I was so upset that I didn't contact him but once a year for five or six years. But we've gotten over it—it's all healed now. He has a fantastic job, running the computer division of the repair service of the phone company down there. His wife's going to take the bar exam next year, I think. They have two daughters. One of them's real sharp; she's going to college next year. I think he made the right decision after all. He's happy.

George never married—says he can't afford to be married. He has a good job down in the city, lives in an apartment there, but he doesn't like the big city, so he comes up here weekends. I don't believe in spending principal, and all my kids are the same way, except George. I said something to him about it once, and he said, "I haven't got a wife. I'm not hurting anybody. If I was married, I wouldn't do it." He gambles a little on the horses. His mother got upset with him a few years ago when he won a big pile one day and lost it the next. He'd started out with $40 the first day, got it up to $3,400, and then had a run of bad luck. His mother said, "You lost $3,400," and George said, "I didn't lose $3,400; I lost $40." George is probably too old to get married now—he's 39—but I wish he had, because he's unbelievable with children. He takes Rick's baby daughter out with him all the time.

Rick is an unbelievable person. He stands 6 feet 5 inches, and he has a big, full beard. He doesn't want to hear a curse or a strong word. Once, when he was about 22, he heard me say "Goddammit!" to Bernice, and he said, "Wait, you don't have to say it that way." He doesn't believe in violence—he really doesn't. He didn't carry a placard or anything during the Vietnam War because he didn't have to go, but he doesn't believe in any violence whatsoever. When anybody gives him a hard time, he says, "Don't get uptight. Whatever you think is wrong, there's an answer to it. Maybe you're right and I'm wrong, but you don't need to get mad at me." He's going to be an unbelievable father—he's married and has a baby girl, like I said. He lives right across the street here, by the way. When we were running the store together, Rick was great—customers young and old loved him. But—another reason I sold out was we started having these punks hanging around the store. They'd filch some cigarettes or a six-pack of beer or whatever it was, and, hey, it was getting to me. They were all from nice families—lawyers' children, doctors', industrialists'—but they were snatching stuff, and it was getting to me. So I got out. Rick didn't take over the store by himself because I didn't want him to. He's not geared for it—he'd have a nervous breakdown before he was 30. He just wouldn't know what to do, because he'd find it very hard to say to somebody, "You're stealing from me." So when I sold out, I gave Rick $10,000 and I said, "Find out what you want to do." He decided he would like to be an electrical engineer, and he's going to school now for that—has a year and a half to go.

I consider myself fortunate. All my kids were married without being pregnant; none of them was ever in jail. Every one of them is normal. Some of them are a little sharper than others—but not really. They're all kind of middle-of-the-road. In fact, I'd say we're way above the average. We have six children and ten grandchildren, and there's not a bad apple in the bunch. They're way above average, I believe, and I'm not bragging.

The Family

We have some friends with children—they make more dough than we do, but making money isn't the only thing in life. I don't think people who make more money take care of their children the way they should. Some of these friends that make big money have had unbelievable problems with their children, because they're too much involved with doing their thing and not enough with their children. I think prosperity has to be handled carefully—money doesn't buy everything. It buys material things, but all the money in the world doesn't make your family, you know.

I was the youngest of five children—four boys and a girl. My father was a newspaperman, as I mentioned. My mother was not socially inclined, and we never had a lot of money. But we always lived in a nice home, and we were always allowed to have friends over to the house. My father was real close with us kids. After dinner at night, we'd gather around and say, "Hey, Dad, tell us a story," and he'd fabricate stories that were unbelievable. He was also quite an artist—he'd draw crazy animals and tell us stories about them. My mother was a seamstress and an unbelievable cook. The friends of mine who were always coming over just fell in love with her.

That was a good family, and the family Bernice and I raised was a good family too. Whatever we did, we did as a family. When Rick was growing up, we'd take him to the rodeo or the mountains or the beach, and the other kids—some of them almost grown—would all go too. We did things all as a family. When Rick went to prep school, we'd take the whole family to parents' day or athletic events. I had to buy a big station wagon to hold them all—they must have thought Rick was born of a harem. I especially liked our family life when the kids were older—16 or 17 or 18—when the girls would be bringing their boyfriends home (they never went out, you know, they always brought them home) and the boys were either working for me or involved in sports and things in school or getting out of school and getting involved in other things. But then I'm crazy about babies too—I take my baby granddaughter with me everywhere. She's part of my soul.

They're all grown up now, but we're still a family. We're in contact with each other every single day, seven days a week. Christmas is a big time when we all get together, of course. We try to do things for the children then, help them along—find out what they need, like a refrigerator or a vacuum cleaner or some cooking ovens. But we don't wait for special holidays to get together. I wouldn't be surprised if before nine o'clock tonight some of the kids won't be down here with the grandchildren. They'll all go swimming and maybe we'll have a cookout. Usually on Sundays the whole clan gets together that way for swimming and a barbecue—except for Dwight and his wife and kids, of course; they're too far away. I tell you, it's amazing. The twins do a lot of things together socially. They're so close. One has three children, and one has two. They baby-sit for each other, and each can reprimand the other's kids. They look so much alike, sometimes a kid will think her aunt is her mother. And the five grandchildren are like that, you know, real close—like five brothers and sisters.

But it's not just my children and grandchildren that are part of the family. My first wife is included to some extent too. She and Bernice have become close friends, and she comes here for Thanksgiving and Christmas. She's always come holidays with the children. She had an operation recently, and I called her once a week while she was in the hospital. I was concerned about the mother of my children. I don't say to the kids, "How is your mother?" I say, "How's mother?" because that's their mother.

Then there's the neighbors' kids and my kids' friends. I care about them almost as much as I do my own. You've just got to love children, and I love these other kids just like I do my own. Most of them are grown up now, and I'll sit down and have a beer with them, or one of them will drop over and have a drink with me and watch a football game. Or if they drop over around dinner time, they're quite apt to sit down and have dinner with us. They come and go through my house as if it were their own—and I love it. Rick lives right across the street, and it's not uncommon on a Sunday that he'll have a whole bunch of guys and their wives and girlfriends over to play volleyball. They'll have a couple of cases of beer and play volleyball until they drop, and then they'll all come over here for a swim. In fact, as far as the pool is concerned—well, for instance, anybody that works in the strawberry fields for us can swim there whenever they get tired. It's quite a family—it's been unbelievable.

All the kids were Bernice's, and all the kids were mine. The girls confided in their mother *and* Bernice when they got their first periods and things like that. They were all close with Bernice—but especially Dwight. I think that he worships her. As for George—Bernice's boy—probably I reprimanded him a little less than the others. I never had to worry about him. I'm sure he loves me. I was pretty proud of him here one time four or five years ago. He never knew his father, but I said to him, "I know who your dad is." He said, "Dad? I don't ever want to know who my father is." His father had left him and Bernice because he felt he couldn't afford to take care of him. In fact, George wanted to change his last name, have my last name. I said, "I'd be more than honored, but it won't make you any more a son of mine than you are now."

The kids have never been jealous of each other about things like cars or homes. Some have cars or houses or clothes that are a little bit bigger or better or nicer than what the others have, but there's never been any bad feeling about it. In fact, I own this block of buildings downtown. Bernice and I have it in our wills that whichever of us dies first, the other owns that property, but Rick gets the income from it, and when we both go, the property goes to Rick. But do you think that was a decision of mine alone or of just Bernice and me? No way. We all got together, and the whole family agreed that this was exactly what should be done. Rick had given up his formal education to work for me—he did it for pretty near three years. And he lives across the street from me and helps me out a lot—takes care of my greenhouse and everything. All my children agreed to this. I left it up to them, and every one of them thought that they didn't need that property and that Rick deserved to have it.

If the telephone rings after 11:30 at night, I've made it known that it means that one of my children or one of my grandchildren is in trouble—and you'd better believe I answer it very quickly. All the time in the back of my mind, that's what it is, you know; if it turns out to be some other kind of call, I'm relieved, but—this is the way. I wish you could see all this family together. They're fun, they really are. They're all sociable—they do whatever they do together, talk together or come over swimming together. They don't have any problems. I don't think that Bernice or myself or my first wife—any one of us—can take credit as a person for what an unbelievable family we have. Once I was divorced and then later married, it was decided that everybody was happy—there weren't any ill feelings. My children have never seen violence or swearing or fighting or bad words. They might have heard me say something if I dropped something on my foot—but other than that, they've never heard that stuff. And their families are that way now. As Rick says, I'm sure that there are other answers than fighting.

John

John has held a variety of jobs, and he now helps run a printing plant for the U.S. government. He was married shortly after World War II, during which he served in the Army. He and his wife have raised two daughters and a son. He is perhaps the only Irish American ever to move out of an Irish neighborhood on St. Patrick's Day!

John and His Parents

Well, I guess the first thing to say would be that I was born 56 years ago of Irish immigrant parents. My mother was born in 1883 and came here in 1900, which made her 17 years old. She came all by herself, not knowing a soul here or anything else. Her parents stayed in Ireland, and she never went back to see them. Think of it! She arrived here 17 years old, didn't know a soul, didn't have enough money in her pocket to pay for a night's lodging. She not only had to get a job that first day—which, by the way, was a Saturday—but she had to get a job with live-in privileges. No money and no place to live. I always thought this was just amazing, absolutely amazing.

She was the oldest girl in a large family—I think there were 11 children. It was a question of economics, her leaving. In those days in Ireland, especially if you lived in the country, when you became of age, your family could no longer keep you. Like they say in the old storybooks, you had to go out and seek your fortune—you had to go out and live and pay for your own living once you became an adult. She chose to better herself by coming over here, because it was just poverty and poor times over there.

My father was born in 1880, and he came here from Ireland in 1902 or 1903. He came to this place in upstate New York—why he went there, I don't know. It's not even close to anyplace. After a year or a year and a half, he moved to the same city where my mother was living—to the big Irish neighborhood there, of course. He met my mother, and in 1908 or 1909, somewhere around there, they decided to get married. Then, for some strange reason or another, my father decided he was going to make a trip back to Ireland—so after being engaged to my mother, he went back to Ireland and stayed there for two years. We used to ask my mother, "Well, weren't you concerned about this? Did you wonder if he was ever coming back?" And my mother would say no, she didn't really care one way or the other. It was hard to imagine her that way, as someone who took things as they came, because as we were growing up, she was a person who . . . there's an expression that would fit her very well: she always had her head screwed on right. She always knew her next step, always knew what was going on. Everything was systematized. I never got over being amazed that when my father went away after the two of them were engaged to be married, my mother couldn't care less about it.

Why did my father stay away so long? I don't know, but he did get a job over there that he liked very much—he worked as a drover. He would buy cattle and cows and pigs and swine in one part of Ireland and take them to another part, to what they called "fair days" over there. He would sell them, and then he would purchase sheep or something that they might have on sale at that fair. My father was quite a gay blade, and I think he liked that job because it allowed him to travel around and have a really good time—he liked his little cup of gin, and he made the most of it. Well, he stopped drinking when he got married. So maybe those two years he spent over there were a last fling before settling down.

My father was the black sheep in our family, I guess—I think that had something to do with why he left Ireland. My father's grandfather and father were tailors—that was the family tradition. So when my father was a young person, they put him into an apprenticeship tailoring, and he served five years as an apprentice tailor. This was what he was supposed to be, but he hated it, so after five years he walked out—never picked up a needle and thread again in his life, except to do his own sewing at home on Sunday morning, which made my mother very mad because she thought he shouldn't sew on Sunday.

When he first came to this country, he worked for a glass company. But he hated that job too and didn't stay in it very long. He went from that into what's probably the hardest job in the whole world—he became a roofer. First he worked for many years for Allan Murphy, a man of high integrity in our neighborhood. Then, around the beginning of the Depression, he went into business for himself. In those times, the great majority of people were not working, so families were together all the time—the father was home because he didn't have a job. But my father was off working every single day, so our family was brought up mainly by my mother. We'd see my father every day in the morning, and we had supper with him every night. And he spent all his spare time with us kids. He worked a lot on Saturdays, but on Sundays and so forth, he would be with us. We were fortunate, because he had money to spend and he would take us to the beach, the amusement park, and places like that. He showed us a good time.

My father and mother were opposites in many ways. For instance, my mother had no love for Ireland at all. She loved only this country. She never went back to Ireland, and she would not have gone under any circumstances. She said that her memories of Ireland were bad memories, memories of a childhood with much poverty and much hunger and much war, and so forth. That was what she wanted to get away from when she left there and came here. My father, on the other hand, had a great allegiance and a great love for Ireland, and he went back there many times before he died. He was an Irishman a hundred percent. Another difference: my father was a great musician—a great singer and a tremendous dancer; my mother couldn't carry a tune in a bucket, couldn't dance a step, didn't know one Irish tune from another. We used to have lots of fun when we were kids growing up and we'd have Irish music on the radio. My father would say to my mother—he always called my mother Kate—he'd say, "Kate, what's the name of that song?" Well, he might as well have asked her anything; she didn't know and didn't give a damn. It was the same way with humor. My father had a wry sense of humor (in the British Isles, they call it a wry sense of humor)—you'd have to catch it real quick, or it went over your head. My mother was just the opposite—she had a good personality and she laughed a lot, but she didn't catch jokes, and she didn't like to kid with people.

My father, God rest his soul, would never show his temper. He would not raise his voice if the house was falling on his head—absolutely would not get excited or lose control. He never showed his emotions. He would only discipline us if we'd done something really wrong. Then we'd get it—he would give you a crack, but he wasn't in a rage when he gave you that crack. And it would be over very quickly. But my mother had a temper—oh, she had a temper. She was more of a disciplinarian than my father. If you did anything wrong, big or little, she would correct you with a slap. She was very quick with her hands—she had a great pair of hands—and she would knock you right off your chair. But it would be over that quickly too.

I think my personality is more like my mother's than my father's. I guess I have the love of this country that my mother had. I don't dislike Ireland, but I'm the only one of my generation who hasn't gone to Ireland, even for a visit. But the main way I'm like my mother is that my temper leans more toward what hers was. I have an appreciation of music and all that, like my father, but as far as temperament goes—and the quickness of it—I'm very quick to anger. Every mistake I ever made in my whole life, I think I made because I wasn't calm enough.

I was the middle child. There were five of us, and I was

number three. The oldest was a boy, then my sister Mary, then me, then my younger brother, and last my sister Jenny—the baby of the family. Being in the middle, and just comparing me to my two brothers, I would say that my father was more strict with my older brother than he was with me, and on the other hand, my mother was more tolerant of my younger brother than she was of me. I probably was put on my own more than my older brother was—got a little more leeway and responsibility than he did—and maybe I also got a little more direction and guidance than my younger brother did.

A Worker

I went to work in December of 1937, and I've never been out of a job for one day, never collected unemployment. I've been a worker, I guess, all my life. My first job was in the printing industry. I went to work as a printer's devil for 25 cents an hour—eight hours a day, six days a week, $12 a week. And no overtime. When President Roosevelt put in the minimum wage law, I felt like a millionaire—I started making 50 cents an hour, plus overtime, and I'm telling you I couldn't spend all the money I was making. The company I was working for mostly printed bills of lading and checks and all the rest of those things, and my first job there was taking care of the numbering machines, putting on serial numbers and progressive numbers and so on. I got a couple of promotions, and then the superintendent really jumped me over quite a few people—as far as seniority goes—and made me a proofreader, which was actually a skilled occupation. The proofreader was quite a responsible person, because it was the proof that he read that the customer was going to give his OK to. If you didn't give the customer a good proof, he might say "to hell with it," and the company would lose his business, at least on that job.

I left that company in 1941, because I got, through a friend, a job that paid more money. I'd only been working there a few months when I got drafted, in 1942. I was in the Army until early in 1946, stationed in this country, working mostly as a classification specialist—meaning that I was one of the clerks who processed the orders about where guys would be sent and what they would do. It was just like a lottery. When I got out of the Army, I went back to the job I'd had for only a few months before I was drafted, because the draft law had a provision that if you were drafted or enlisted during World War II, then wherever you were working before you went in had to take you back.

I joined the union then, and part of the contract that our union got was an incentive system—we didn't agree to piecework at all, but we did have in the contract this incentive system for whatever you produced above and beyond your guaranteed base wage. The incentive scale was arrived at partly by time studies, so the union needed a union person to be in on these time studies. Why I don't know, but I was chosen to be the union time-study man. When a grievance came up about the incentive rate on a particular job, my job was to make a time study, along with the company's time-study man, and then to bargain with him and come to an equitable incentive rate. I got along pretty well at that job.

I got married in 1948, and I left this job in 1949, when my wife, Teresa, and I were about to have our first daughter, Rosemary. I had a chance to make more money working for a laundry company as a driver. As things have turned out now, I don't regret the decision I made then, but I did dislike this new job, and I had really liked the job I'd quit. I stayed at the laundry until November of 1952, a few months after our second daughter, Diane, was born. Again, it was a question of earning enough money to support my growing family. I went back to being a printer, this time for the U.S. government. Because I was an experienced, skilled printer, I was able to dictate my own terms when I started there, and they were very good terms—I started at a good rate. I worked as a printer in the plant there for about 20 years, and for a time there when the kids were teenagers (we had our third child, our son, Matt, in 1955), I also did some moonlighting—drove a cab and worked as a night watchman.

It was again a case of economics. My wife is the one who handles all the money, and she does a tremendous job of budgeting and buying the food and clothes and all that. When she presented the whole financial picture to me, I saw there was no other recourse. We were spending so much for food and so much on the mortgage and so much for maintenance, and so forth, and I wasn't making enough to cover all those expenses. Teresa couldn't go out to work and still bring up three children, so it was up to me, the bread-earner in the house, to bring in more dollars in order for us to live the way we wanted. I was very pleased with the life we were living—it was nothing extraordinary, just ordinary good living, but I enjoyed it, and I wanted it for my children. If I had to sacrifice and work a little bit harder so they could have it, why sure, I'd make the sacrifice—absolutely. At the time I was working overtime at my regular job—four or five hours every night and Saturdays—so my time at my extra job was Saturday nights, Sundays, and holidays. I didn't really miss out that much on time with my family, though, because the kids were getting to the age when they liked to spend their leisure time with their friends. And on holidays we'd always have our big meal or whatever after I came home.

About four-and-a-half years ago, I got promoted to a supervisory position at the printing plant. I've gotten along pretty well since I was promoted, because I think those men are a tremendous group of people to work with. That's how I think of it—they don't work for me, I work with them. I'd been with these workers for some time—always liked them and been one of their buddies—and I've tried to be the same way since I got this new position—tried to treat the men just the way I always wanted to be treated when I was a worker there.

It's funny, but I think the fact that I was number three in a family of five children has really helped me in doing this job as a supervisor. I can think of two guys that work for me that are only children and a couple of others that are from large families, like me, and I can really see the differences. I think someone who is an only child, or comes from a small family, becomes more critical, has a narrower viewpoint, than a person who is from a large family. The only child hasn't had as much of a chance to learn about getting along with many different types of people. The person from a large family will maybe be more tolerant of different people and different points of view.

Getting Married and Finding a Home

You might want to hear about how I got married. I was hanging around with this guy Ralph, and Ralph was dating Teresa's sister, Mary Ellen. He couldn't drive, but he wanted to take Mary Ellen to Vaughn Monroe's ballroom, out on Route 6. He also wanted to get a date for Mary Ellen's sister—namely Teresa. So the arrangements were that if they wanted to go out, why didn't he get a friend that drove a car to take everybody—namely me. So it was to be a blind date with Teresa, you might say—that's what they call them. Now I wasn't too keen about going on a blind date because I had been stuck a few times, but I finally said, "OK, here's your ride." We did go out to Vaughn Monroe's place and had a very nice time. And from there, it was just a hop, skip, and a jump before she grabbed me.

We were engaged for about a year—in those days a year was no time at all. We wanted Mary Ellen to be the bridesmaid at the wedding, but she was working for the government in Bermuda. We had planned to go to Bermuda on our honeymoon anyway, so we decided to get married down there and have Mary Ellen for the bridesmaid after all. We got permission from the Church and went down there and got married—and I hated Bermuda. Teresa's going to kill me for telling this story, but it seemed to me we spent all day, every day, just trying to eat. Oh, it was terrible. To get lunch you had to hire a car, and in order to get a car you had to call up for it the day before you wanted it. Then when you got to lunch, the car wouldn't stay there and wait for you. You had to call them when you were finished and wait for them to come and get you. Lunch would take about four hours. I couldn't stand it, so I said, "Let's get the hell out of here and go back to New York." And we did. I think we disappointed Mary Ellen, and Teresa said at the time it was thoughtless, but I just couldn't help it.

This was in November of '48. Rosemary was born in February of '50. We were living in my old neighborhood, in a housing project, and neither of us liked that very well—partly because it was a project, and partly because a number of the other families used to drink and carouse a lot. Rosemary was a little child, and we just couldn't see bringing children up in those circumstances. So when Diane was on the way, and we needed more room anyway, we decided to look for a house and make our move once and for all. Teresa was actually the one that found the house—she saw an ad in the Sunday paper, came over and looked at the house, liked it, brought me over, and I agreed. We bought the house, and we've lived there ever since. We've never regretted it. It's been a very happy home for us—we've had good neighbors and just a real good time.

We bought the house in December of 1951, but we didn't actually move in until the following March 17th, just a few days before Diane was born—I moved out of my old Irish neighborhood on March 17th, St. Patrick's Day! It was on a Friday night in a big rainstorm. A friend of mine was helping me. So there I am—it's about eight o'clock at night, and it's raining like hell, and we're carrying things down, and here's this guy sitting on the front of the truck, drunk as hell, and he says, "Hey, what the hell are you guys doing!" I was short-tempered, you see. "Get the hell outta that truck, or I'll drop this bureau on your head." He's still going, "What the hell are you doing?" So finally it's, "What do I look like I'm doing? I'm moving." "Jeez, you can't move out of here today! It's St. Patrick's Day!" He called me everything—I was a traitor, and I was this, and I was that, and I was an SOB and everything else.

John, Teresa, and the Kids

All the time the children were growing up, Teresa was with them eight or ten hours a day. I was only with them two or three hours a day. I worked all day; I got home at five o'clock at night or six o'clock at night—whenever it was. We had supper together, and the kids did their homework, and then they went to bed. So how long did I have with them?—two or three hours in the day, and that was it. But I got my licks in. Sometimes we played games in the evening. Matt loved to play cards, so I taught him how to play cribbage. I forget some of the other games—pick up sticks, we played that. There'd always be a little bit of cheating going on—somehow they always managed to beat me. Also, I was usually the one who helped the kids with their homework—at least I did until they got into that new math. The kids and I would work on homework out in the kitchen while Teresa was washing dishes and ironing, getting the kids' clothes ready for the next day. Yeah, they taught me a few things—we used to have a lot of laughs. Those were good times.

Believe it or not, one of the kids' teachers, a Sister, used to send me home schoolwork to do every night. She'd give Diane a shopping bag to bring home, and she'd say, "Have your father cut out 12 stars this size and 13 apples that size and 14 bananas and make a group of R's on the top of this paper and a group of P's." Diane was in second grade, and the kids were just learning how to put words together, and so forth. The Sister had picked me out to make materials for the class. I used to say to her, "I'm not in the second grade. When are you going to promote me?" And she would say, "Don't talk silly! Now I want three apples by tomorrow night and four bananas. And you must have some roll paper and some red paper up there at your printing plant. You'd better bring some of that home." She was a very strong-willed woman—no matter how many times you said no to her you always ended up saying OK. I don't know why, but I think I was the only father she roped into doing homework.

We sent our kids to parochial schools. We lived here for three or four years before our children actually started school, so we had a chance to make our own observations, and we just felt that the kids in parochial school came out with more learning and came out being more polite and more considerate. We wanted our kids to have teachers like the Sister who made me do that "homework." She had dedicated her life to the children—she'd spend time with them in school, of course, but also on Saturdays and Sundays in their homes if they needed more of her time. She gave so much of herself—Sisters who taught in the higher grades have told me that there was never a child she ever taught that ever flunked. That was the sort of person we wanted teaching our kids.

When the kids were older, we let them call the shots themselves about where they would go to school: Rosemary went all the way through high school in the parochial schools, but Diane switched to public school in the ninth grade, and Matt did in the seventh grade. We always encouraged the kids to make their own decisions, but Teresa was better at that than I was. I was more the type to shelter them. When Rosemary decided to enter the convent—which was when she was about 16—it was a shock for both of us, but Teresa wasn't shocked quite as much as I was, because prior to this she had treated the children more on the adult level than I had. Rosemary just bombed us with it one night at the supper table. She said it like she was saying, "I'm going down to the movies tonight," and that was that. I just couldn't believe it, and it took me quite a while to get used to the idea. But it was an awakening for me—I began to see that these kids of mine were growing up and becoming capable of making important decisions on their own.

It was the same way when Diane got out of high school. She decided to go to a college here in the city, but she wanted to live over there instead of here at home. That shook me up at first, and I was opposed to it—I thought of it as leaving the family. But after a while I said, "Gee whiz, Diane's an adult. She's doing all right." Then when Matt, the youngest, wanted to go out of state to college . . . well, I would have preferred that he stay here at home, but I really didn't mind it very much. I said, "If that's what you really want, it's your decision, and I'm all for it." So I did learn—gradually—not to be so strict with the kids.

I think there are so many factors that are beyond a father's and mother's control. I've learned as I've gotten older that no matter how great the parents are with their children, 15 minutes outside the home with the wrong person, the wrong environment, can take away 20 years or 30 years just like that. A lot of mothers and fathers put themselves in the grave asking, "What did I do wrong?" They didn't do anything wrong. It's just that something happened in the wrong place at the wrong time, and away the kid went. You just have to hope your kids have learned to think for themselves. I think one of the main troubles in the world today is that too many people are led by too many other people. As your kids get older—15 or 16 or 17—if they haven't learned to think for themselves, and they're the followers of somebody else, and the person who's leading them starts doing the wrong thing, then you've got a real concern. I've learned, with Teresa's help, to say to the kids, "You're intelligent people. God has been good to you, so use your heads! Don't be led."

I think Teresa has a better personality than I do—she's more patient and tolerant. She did an excellent job of raising the kids, and I think they now show more of a reflection of their mother than they do of their father, in their temperaments and thinking and behavior. For example, they're more tolerant than I am, like their mother. Thank God!—I do really and truly thank God that none of my children have a quick temper like mine. They can very well do without it.

A Way of Life

It wasn't until I got married and had children of my own that I really began to think about my father and how much I admired him. I mentioned before that though he liked a good time, he cut out drinking altogether after he got married. I never saw my father take a drink. I'm not sure of this, but I think maybe he got very serious and said to himself, "My first mission in life now is to raise my family and provide a living for them." When I got married, I did the same thing as he did. When I was young and single, I liked a good time as much as the next guy, but I haven't had a drop since my first child was born.

Please don't misunderstand. It's not that I'm a prude or anything else—like my father I have liquor in the house, and I often offer a fella a drink, "Hey, help yourself, please." My wife will take a drink, and my children will take a drink—good luck to them! But I don't think I can be the type of person that I should be if I drink. I see it in other people. I'm not saying that about everyone who drinks, but I have seen some men that I think would be better providers and better family people and better fathers if they didn't drink. Marriage and bringing up a family is at best a hard job. It requires a clear head and so forth. I can't do it as well if I drink. Money comes into it too. I'm very conscious of money because I was young during the Depression. If I've got a choice between a buck for booze and a buck for my family, I'll choose the family—I'll put it into the house or something.

My father was a great provider for the family—just a great provider. I think so often about how hard he worked, and sometimes I just can't believe it. I know what I'm talking about, because I worked for my father for a while off and on, and I hated roofing with a passion. But he did it for years. You have no concept, no concept of a person standing out on a roof, sometimes when it was as cold as ten below zero, working for 8 or 9 hours a day—standing out on a slate roof, or a tile and gravel roof, or on an asphalt roof, at 100 or 110 in the summertime, for 12 or 14 hours a day, six days a week. There's no concept—you can't put it together! How could he stand it? I'd see him come home with holes burned into his overalls from the heat—and he never complained. He was doing it all for us.

Everybody liked him. He loved doing things for people. If anybody was ill, he was concerned about them and helped them out. In those days there were families in our neighborhood where the fathers had died, and it was just the mothers trying to bring up the children. He would help these families—paint their ceilings, fix the roof, do simple plumbing and carpentry for them. Widows on the street and so forth, he'd help. He'd help people at the Church. If anybody he knew died, he went to the funeral. He went to wakes; he went to visit people at the hospital; he went to see them in their homes. He had a brother, for example, who lived not far from us, whose wife died in childbirth. The brother was left with four girls to raise all by himself—the oldest one, at the time his wife died, was six or seven. My father was very concerned about his brother's welfare and that of the children. He would tell my mother on Fridays, "Kate, when you go shopping tomorrow, why don't you pick up a smoked shoulder or a corned beef or something for Stephen?" And then Sunday morning he'd run up there with it. Yet with all his hard work and all his helping people out, if we wanted to go someplace or if we wanted him to play with us, my father never said he was too tired.

I learned to do things my father's way. During the Depression, when I was 17 or 18 and just starting to go to work, my older sister's husband got laid off—they already had a child at the time. One night when I got home from work, my father said it would be a nice gesture on my part if I helped out my sister and her family. He said, "From now on, instead of bringing your week's pay home here, stop at your sister's house and give it to them." And of course I did it—I was never resentful, and I never thought I was doing anything great. It was just that they needed me and I helped them. If the day had come when the roles were reversed, I'm sure they would have done the same thing for me.

So when I had to do that moonlighting I told you about, it was no big thing. It was just like eating three meals a day—all the more so because I had a family. If you get married and you want children, it's your duty as a good father and a good provider and a good husband to work for them and just do the best that you possibly can—absolutely. I'd do it again today and wouldn't blink an eye at it. I don't think any father or mother should get any special accolades for doing it. I think working hard for the family is part of the thing that a parent wants to do in the first place. I get a great inner satisfaction out of being able to provide for my family—I like to see my children have things, and I would do anything I could to see them forge ahead.

I've heard people say, "Oh, when a child gets x number of years old, that's it." I don't believe in that baloney. I'm a helper—I'm a helper to the guy across the street or the guy up the street, and I don't think anything of it. If I can help my own children when they're 50 years old, I'll do it. I don't sever the cord just because a kid of mine is 21 years old. I don't say, "That's it, you're on your own—don't ask me for financial help or anything else." I'd feel the same way if one of my children did something wrong. If you throw that child out of the house, you've lost that child forever. As long as you have the kid around to talk to, there's a chance that you can do something about it. But if you close that door, pal, that's the end of it.

My family and Teresa's family and our immediate family— we're a very close-knit organization. When Diane was very, very small, she had a touch of polio or something, and it gave her a fibrous bone condition that she still has—one of her legs is like a honeycomb; it's not solid bone. All through her childhood and teenage, we took her to I don't know how many doctors—one would tell us one thing, and one would tell us another. Teresa, Diane, and I, the other two kids, Teresa's side of the family, my side of the family—all of us were involved in the whole thing, trying to figure out what the hell the doctors were saying, and just trying to help Diane get along. I don't think she ever realized herself that there were little telltale signs that would let us know her leg was tired and was bothering her. We'd see those, and we'd try to plan an activity that would quiet her down and give her extra rest. Teresa had read that eggs would build up a person's bones, so since Diane wasn't an egg eater, she would camouflage the eggs in a frappe or something. I don't think Diane knows even to this day how many eggs she ate under camouflage.

My way of life, the way I was brought up and the way I've lived—the people in the family help each other, and they enjoy each other. I can't understand people who say, "It's tough being a parent. It's tough bringing up a family." God help us! One of the most enjoyable things in life is being with your own family and bringing up your children, and people tell me how tough it is! I guess I'll take my way of life to the grave with me. I haven't seen anything yet that can take its place.

I don't see people today helping each other out and enjoying each other the way they did 40 or 50 years ago. I don't know why—maybe World War II had something to do with it. I know family life never went back after World War II to what it was prior to World War II. You can see it in religion. When I was growing up, the family said a rosary together every night. After a while it became drudgery to me to go through that every night, but as long as I was living in my parents' house, I respected their customs and I went through it. When our own kids were growing up, though, Teresa and I didn't say a rosary with them every night. We did like to go to Mass, and we took the kids with us. But I don't think our children enjoy going to church now as much as we did and do.

Still, I think that in their own way my children are leading lives as good as mine—probably better. I'm very pleased with all three of them. We did live a good Catholic family life, and I think it rubbed off on the kids to some extent. As a Catholic, I've always been taught, from age number one, that someday I'm going to die and that when I die I'm going to go to heaven. I'm going to go up there for the first time, and there's going to be a man up there whose name is God, and he's going to judge me for all the things I did in my life. But I have a philosophy about it. I've said to my wife, and I say to my children: "My thinking in this life is that the most important judgment I'm going to have made on me is how I brought up my children and what I've done for them and what I've done against them." Because this is the great trust that God has put upon me, bringing up and raising my children. And this is strictly my responsibility—nobody else's. It's 100 percent my responsibility. I'm very concerned about saving my soul—I want to go to heaven—and I think this, how I've done by my children, is the big thing I'll be judged on.

Randy

Randy, age 36, served in the Marines, married and had a son, and worked for several years on construction jobs. Convicted of second-degree murder when his son was six years old (his case is still under appeal), he is now serving a life sentence in prison and maintaining close ties with his wife and son. Prison officials failed to respond to our several requests to interview him with a tape recorder, and even made it difficult for us to visit him at all. As Randy says, "Prisons are designed to keep people out; not people in." But Randy was as eager to talk to us as we were to listen to him, and so he told us his story in the following letters.

6/13/77

Hi Keith:

I received your letter today and figured I'd try to put down into writing what would be to the point of exactly what you are trying to put together.

First of all, I was born in 1940 and was the fifth born of the nine children in my family. My father was a typical Irish Catholic with one big exception! He's one of the few Irishmen I ever met that never drank! I can't remember him as being any kind of influence on me because being born during World War II and him working two jobs, I very seldom saw him, but I can remember him as always being a man who loved and cared for his wife and family. Most of the discipline administered to us was done by the oldest brother. I have six brothers and two sisters and the oldest brother, who was very tough, gave us the whack on the ass when we started bugging our mother. I can't ever remember getting into any kind of serious trouble when I was young, and having three older brothers, the oldest being 11 years older, kept us more or less in line as the old saying goes. I was sent to Catholic schools. That was mandatory in our family. We didn't exactly have it easy and money was tight, but I lucked out! My father was very religious and I took an entrance exam to the Catholic high school, which cost $150 a year in 1954, and passed with a score high enough to get me a scholarship. This made my father and mother very happy to finally get one out of the nine into a Catholic high school. In the tenth grade, things started going bad. My mother, who I can honestly say I loved more than anything else, became ill with an incurable disease. She refused to let anyone but her sons touch her and she had to go to the hospital for X-ray or radium treatments, and she always wanted at least two of us to take her to the hospital for her therapy treatments. She knew and we knew that it was only a matter of time but they gave her six months to live and she lasted until 1957, which was two years more than they predicted. During this period of my life in between 12 to 16 years of age, I started working out with weights and fighting both in the ring and out of the ring, but nothing serious, just enough to get me thrown out of the Catholic high school for punching a teacher in the face. He had snuck up on me from behind and hit me over the head while I was fistfighting with another kid and I got expelled and transferred to the public high school. One thing about the difference in schools was that I was like a year ahead of the public school so I started goofing off, skipping school, and just lost interest in everything except sports. I played just about every sport that was played in those days. My mother was my biggest fan! She never missed a ball game; whether it was raining or not, she was there and let everyone know that we were *her* boys! When I wasn't playing sports, I was working since I can remember. I started with the paper routes and when I turned 14 I was strong enough and tough enough to start working over at the docks. My father got me the job in a freezer 30 degrees below zero for $1.25 an hour. My father was a checker at the piers and everyone knew him so I really didn't have too much trouble. All monies earned in those days went to Moms and I didn't mind giving her the whole check because I loved her. What she didn't know or at least I don't think she knew is that I was, we'll say, borrowing frozen shrimp and lobsters and selling five-pound boxes of them to the Italians over at the market for $5 a box. I won't mention how many of the boxes were borrowed but I never lacked for spending money. Even though I saw everyone I knew doing this, I made sure my father never saw this because he wouldn't even take any of the graft from the trucks that got lost on the docks. In fact, I think he would have hurt anyone who offered him anything illegal. My father used to get nervous because of all the blacks working where I was working because most of the blacks were young girls and he caught me with them a few times, and it's the only time I can remember him getting pissed off at me. I worked there every summer until I was 17, and by this time my mother was just about dead. I had been thrown out of school for missing so many days even though I spent quite a few taking my mother to the hospital. Right up till the end, she still refused to let any attendant lift her out of a wheelchair onto the table for her treatments. I watched her rot for three years with this disease and maybe it did do something to me, because I started fighting a lot, and when she died, I think I was the happiest of all of us because she was that sick that I didn't want her to live. I kicked around after that for about two years and was persuaded by the police that if I wanted to fight anymore and not go to prison that I had best go into the Marines. I was in the Marines from December 1959 to August 1964 and on that alone you could write a book. Without any exaggeration, I had over 100 fights with bare knuckles, clubs, knives, and anything I could get my hands on as long as I won. I was court-martialed five times and was on the chain gang twice and every charge was the same, assault and battery. It took me until 1964 to finally get thrown out of the Marines with a bad conduct discharge. Although I had signed up for only four years, I spent four years and eight months and did the last year in a naval prison for almost beating a guard at a Marine brig half to death. That's when I found out that I was an "alcoholic!" The Navy psychs explained to me that even though I was only 23 years old, I was and always will be an alcoholic and they recommended a medical discharge, but the Marines said that I beat on people while I was sober and they couldn't comprehend that alcohol causes brain damage and that was why I was so short-tempered and couldn't remember half of what I did! Here's the best part—I didn't believe them until after I got married and ended up in an alcoholic ward and almost croaked. I'm getting a little ahead of myself, because before that happened I met Francine and we had Randy Jr. It still took me eight more months to find out exactly what an alcoholic is and here's a good point—I quit drinking to stay out of trouble and haven't had a drink since 1967.

Take Care,
Randy

6/14/77

Hi Keith:

I left off yesterday about the Navy doctors trying to explain "alcoholism" to me, and being 23 years old, my conception of an alcoholic was a wino lying in the gutter, so now you have to picture a young man, 23 years of age and very bitter about being thrown out of the Marines because the Navy docs said that I suffered from a pathological personality disorder. In July of 1964 while I was in the brig, I asked to be sent to Vietnam, because if they sent me back to duty, they would have to give me an honorable discharge, but they refused and accused me of shooting 20 rounds of M-14 caliber ammo at a gunnery sergeant while we were in Cuba during the Missile Crisis. So in August of 1964 my U.S. senator read all my court martials and saw that I had never been AWOL. So he cut my sentence and told them to discharge me. As I told you earlier, I had three older brothers and three younger brothers and the oldest one was now a foreman ironworker on structural steel. The next two older brothers were all installing elevators and they got me into the elevator construction union. After six months on probation while waiting to get into the union, I met my wife. I met Francine in October 1964 and fell in love with her for two reasons; she was pretty and built like a brick shithouse and she never tried to tell me to cool it on anything. I couldn't understand why Francine loved me so much because when I first met her, I was still very bitter and hurt a few guys over her just for looking at her or saying something to her. I'm the possessive type and refuse to give up on anything that I want. The first three years with Francine were the best years of my life—that was '65, '66, '67, with the exception of the time that I spent in the hospital for "alcoholism." We were married in the first part of 1965 and my son was born December 30, 1965 which I would have to say was the best day of my life. Francine knew that I wanted a boy, but I told her that I wanted a girl, but it really didn't matter as long as the baby was healthy. I was 25 when Randy Jr. was born and drinking more and more but still working and making good money. Unions don't care what kind of discharge you have—it's who you know and also you had to be able to walk the open steel. Our first year of marriage was beautiful; we went out a lot dancing, which used to be my way of meeting girls; you know, I needed some kind of advantage to meet the nice-looking girls like Francine so I perfected my dancing, especially my cha-cha, because every time the band played a cha-cha I noticed all the men sitting down and the girls dancing with each other! You have to take into context that my face was just a wee bit distorted from all the fighting so I needed my dancing ability to break the ice. It worked out good for me because Francine is a wonderful dancer and it was good exercise for her while she was carrying Randy Jr. The first year with my son was beautiful for me and easy for me. I came from a big family, and by this time I had all kinds of nephews and nieces and learned from them about the basic fundamentals—changing diapers, feeding, etc. Francine is or I should say was the showcase Mother. She kept Randy Jr. almost too clean but I was proud of the way she took care of him, and my day for taking care of him the first years was Saturday. Francine always went to the hairdresser's on Saturday and that gave me the time to just get all my hugs and kisses as I called them. Of course Francine's mother just happened to drop in every Saturday morning to check on "her" baby. She was a little doll and wouldn't hear of a man changing a baby's diaper and washing him up and powdering, so Randy Jr. used to get cleaned and scrubbed whether he needed it or not. Francine I think was glad that I was able to take care of Randy Jr. the way I could, but the best part is when he started walking. I think I spent more time on the floor than he did, just playing with him and kissing him. He had those big fat cheeks and was very active and enjoyed the goofing off with Dad. I really don't go in for those playpens but they are needed when it's time to clean up. Another thing I enjoyed doing was feeding him. Randy Jr. would eat better for me, or I should say eat the things that he wouldn't eat for Francine. After the first year I found myself drinking more and more and the last six months of 1966, I was really hitting the bottle and didn't spend that much time at home because I was either in a barroom, working, or asleep. Then the New Year's party of 1966–67 was my last drink of whiskey. It wasn't my idea, it was the doctor's! New Year's Day of 1967, I fell flat on my twice-operated-on nose and started convulsing and ended up in the alcoholic ward. I didn't remember much of anything for two weeks and was convulsing and withdrawing and I was told that I almost died. The doctors there told Francine that the only thing that saved me was my physical condition and my age (26) but if I persisted in drinking I would be dead in five years at the most. The doctors explained to her that alcoholism was a disease and that maybe one out of a hundred can stop. I read everything I could get my hands on about alcoholism and figured out they were right, so I quit! The doctors said that I would never make it on my own and that I would have to join A.A. I have nothing against A.A., but I was always a loner and I took it as a challenge and I'll pat my own back by saying that I haven't had a drink in over ten years. Of course the last six have been in prison, but four of them were out on the streets. Now Randy Jr. was only two years old when all this happened and he still remembers, because he got a few whacks on his ass while I was drunk, but never hard enough to hurt him. I figured that a kid of two years old would never remember anything that far back but Randy Jr. is 11 years old now and if I ask him about it, he just says "That's all right Dad, you were drunk and I know that you didn't mean it!" Now this showed me that children's memories can maintain certain experiences at a very young age. While I was recuperating from the booze, I was still getting my check for workingman's compensation for a fall I took just before I went to the hospital, but it wasn't enough so Francine went to work and I took care of Randy Jr. He was two years old, and we spent most of the time wrestling around on the floor and just roughhousing. I played just a little bit tough with him to make sure he was to be more aggressive. Like sometimes I'd make like he hurt me just to get the kisses; he always gave you the kisses after he thought that he beat you up enough. During this time, I'd take him to the beach because he loved the water, and that's another thing instilled into young children—"Fear of Water." I just let him go into the water by himself but I stayed close enough so that I could reach him in one jump. The only trouble I had with Randy Jr. and the water was getting him out of it. Now at age 11, he water-skis and goes to the YMCA to swim if he can't find a lake or ocean to swim in. One thing I used to make Randy Jr. do at age two that nobody liked was to have him light up my cigarettes for me, *but* I had my reasons. In the Marines, they brainwash you to be what they want you to be, and what I was doing to Randy Jr. was on the same idea and I don't care who likes it. After about two weeks of lighting up my cigarettes, Randy Jr. would get bullshit if you even blew smoke near him and if he got the chance he would put them out if you left them in the ashtray. As I say, you can call it brainwashing, but at 11 years of age now, he'll ask you politely not to blow smoke in his face!!

Giving up the booze gave me more time to play with him, and I used to do a lot of push-ups and sit-ups. He was three years old so I used to let him lie on my back while I did the push-ups, but all I was really trying to do was to get him to do them himself. Naturally like all young and new fathers, I bought him the usual paraphernalia of footballs, hockey stick and puck, baseball bat and glove, and just more or less got him to use them by seeing me use them. I played all three sports, but when I was young I never had any equipment to play with and I made up my mind that no matter what, he would have whatever sports equipment he needed. At the age of four, Randy Jr. showed more interest in the hockey stick and baseball bat, so I started showing him how to hold the stick and bat. He really dug the hockey stick and puck but he told me that they use them on ice, so I said "Let's go buy some skates!" If people only understood the importance of starting a youngster in something he shows an interest in at an early age. Francine thought I was nuts because I spent $60 on the best skates I could get. I knew he would grow out of them in two years, but he got his $60 worth out of them and so did I just watching him. When I saw just how much he liked skating and playing hockey, I thought it would be a good idea to enter him in a league; the "Pee Wees;" but I was rudely interrupted by the authorities on an alleged murder charge which I will say very little about but will explain what it has done to Randy Jr.

Later,
Randy Sr.

6/15/77

Hi Keith:

I left off yesterday by saying that I was rudely interrupted by the police on that alleged murder charge, but we also have to say that I was convicted of second-degree murder, which means that I have to do 15 years before I am eligible for parole. This part here is tough for me to write about because when this alleged murder took place, Randy Jr. was five-and-a-half years old and had already been to that Head Start school and could read good enough to read all the newspapers. That was one thing that Randy Jr. excelled in, his reading, but then he had the Head Start teacher and his mother who is very intelligent helping him to start when he was four years old. You're probably wondering why I'm putting so much emphasis on his reading? Well, the papers bombarded me for almost a year straight and naturally they work on sensationalism to sell papers, so I knew my son was reading them. I was trying to figure out what to tell him and figured that I'd just tell him like it was! Now, we have to use the word "alleged" because this is still under appeal. I had to explain what happened to my son because the newspapers blew everything out of proportion. The newspapers put it like this: Man robbed and stabbed several times returns two hours later all bandaged up and "allegedly" shoots the man (who stabbed him) in the lower stomach and then beats him over the head five times with the shotgun while he lay there in a pool of blood! At least they said "allegedly," and that's the first word I explained to my son—"allegedly!" This is when I found out exactly how much Randy Jr. loved me. I knew that he depended on me—like when he had to go to a dentist or a doctor, he always felt safer. I never asked him why he felt safer with me but it used to crack me up because he would not cry in my presence. Like if Francine tried to take him, she couldn't do it because the little guy put up a fight with her and she couldn't handle him physically. Maybe it's because of the time he got hit by a laundry truck. The minute I found out he was all right, I beat the driver of the truck half to death and told him (Randy) to not ever run into the street like that again and that as long as I was with him no one would ever hurt him. I guess he just wanted to show me, like at the dentist's that he could sit there and get fillings etc. without moving or making a sound; same thing with the doctor's when he needed stitches, not a peep out of him. Both doctors asked me how I did it, and I told them that I told Randy Jr. that only little "girls" cried, not big boys like him. When he was about four, his favorite story was how his Daddy beat up the elephant at the zoo! What I did was punch the elephant in his trunk when he grabbed the bag of peanuts. Next thing I knew was that he wanted me to take his friends so they could see me do it. Children are more fun and are so trusting that I find it impossible to believe it when people say they hate them or don't want any!! My wife and I tried to have more, but I think something happened to me on the booze thing because I ended up with prostate gland trouble at age 27! Back to when I found out that Randy Jr. loved me. He knew I was in trouble because I was in jail and he read something in the paper about his Dad. When he saw me (through a screen) all bandaged up, he started crying and kicking and punching the guards because they wouldn't let him sit with his Daddy. I asked him if he knew why I was in jail and he said yes but he wasn't sure what it meant. When I explained it to him, leaving out some of the details, he said good! He knew that it was wrong to steal and kill but when he saw all the blood on my bandages, all he asked was if I was going to die! I told him no and that in a few weeks I would be all healed up. Now, here's a five-year-old boy that sees his father all chopped up and they (the jail officials) would not let him sit with his father. I tried to explain to him why they had screens in between us but he couldn't or would not accept their rules. This went on for a year while awaiting trial and even though I had not been to trial and found guilty, the *fallacy* of being innocent until proven guilty is proven here; it's just the opposite—guilty until proven innocent! At least that's what my son told me and believe me, he could explain to you right now more about prisons than 90 percent of your psychiatrists and penologists! In that first year, I was transferred 13 times because I was accused of starting several riots and numerous assaults on Correctional Officers. My son could only see me once a week through a screen but was not allowed any physical contact, not even a kiss or hug, and he developed a hatred which even now, six years later, he still holds for them. Now in prison: for the first two years everything was cool—he was allowed to visit me and no screens to separate us.

Later,
Randy

6/19/77

Hi Keith:

Today is Father's Day and believe me when I say Sunday is a drag—it is! Most of the guys in D.S.U. lockup sleep until 12:00 or dinner time with the exception of a few of us. Don't forget that we're locked up 23½ hours a day and the routine varies very little. We are fed in our cells and are let out of our rooms just for a shower or a visit. Most of us are kept here for, as we call it, "Prison Politics" and I have spent more than four of the six years here in either D.S.U. (Disciplinary Segregation Unit) or A.A. (Awaiting Action). Now A.A. is used to keep men in a segregation unit until they can think up a good enough reason to put them in D.S.U. by saying, e.g., "He's a 'threat' to the inmate population; therefore we have to keep him segregated from the rest of the population!" The reason I'm telling you this much is because while in D.S.U. or A.A., the visiting rules are totally different from the rest of the population. Such as there is a screen in between visitor and inmate. Now they have switched up on us every now and then to see what kind of reaction they will get from us. Like for two years straight, my son was not allowed to sit on the same side as me and when I asked them why, they came up with their favorite answer to everything: "Security." Prisons are designed to keep people out; not people in—stop and think about this, e.g., why the press isn't allowed in unless it is controlled by prison authorities. Again, "Security" is their answer always! It's like a Catch 22! Now, D.S.U. is designed (the visiting area) so that your people are harassed and intimidated because of the different rules set up just for our visits only. We are allowed only three one-hour visits a week and out of that one hour, 20 minutes is used up by the authorities on Security; e.g., all visitors may be asked to be strip-shaken, which is to take off all of your clothes so that the prison officials may check out every orifice or opening in said human's body such as mouth, vagina, or anal passage! They will do this if they know they can get away with this, and a lot of people don't realize that it's against the law. Their main reason for doing this is to discourage your family or friends from coming up. Now, the administration has me down as a Negative Inmate Leader and that I'm allegedly involved in an Irish-Italian "gang" along with being on the board of directors for the N.P.R.A. (National Prisoners Reform Association) which the administration has stopped by locking up the entire prison and taking the 21 board of directors and putting some in D.S.U., some in the Maximum End of the prison, and some in the Minimum. Anyway, they destroyed it and have kept members separated from the new inmates so that they can maintain their "Step Program" which right now is in high gear, and that's the main reason that this place now has three prisons all in one. The Step Program has been slowly worked in on us over a period of three years, and it's part of (or I should say just another name for) "behavior modification!" The inmates are not the only ones that go through this; the visitors also go through it! You go from the small visiting room in Block #10 D.S.U. Prison that we'll call Prison or Step I to the Maximum End, or what we'll call Prison or Step II, which holds approximately 300 inmates, and they go through the same thing as D.S.U., except they get two hours' exercise in the morning, afternoon, and night, but the visiting room is large enough to hold 50 people, and they have a ventilating system— from there you go to Prison or Step III, which is the Minimum End of the prison, and you can work in the shops or foundry, laundry, etc.; go to school (if they have any) and have five visits a week in a large visiting room with a huge yard with swings and toys for the children. This part of the prison is where 250 to 300 inmates are kept but they have the threat of being sent back to Step I or Step II if they commit any infraction of the rules. Now, the children one day or night might be visiting their father in the large yard playing catch with a football while Mama is having a cup of coffee, and then the next day they're sent to visit him in the ten-foot-by-ten-foot visiting room with screen, and if they ask why, they can be given a hundred different reasons such as suspicion of being suspicious! How do you explain this to a child of five to ten years old? He or she knows that something is wrong and they want to know why they can't play football like we used to, Daddy? This was asked of me by my son when he was eight years old. One day he was playing catch with me and just lying down in the grass with me and Francine, talking about his hockey and his trip to Canada to play the kids up there and how he was going to take Mama with him because I told him that he's the man of the house and it's his job to take extra good care of Mama for me! Then on June 20, 1975, he's told that I'm not allowed any visits and that he and Francine will be informed when they can visit me again! In a matter of 24 hours, he's turned around from his visit in the yard to no visits for six weeks to visiting me in the ten-foot-by-ten-foot screened-in visiting room. Now, he doesn't really care for their explanation; all he knows is that they are making his mother strip naked and that he can't sit on the same side with me and he doesn't like it at all.

Later,
Randy

6/23/77

Hi Keith:

Got your letter today and I'll try to keep it going like it is; it's hard because they keep moving me around. I think I left off talking about how Randy Jr. hated this visiting setup for more reasons than one. Even though I'm allowed three one-hour visits a week, we are allowed only one visit on the weekends. So that means that I only get to see him once a week and the screws waste 20 minutes of that on security which means that I only have 40 minutes a week to talk to my son, and when he visits it's all set between myself and my wife that I spend the entire visit talking just with him. If I have something for my wife to do for me, I tell her on the other two visits. We talk and fool around for 40 straight minutes and even though it's only once a week, I figure that we talk about more things in those 40 minutes than most fathers and sons do in a week! How many fathers just sit down and rap with their children for five minutes or more out in the so-called normal world? Naturally my situation is extremely difficult because there are so many things that I want to talk about and do with him, but I'm restricted to talking about what he wants to talk about and I usually save the last five minutes to give him his usual reprimand on his behavior. This is always the part I hate because I have so little time with him that I don't want to spend any of it reprimanding him. Francine asks me to do it because, as she says, "You're the only one that he pays any attention to!" She tells me that he behaves himself perfectly when he's at someone else's home, but the little things he does to bother her at home remind her of me. I was always teasing Francine and bugging her and Randy Jr. saw this and figures that if I can do it, he can! That's when I really started on him. I told him that the only thing that I won't put up with at all is for him to hurt his mother's feelings! He's never done anything really serious enough to warrant me to hit him. I realize that a lot of people feel that to give your kid a whack is bad, but I did it about the same time that I used that brainwashing tactic with the cigarettes. He always got a good belt across his ass with my hand when he did something wrong, but I always told him why he got the whack and believe me, sometimes I think he did it on purpose just to see if he would get away with it. I figured that it was normal, and naturally I knew when he was fooling or he really screwed up because like any other child, his face gave him away. Also, the slap across his ass hurt his feelings more than his ass. I think the last time I had to punish him like that he was about three and a half years old. After that, just Francine telling him that she was going to tell Daddy was enough to get him to stop doing what he was doing. I consider myself very lucky to have him and I love him and I show him that I love him and I'm not afraid to tell him that I love him. Like when he visits me, the first thing I do is pick him up and give him a big hug (I always hugged him tight) and kiss his fat cheeks! He's never got embarrassed by this until the last couple of years. You see, a lot of my friends in prison don't have any kids and they think of Randy like he's their nephew, and when he was five years old, they used to give him a hug and a kiss. We explained the facts of life to him when he was seven years old and I had a blast doing it! Francine at first got mad because she said that he was too young, but he's a "reader!" I couldn't believe that a kid of five could read a newspaper and he even read the editorials, which I didn't even read, but then came the questions. I never once told him that he was too young to know what he was reading and explained as best I could what he was reading. At first it cracked me up because he looked like a little old man because the paper was as big as him. Francine started helping him with his ABCs when he was three and we had him in the Head Start Program and he loved it. Since he started regular school, he's been on the honor roll and his highest mark was always in reading! He never asked me about sex, but I knew he knew something about it so I decided to explain it in detail at age seven.

Later,
Randy

6/24/77

Hi Keith:

The summer of '74 Randy Jr. was almost eight years old and it was the best time we had considering the fact that I was seeing him three or four times a week, which meant that we could talk about things such as prison and he also learned quite a lot just by listening to why other guys were in prison. When we weren't playing football or he wasn't on the swings, he noticed that for the first time since I had been locked up in 1971 there weren't any Correctional Officers around. He knew quite a bit about prison procedure by now because he used to go with his mother who was on the board of directors of a group of people whose function was to provide people who had loved ones in prison with information about how to get rides to different prisons and houses of correction or get them lawyers if they needed legal assistance for some problem they may have had while visiting their husband, wife, or family member. Randy Jr. spent enough time around this group to see and hear more problems than most psychologists could hear in a lifetime! When he noticed there weren't any Correctional Officers around with the exception of a few that worked the control rooms so they could lock up the inmates at night, he wondered what was going on. I took the opportunity to take Randy Jr., age eight, into the prison and gave him a guided tour! I could do this because the Correctional Officers had actually gone out on strike because they decided they weren't getting paid enough to work in the "most dangerous prison in America," as they called the joint. During this strike, guards were still manning the gun towers but the internal security of the prison was run by the board of directors of the N.P.R.A. Someone of the N.P.R.A. got the idea that we should show our loved ones how the prison was "inside" and that's how I got Randy Jr. his guided tour, and he didn't like what he saw at all and only stayed for about five minutes. I didn't take him in to scare him and he knew most of the guys, and at first he was acting like any normal eight-year-old boy or girl would until he heard some doors closing and being opened and how there wasn't any windows or privacy! That's when he told me that he wanted to go back out and stay in the big yard and visit with me there! The reason I'm running all of this down to you is because people always say "It can't happen to me!"—at least that's what I always said!

When the guards ended their strike, they knew the first thing to do in order to regain control was to lock up the now quite controlled (for three months) inmates and get them mad enough to start killing and stabbing each other. They succeeded by letting P.C.s out in the inmate population and getting them killed. P.C. means Protective Custody—a P.C. is an informant and has many enemies in prison! Now this gave the guards what they wanted, sensationalism for news coverage! Now they could say they needed more money for "Security" with steel walls separating one prison into three prisons in which to implement their Step Program, which brings us back to my seminormal relationship with my son because naturally they have to separate those violent inmate leaders on the board of directors of the N.P.R.A., which I just happened to be one of, and put me into the D.S.U. unit in Block #10 because I'm allegedly an inmate who is as they call it a Negative Inmate Leader! So we go from one extreme to another, from the large visiting room to the ten-foot-by-ten-foot screened-in room, no more personal visits but restricted visits, which bothered all three of us!

Later,
Randy

6/28/77

Hi Keith:
I left off the last letter talking about how in '74 the adminis-tration turned this whole place upside down. Now, when the

Pigs say they are locking you up for "Control Purposes," why take it out on the inmate's family? I'll answer my own question; they do it in order to maintain a higher degree of *control* over the inmates. You can take just about anything except them harassing your family and they know it! Now, they also realize that by doing this they are putting the line guards' (Correctional Officers that work on our tier, like to feed us, sweep the floor, pass out medication???) lives on the line. I'll use my own experiences on this subject. I know that I can't get at the guards that are responsible for harassing my visits, but I can get at the guards who work where I'm locked up because the visiting room is right in our Block #10 D.S.U. at the end of the tier we sleep on. Now, these guards are very paranoid because they are told by their superiors that we will attack them for no reason at all. Let me explain. All the Correctional Officers that work in Block #10 D.S.U. are new guards! They take young and new officers that don't know us and sort of break them in by having them unlock the doors so that we can go to our visits. In order for us to get to our visiting room, we only have to go a maximum of 30 feet and we reach the first gate, which is unlocked by a rookie screw and a few older guards ready to run for reinforcement if we jump him! Yes, they let the rookie take the full brunt of all the harassment which the older guards know about and the rookie doesn't! Now if nobody jumps the new guard, we go into our ten-foot-by-ten-foot visiting room at the end of the tier and have our visits. The first thing I ask my wife and son is if they were bothered on the way in, and my wife will only tell me when they really harass her, e.g., making her strip nude etc., but my son who witnesses all of this just looks me right in the eye and says no they haven't bothered him! I found out from my wife why he will not tell me when they bug him. He told my wife that Daddy beat up the last screw that bothered him and then he couldn't see Daddy for one month! So what it comes down to is that they use your wife and son as a *weapon* to control you! Now, the only way to combat this is to take away their weapon! After June 20, 1975, I went until September of 1976 having my visits harassed and myself being threatened by the administration with the threat of losing my visiting privileges (which I did lose for a period of over six months all told) and figured the only solution was that I would have to permanently damage if not kill one of the Correctional Officers. I wrote my lawyer and explained everything to him and also to cover myself if anything drastic should happen. All of this was nullified by a car accident in which my wife was hospitalized for several months, and true to form I was never informed by the Correctional Authorities of this accident because, as they put it, "He'll only get upset!" so they waited until a friend of my wife's came up to tell me.

Later,
Randy

6/30/77

Hi Keith:

I left off when Francine had the accident in August 1976, and she was hospitalized for about a month and pulled through physically; but with all the harassment from the administration here, coupled with working and doing errands for myself and my friends, Francine decided she needed to go west for a rest! Francine is one person in a million! How many people do you know that are trusted by all of the so-called animals in this joint, especially my friends??

This car accident she had put another crimp in my seeing my son because of where I'm kept (Segregation) but Francine had one of her girlfriends bring Randy Jr. up. At first, the Administration "balked" about this because her husband is doing time in another prison. That lasted for about four visits in which I laid down the rules for his trip west. At first, he didn't want to go because he would have to leave his friends, his hockey team which he's been with for five years, and last but not least, he wouldn't be able to see me. It wasn't easy for me to tell him he had to go because he's my only son and I knew I'd miss him, so I told him that if he didn't go, who would take care of Mama? This always cleared everything up between us because I drilled it into him that it's mandatory that he takes care of Mama for me. Francine has remarked a few times to me that he was overly inquisitive about where she was going, who she was going with, and not to stay out too late. He took what I said very serious about his taking my place as the man of the house but he did get on Francine's nerves, which I consider normal. You might want to know how I solved the problem of Randy Jr. spending too much time in an all-female environment. First of all, he plays both organized hockey and organized baseball during the summer. Also, he spends a lot of time with two of my brothers-in-law, one who owns a boat and since he has no son of his own, he takes Randy Jr. with him water-skiing and swimming. My other brother-in-law has a son five days older than Randy, and those two hang around together like they're brothers, and Randy stays over at their house, eats there, and swims in their pool, and just goofs off with his pal and cousin until Francine gets home from work or from seeing me. Randy refuses to miss school to come up to see me because I've put more emphasis on his school than sports! I'm pleased that he likes sports like he does, *but* school comes first and as it turns out, he likes school and his marks show it. I don't like to impose Randy Jr. on anyone so Francine tries to split it up, but my sister and brother-in-law love him and like my sister says, "It's like having twins"—as I told you, there are only five days' difference in their age. My partner's sister who visits her brother the same time as Francine visits me is married and has three children, all girls. Her husband takes Randy Jr. at least once a week to his karate school where he teaches a couple of times a week, while his wife visits with her brother and Francine and myself. The guy is really interested in Randy Jr. because Randy is athletically inclined and very aggressive and I guess all the kids are into this karate thing now; but as usual Randy Jr. takes it very serious and this friend teaches him as much as possible. Francine saw him and Randy Jr. working out and got a little scared at what he was learning, but I told her not to worry because he's into organized hockey too heavy to have the time to really master karate. That breaks it down to three mature men that I think play a very important role in Randy Jr.'s growing up. Two of them are in their late twenties and my brother-in-law and sister consider him as one of theirs, and my sister says that her husband, who is one of those good-natured slobs who always goofs off with the kids, really digs Randy because Randy likes his jokes?? I know Randy likes him and every joke he hears, I hear at my next visit!! If I had to pick a surrogate father for Randy, it would have to be my brother-in-law. He may not be into sports as the other two are but he takes real good care of his family and thinks that Randy is so smart. When he talks to me and tells me that Randy Jr. got straight A's and plays all those sports and is so well behaved, it sounds like he's talking about his own son! I seriously think that Randy Jr. has been around Pete so long that Pete does think of Randy as his own which I like!

Later,
Randy

7/8/77

Hi Keith:

Francine and Randy Jr. got in a few days ago, and I've been deluged with visits etc. The part I ended on (I think) was the old "Father and Son" talk about girls! I started like I said when he was seven, explaining the difference between the sexes! Needless to say, he already knew boys had a penis and girls didn't, so I told him that both sex organs had dual purposes, e.g., urinating and why a girl sits down and a boy or man stands up or sits down if he prefers that way. Also, that in a few years he'll reach "puberty" and that I would explain that when he's 11 or 12 or sooner if he asks. I knew that he had read books on sex and they now teach it in school, but I figured I'd fill him in early on why his penis gets hard while sleeping (it only gets hard when he sleeps—age seven to ten). I told him that the reason his penis gets hard is because the penis is a muscle that gets larger and stiffer by blood pouring into the penis and making it that way because he might be dreaming about something that he doesn't understand yet. He told me that he had already read about this. He then turned around to me and ran down the complete functions of both male and female sex organs and that babies are made by male and female "copulation!" When he was ten years old he started showing an interest in girls—not much, but he stopped that look of "girls are a pain in the arse!" Also, he was out west and making friends, male and female, and wrote and told me that he was seeing one girl who went to the hockey games and Little League games with him and he carried her books and said she was all right for a girl! I made the cardinal mistake of teasing him about girls when he was six years old and caught myself in time and forced myself never to embarrass him about girls in front of ANYONE! He's now at home and I had a one-hour talk about girls with him and his cousin-pal Billy. Now, Billy is a "wolf" and loves the broads, so half-assed teasingly I said "Seems how little Randy's been gone for a year, Bill. Would you have an extra girl for Randy?" Billy said that Randy already had met a girl who is a friend of Billy's girl-friend and both of them had big shit-eating grins on their faces! Neither one of them was embarrassed and there were several girls present when this was said, so I didn't make any big thing out of it (even though I was very excited about it) and changed the subject to baseball. Now, I think I'll just let nature take its own course but I intend to keep a very close eye on this subject! After schooling, sex I think is very important for a young person to know "everything" about!

The way the children are now, I think they know as much as we do!!

Later,
Randy

7/12/77

Hi Keith:

Received your letter and sorry that we had to do your book this way (by letters). Like I forgot to mention the reason why Francine and Randy Jr. went out west in the first place! After the car accident, she was very disoriented, and the specialists she was seeing prescribed rest and relaxation! Francine was offered a job which paid very well considering there's a "RE-CESSION??" on (when she started work, right away she started buying bonds for Randy's college days). The area she went to was ideal for her to recuperate in. Actually, it gave her the chance to lead a normal life for the first time in five years. She checked out the schooling and sports setup for Randy Jr. to

make sure that it was up to par! Naturally, neither of them
wanted to leave, but then we all have to do things that have to
be done. They spent eight or nine months out there before
coming home the first of July. Francine had two weeks' vacation
so that meant she could stay back here for 17 days. We were
only allowed six visits, but then who wants to keep an 11-year-
old boy caged in a room ten feet by ten feet for more than one
hour at a time?

Randy Jr. seemed to want to know more about my appeals
that are still pending in court because he still feels that I'll be
getting out and be able to do things fathers and sons do! Like on
our last visit, he had Billy with him and asked him to look at the
knife wounds in my back and chest and the three-inch-by-half-
inch-wide scar on my arm which I got blocking a slash at my
throat! Evidently, they must have been discussing the aspects of
the case so I told them right out in plain English that I survived
and the other guy died. I left it up to them to figure out if I was
right in doing what I did! To clear this up, in case any citizen
feels that a person convicted of second-degree murder must be a
murderer! My case is open to the public to read if they so desire,
as all cases are once they have been judged by a jury of their
"peers" (that's a laugh) but they will never get it straight from
the shoulder like I'm going to explain it! I'll tell it to you, the
same way I explained it to my son six years ago. I'll make it
short and to the point! Six years ago I went to a party and
during the party, $400 was stolen. The only person that could
possibly have taken it was the deceased, so I went up to his
apartment at 8:00 A.M. the following morning because he was a
junkie and $400 goes fast! Myself and a friend knocked on his
door, and his girl answered and I entered without thinking that
he might be armed and scared. When I entered the room, I was
stabbed in the lower back but—and this saved my life—the knife
got stuck in my rib cage, which enabled me to spin him around;
as I did so, he slashed at my throat and I blocked the knife with
my left arm but sustained a severe cut just above my left elbow,
but my left arm slowed the slash down enough so that the knife
just barely entered my upper right chest. While this was happening, his girlfriend tried to put a butcher knife through my

back (all of this is in the transcript) but my friend punched her
in the face, knocking the knife out of her hand. My friend then
pulled me off of the junkie and half carried me to the hospital to
get patched up. He thought I was dying because of all the blood
but after two hours in the hospital, I was stitched up and X-
rayed and my left arm was put in a sling. Naturally, the police
wanted to know who did it but this was not the first time that
I've seen our finest at work! I knew they would arrest him, but
now you have to think as I thought. If I told them who did it,
they *might* lock him up! I say "might" because legally, I was in
his house and all he had to say was that I attacked him and that
I was physically stronger and an intruder who was trying to kill
him! Even if they locked him up, bail would be set at Personal
Recognizance. In other words, he would be out of jail before I
was out of the hospital! I had a friend of mine call him and tell
him that it was a mistake and that someone else had taken the
money. Now, I knew he took the money because my friend said
he was high and he didn't have a job, so where did he get the
money to get high?? The next statement cost him his life (by
accident). He told my friend that he was going to finish off
"tough guy" the first chance he got. When I heard this, I
grabbed a 12-gauge shotgun and had someone drive me to his
house. I kicked in his door and told him that he shouldn't have
warned me, but he was so high that he actually attacked me
with his knife! I aimed at his kneecap in order to disable him
until I myself had time to heal up. The round hit him in the leg
severing the femoral artery, which caused him to bleed to death.
I feel in my own mind that I did right but I had no intention of
taking this man's life. Money cannot replace a human life but a
man or woman has every right to protect his own! Now, my son
saw the knife wounds in my arm, back, and chest and that they
were all infected, and I told him what happened. He was too
young to really understand what was happening; all he knew
was that his Daddy was hurt and that he couldn't see me when
he wanted and that his Daddy had to stay in jail. He was also too
young to understand about the taking of another human's life,
but in the past six years he's had a double education! One on
what happens when you break one of "society's" laws and the

other, his regular schooling! When I talk about Randy Jr.'s prison schooling, I'm talking about all the different friends of mine he's met and why they are in here. He found out that some of my friends couldn't read or write and at first he couldn't believe it because he thought that everyone could read and write. Like there's 90 percent of them that were in foster homes or some kind of reform school or "detention" homes for so-called disturbed children. This gave Randy Jr. a chance to compare what he has and what could have happened to him if he didn't have the love generated by his mother and myself and our families. At first it was hard for him to understand that nobody wanted these guys when they were his age, because all Randy remembers of his early childhood is being kissed, loved, rough-housed, and just out-and-out being loved and feeling secure. He has not only talked with my friends but has traveled to these houses of detention with Francine while she was driving parents to see their children *that they themselves had put there!!* At first Randy couldn't believe that my friends' fathers never took them to the zoo, ball games, ice skating, or just playing catch with the football or baseball. He thought every kid played sports, and that's what I meant by having two different kinds of education!

Francine and Randy will be going back west the 17th but may only stay a few more months. We write every chance we get and I keep him up to date on the teams here, and he lets me know how his schooling is and how his Pee Wee teams are doing. We have our secrets like girls; he's at that age now, so maybe the letters will get juicier! I'll end it this way; at least I know my son loves me and does what I say and his mother is one in a million!

Take Care,
Randy